In the Spirit

Reconstructions in Lutheran Doctrinal Theology

This series will explore what contemporary theology in the tradition of Luther "should believe, teach and confess" about the God of the gospel. The series will critically engage, explore, and freshly formulate a wide range of topics in dogmatic theology. Every study will ground itself in the doctrinal tradition stemming from Luther's Reformation theology and accordingly will be explicitly focused on the knowledge of God given to faith by the Holy Spirit in Christ according to Luther's pregnant formulation vera theologia et cognitio Dei sunt in Christo crucifixo. The studies will articulate the content of faith in formulations which as such propose to be binding upon the contemporary community of faith.

Series Editor:
Paul R. Hinlicky

Editorial Board:
Matthew Burdette
Jennifer Hockenbery
Lois E. Malcolm
Derek Nelson
Piotr J. Malysz

In the Spirit

Human Subjectivity Under
Law and Gospel

Candace L. Kohli

 CASCADE *Books* • Eugene, Oregon

IN THE SPIRIT
Human Subjectivity Under Law and Gospel

Reconstructions in Lutheran Doctrinal Theology

Copyright © 2024 Candace L. Kohli. All rights reserved. Except for brief quotations in critical publications or reviews, no part of this book may be reproduced in any manner without prior written permission from the publisher. Write: Permissions, Wipf and Stock Publishers, 199 W. 8th Ave., Suite 3, Eugene, OR 97401.

Cascade Books
An Imprint of Wipf and Stock Publishers
199 W. 8th Ave., Suite 3
Eugene, OR 97401

www.wipfandstock.com

PAPERBACK ISBN: 978-1-6667-3663-2
HARDCOVER ISBN: 978-1-6667-9527-1
EBOOK ISBN: 978-1-6667-9528-8

Cataloguing-in-Publication data:

Names: Kohli, Candace L., author.
Title: In the spirit : human subjectivity under law and gospel / by Candace L. Kohli.
Description: Eugene, OR : Cascade Books, 2024 | Series: Reconstructions in Lutheran Doctrinal Theology | Includes bibliographical references and index.
Identifiers: ISBN 978-1-6667-3663-2 (paperback) | ISBN 978-1-6667-9527-1 (hardcover) | ISBN 978-1-6667-9528-8 (ebook)
Subjects: LCSH: Theological anthropology—Christianity. | Lutheran Church—Doctrines.
Classification: BX8065.3 .K65 2024 (paperback) | BX8065.3 .K65 (ebook)

VERSION NUMBER 11/13/24

For June and LaVinna who paved their own paths;
To Emma, that you may be bold and do it too.

Contents

Series General Introduction | ix
Acknowledgments | xv
Abbreviations | xvii

1. Introduction: Rethinking the Human Subject in Martin Luther's Theology | 1
2. Medieval Roots | 30
3. Law/Gospel and Human Experience | 45
4. Purgation and Prayer "in the Spirit" | 100
5. The Human Subject After Justification | 148
6. Conclusions: Human Agency in the Spirit | 187

Bibliography | 195
Index | 213

Reconstruction in Lutheran Doctrinal Theology

Editor in Chief: Paul Hinlicky

Associate Editors: Derek Nelson, Lois Malcolm, Jennifer Hockenberry, Piotr Malysz, Matthew Burdette

General Introduction

PRINCETON PHILOSOPHER OF RELIGION Jeffrey Stout reflected not long ago on the sorry fate of Christian theology since Barth. He wrote of a doubly cruel loss: both of audience and of theme. Fear of the future, or fear of being left behind by it, cannot but sap theological nerve in a culture for which History-Written-by-Winners is the de facto deity. This failure of nerve must threaten all the more where and when theology still arises in faith alone at the improbable word of the resurrection-vindication of the crucified Jesus. All this points to a crossroads at which the tradition of Christian theology stemming from Luther in particular stands. It does not take much effort or insight to observe how Lutheran theology today either dwindles into irrelevance as the mere defense of an ever-shrinking piece of ecclesiastical turf or dissipates into revisions increasingly distant from, if not antagonistic to, its source. Consequently, it takes *courage* to venture the relevance of this tradition of Christian theology and to pursue its reconstruction in forms that are fresh yet recognizable developments of core affirmations going back to its genesis.

This series of books, therefore, boldly explores what contemporary theology in the tradition of Luther "should believe, teach and confess" (as *The Book of Concord* once admonished) about the God of the gospel. The studies focus explicitly on the knowledge of God in Christ given to faith by the Holy Spirit according to Luther's pregnant formulation, *vera theologia et cognitio Dei in Christo crucifixo sunt* ("true theology and knowledge of

God are in Christ crucified"). At the same time, the studies do not ignore, mischaracterize, oversimplify, or otherwise run roughshod over the context in which retrieval takes place. The "theological production of doctrine" (C. Helmer) articulating the knowledge of God is consequently an enormous challenge today after the cultural "death of God" announced by Nietzsche's Zarathustra at the turn of the twentieth century. A century later, the ripple effects—varied and far-reaching—of Zarathustra's discovery have hardly subsided. Not only courage, then, but also *insight* into the dramatically transformed spiritual context of "post-Christendom" in the contemporary West is requisite to the theological task today.

With courage renewed, this is a challenge which theology in Luther's tradition can and must undertake in that it has no other claim but that it knows God in the Christ who was once for all truly "crucified, dead and buried"—knowing Creator, and so also creation, only in him, with him, and through him. The theocentric focus on knowledge of God by way of the scandalous "monstrosity" (Hegel) of Christ *crucified*, the Son of God *incarnate*, for the interpretation of topics in doctrinal theology thus demands *critical* retrieval; critical *retrieval* in turn effects a contemporary *pruning* of an overgrown tradition and of necessity entails disciplined experimentation.

A few words by way of introduction to these claims: Lutheran theology flourished in the time of Christendom when Christian theology, including Lutheran theology, undertook the task of promulgating a comprehensive worldview. But Christendom slowly withered under a variety of assaults for this overreach during the Enlightenment. It was buried in the ashes of the twentieth-century experience of Hitler, Hiroshima, and Stalin, moral catastrophes that were perpetrated on the soil of Christian civilizations. Only in retrospect can it be seen how much the enlistment of Lutheran theology in the project of Christendom blunted its critical edge and explosive testimony to the God of the gospel. Nostalgia for those so-called "glory days" of Lutheran theology should also be buried. Let the dead bury the dead.

As may be seen in the twenty-eighth article of the Augsburg Confession, the Lutheran Reformation challenged the medieval understanding of Christendom as the political polity of the Christian people under the governing alliance of pope and emperor. Yet as a "magisterial" Reformation, it conceived of itself as the proper renewal of the polity of Christendom, although historically this tended, without pope, to a new "Caesaropapism." The church became an instrument of the emergent modern nation-state, a "people's church" as opposed to a "confessing church." So a root issue of ecclesial self-understanding was posed during the German church struggle in the 1930s. But with the post-war collapse of Christendom, whether in Protestant or Catholic iteration, the Lutheran version of, and lingering aspirations for, a renewed alliance of throne and altar has become an albatross around the necks of all who would continue Christian theology with insight drawn from Luther. Thus the task undertaken in this series turns upon a core assumption about the contemporary cultural-spiritual context of *post-Christendom* in Europe and North America, an unprecedented situation which both elicits and requires theological renovation.

Today we reckon with the rise of the natural sciences but also with the conceits of Enlightenment modernity, which ideologically justified extractive colonialism with the racialism of white supremacy, exploitative forms of industrial capitalism, murderous forms of socialism, total warfare, and now the threats of economic and/or ecological collapse. The list of disasters on the soil of Christendom could be multiplied, while the real but tottering achievements of the modern order are today staggering under these accumulated pressures and in danger of disintegration. We enter into a multipolar world no longer dominated by one superpower; willingly or not, we become data sources for the control, manipulation, and prediction of surveillance capitalism, whether in alliance with the national security state pretending to defend "democracy" on one side, or, on the other side, with emergent autocracies, bold and powerful, which disdain any very pretense of "democracy."

The forms of Lutheran theology inherited from the passing era of modernity, then, have become not only dysfunctional, but deservingly discredited along with dying Christendom itself. Lutheran theology in the epoch of emergent modernity had oscillated between "modernist" forms of accommodation to rising secularist ideologies and "fundamentalist" forms of resistance to them. Both of these strategies are today in disrepute because each in its own way sought the rehabilitation of the political order of Christendom. Persisting in these lost causes only inhibits theology from facing up to present and future dangers, seeking and finding salutary ways forward.

As Dietrich Bonhoeffer saw from his prison cell, the polity of the Christians, *corpus christianum*, has now dissolved into its components, the body of Christ and "this world," indifferent to "Christ existing as community," if not hostile—yet astonishingly loved by God! The studies in this series take for granted this contemporary cultural-spiritual context and see no particular need to advocate, especially in our Euro-American post-Christendom, the need for a new synthesis. Instead contributions stipulate each respective author's understanding of this context and proceed to the critical and constructive task of the production of doctrinal articulations of Christian faith's knowledge of God. To be sure, authors will understand this context and the path forward in varying, perhaps even *contrary* ways. But we have sought some measure of coherence for the series by asking authors to give attention to one another's work in constructive dialogue, patient elaboration, and charitable critique.

The series attends to the challenges of the world's plurality and multipolarity in two ways. First, the notion of what constitutes legitimate subject-matter of dogmatic reflection has been opened up. Thus, books in this series critically engage, explore, and freshly formulate traditional topics in dogmatic theology but also some newer ones. Second, the theological tradition stemming from Luther is not the exclusive preserve of nominal "Lutherans" but bears from its origins an ecumenical intention, appeal, and to some extent influence. Accordingly this series has deliberately enlisted authors beyond the boundaries of denominational Lutheranism who intend in their own fashion to continue what Luther started. Thus, while every study grounds itself in the doctrinal tradition stemming from Luther's Reformation theology, each proceeds as a critical development of it.

The series has not solicited theologians from the Two-Thirds world, though we think our series will be a richly informative for those who find the complexities and partisanships in current Western theology baffling. The rising generation will happily see a flowering of indigenous Lutheran theologies across the globe which wrestle with problems not identical to the Euro-American context of the demise of Christendom. Perhaps our wrestling in the series can serve as a cautionary tale in certain respects for global partners in the Lutheran theological tradition. Perhaps these new␣utheran theologies will shed light in turn upon our own Euro-American perplexities.

The situation of post-Christendom, in parallel to "post-modernism" but not identical with it, thus forces a winnowing so that what is essential for theology as a discipline is clarified as knowledge of the God of the gospel such that other dimensions of Christian doctrine are clearly developed as corollaries of the saving, therefore essential, knowledge of God. In arguing cognitive claims about God, the studies articulate the content of faith in formulations which as such propose to be binding upon the contemporary community of faith in that they are integral to the gospel of God that authors and authorizes Christian faith, community, and mission. Such proposed formulations neither repudiate nor repeat formulations of the past but seek freshly to articulate their pertinent content, rationale, and relevance.

This series originated after the publication by Cascade Books of Paul Hinlicky's *Lutheran Theology: A Critical Introduction*, when Cascade queried whether he would be willing to edit a series of books on Lutheran theology. Hinlicky gathered together theological colleagues, most of whom had worked with him on the *Oxford Encyclopedia of Martin Luther*, to form an editorial advisory group. He also recruited an editor who would reflect the series' ecumenical orientation. The group brainstormed prospective authors and topics and began solicitation of interest. The response has been overwhelming as the series launches with thirty-some authors with topics under contract to appear over the course of the next seven years. We have deliberately sought out a rich mix of senior and junior scholars from a variety of backgrounds holding to various positions within contemporary systematic theology, experimentalist *and* retrievalist, deliberately breaching denominational walls and crossing old battle-lines.

Systematic theology is, even at best, an ambiguous good, reflecting our status as wayfarers on a pilgrim way. In a better world yet to come, we would not labor to articulate the knowledge of God but simply worship the God of the gospel who in the cross of Christ has sought and found *us*, and so come to *know* us. But here and now, between the already of the resurrection-vindication of the Crucified and the not yet of his final victory for us and for all, we write *about* the God whom *we know as knowing us* that we may serve *intelligently in this fateful interim time*. Such is our task, neither hankering after the fleshpots of Egypt nor storming the kingdom to take it by force. In the end (pun intended), true theological statements are doxological, finding their correction and vindication in the great doxology of the creation rescued and fulfilled at the Pauline "redemption of our bodies." In this confidence we offer this series to the glory of God and for the edification of the Body of Christ in its mission to the world.

February, 2024

Paul R Hinlicky with Matthew Burdette, Jennifer Hockenberry, Lois Malcolm, Peter Malysz, and Derek Nelson

Acknowledgments

IN 2007, I KNOCKED on the door of a Harvard Divinity School professor who was teaching a class on Luther. I wanted to know more about her class, I said. Little did I know, that seemingly inconsequential moment would set the direction of my life for nearly twenty years. Christine Helmer, my *Doktormutter*, introduced me to a figure who would captivate my curiosity, disturb me, and make me laugh at his ridiculous banter. Christine gave me permission and courage to call into question entrenched interpretive paradigms in Luther scholarship that just did not seem quite right. She modeled scholarly rigor. Echoing Marilyn McCord Adams, she encouraged me to "take the sunglasses off" and pointed me toward the resources and knowledge I needed to sustain my interventions. In doing so, she helped me to find my voice. Christine has handed me opportunity after opportunity. When life knocked the wind out of me, she reminded me of my passion. Thank you, Christine.

After years of reading book acknowledgments where authors thanked wives or secretaries for typing their books, it seems only fitting to turn the tables. Christine's husband, Robert Orsi, has indelibly shaped my scholarly intuition. A scholar of American religion and a narrator of the religious experiences of ordinary people, he encouraged me to cultivate my inner social historian who he saw coming alive in the pages of this text. Where I manage to portray the real-life experience of Luther's day, there is Bob Orsi. Cristina Traina taught me theological ethics and helped me see the philosophical constructs Luther deployed. She encouraged me not to be afraid to point to Luther's Catholic inheritances so long as they were really there. Her guidance, encouragement, and mentorship nourished my humanity.

ACKNOWLEDGMENTS

Funding for this research was generously provided by the German-American Fulbright Commission and Aarhus University's Visiting Graduate Student Grant. My international hosts—Volker Leppin, then in the *Evangelisch-Theologische Fakultät* at Eberhard Karls Universität Tübingen (Germany), and Bo Kristian Holm, in the School for Culture and Society at Aarhus University (Denmark)—have stimulated my thinking and become valued mentors. Like Christine, they proved themselves to be sources of critical feedback, compassionate encouragement, insightful guidance, and chocolate cake.

In many ways, research and writing are monastic practices. Yet, I have been truly blessed by the relationships I developed while this project was underway. My Northwestern University colleagues were instrumental in shaping my thinking and bringing me joy: Stephanie Brehm and William Caldwell, above all. Matthew Robinson, Aaron Moldenhauer, Kristina Knowles, and Kate Dugan were grounded resources for advice and feedback. Sasja Stopa became a cherished friend. Traci and Teri brought chortles. My colleagues at the Lutheran School of Theology at Chicago have been supportive, encouraging peers. The excited question at every faculty meeting, "Is it done yet?!" spurred my progress. Paul Owen at Montreat College has mentored me since I was eighteen and sitting in his Greek class. I owe him more than I can ever repay, not least a few dog songs.

My family supported me with their pride; my dad with his only half-joking requests for a *signed* copy. Emma, Noah, and Landon made this world bright merely by their existence in it. I love you three more than you will ever comprehend. My chosen family, Dottie and Eric, visited me the world over and gave me the most wonderful fun and memories. Jeff and Adam offered camping trips, paddleboards, and the moral support of family. Abe, my sweet houndy-boy, laid at my feet for every single word in this book. I honor his existence in these pages.

Abbreviations

CR   *Corpus Reformatorum.* 101 vols. Halle: Halis Saxonum with Schwetschke and Sons, 1834–1907.

LW   *Luther's Works: American Edition.* Edited by Jaroslav Pelikan and Helmut T. Lehmann. 55 vols. Philadelphia: Fortress; St. Louis: Concordia, 1955–1986.

NPNF   *A Select Library of Nicene and Post-Nicene Fathers of the Christian Church; First Series.* Edited by Philip Schaff. 8 vols. 1886–1900. Reprint, Grand Rapids: Eerdmans, 1989.

PL   *Patrologia Latina.* Edited by Jacques-Paul Migne. 217 vols. Paris: Migne, 1844–1864.

WA   *Luthers Werke: Kritische Gesamtausgabe: Schriften.* 65 vols. Weimar: H. Böhlau, 1883–1993.

WA BR   *Luthers Werke: Kritische Gesamtausgabe: Briefwechsel.* 18 vols. Weimar: H. Böhlau, 1930–1985.

WA DB   *Luthers Werke: Kritische Gesamtausgabe: Bibel.* 12 vols. Weimar: H. Böhlau, 1906–1961.

WA TR   *Luthers Werke: Kritische Gesamtausgabe: Tischreden.* 6 vols. Weimar: H. Böhlau, 1912–1921.

Chapter 1

Introduction: Rethinking the Human Subject in Martin Luther's Theology

In 1527, plague came to Wittenberg. In a moment where one might expect pastoral care as comfort and consolation, Martin Luther approached the plague's arrival in terms of the Christian moral life. "Godliness," Luther wrote in "Whether One May Flee a Deadly Plague," "is to serve God. To serve God is to serve the neighbor."[1] Luther's connection between godliness and service assumed a kind of interplay between the human soul and body. The godly soul must relate in some way to the body such that moral action in service could occur. Yet, Luther's (in)famous 1517 intervention in the medieval penitential practice of indulgences supposedly problematized this very premise. The problem was sin, which had so corrupted human intellectual and volitional powers as to render them totally powerless in producing good works as godliness or righteousness.[2] How could the Christian, plagued by the effects of sin, produce godliness through service?

A few years earlier in 1520, Luther had attempted an answer. After explicating a new concept of Christian freedom through the soul's passive reception of Christ's righteousness in justification in *The Freedom of a Christian (de libertate Christiana)*, Luther turned to talk about the outer person and the body. This outer person was the domain where the effects

---

1. WA 23:359.15–17.
2. WA 1:225.37.

of sin on the Christian's mind, will, and desires could be felt and seen. Nevertheless, Luther insisted that this was precisely where good works began as the Christian sought to subdue the body and the inner effects of sin it represented, bringing this "outer person" into moral alignment with the new righteousness of the soul. But Luther had a logic problem. If the soul's new righteousness was Christ's and not really its own, how could the "righteous" soul move the sinful body, or outer person? Luther determined that the Christian, caught in this paradox between sin and righteousness, does works "out of spontaneous love."[3] But how does this occur? In the context of late-medieval Scholastic moral theologies that offered highly detailed accounts of the movement between soul and body for moral action, Luther's response was cryptic.

This study takes up this problem of human moral subjectivity after justification in Martin Luther's theological anthropology. In philosophical and theological anthropology, human agency, or subjectivity, involves the human intellect and will working together to motivate and drive human action. Luther's concept of justification by faith alone caused a rift in thinking about the human moral subject in the Christian West. Luther rejected later-Scholastic theologies from the twelfth to the fifteenth centuries that posited a divine-human relationship on the basis of human merit.[4] Luther agreed with the Medievals that God places a moral demand on human persons in the law. God commands love of God for God's own sake above all else. However, Luther thought that original sin rendered the human person capable only of self-love. This incapacity negated law obedience for human merit and endangered the God-human relation. Instead, Luther established more certain grounds for justification in divine activity alone.[5] He determined God's command articulated in the law exposes the human person's sin, accuses her as sinner, and drives her to Christ, who graciously fulfills the law on the human person's behalf. The "justifying God"[6] does everything in the God-human relationship. The human is purely passive.

Luther's theological focus on divine agency appears incompatible with notions of human agency and subjectivity for another reason. By maximizing God as agent, Luther also annihilated the anthropological features that make moral action philosophically possible, namely, human

3. WA 7:60.28.
4. WA 1:224–28.
5. WA 1:364.4–16; 365.2–20.
6. WA 40/2:328.26.

reason and will. The basis for Luther's rejection of human merit in the God-human relation was the ravaging effect of original sin on human moral powers. Sin corrupted the core of the human person. While she remains able to produce certain kinds of acts, like using reason to form judgments or the will to feel and choose certain affections, these acts are corrupted because the person producing them is corrupted. Thus, the human person under sin is unable to judge rightly using reason or to choose the good through the will.[7] Even if reason could judge rightly, Luther thought the human will was bound to its own affections. It could only ever choose to love itself, to satisfy its own pleasures.[8]

This castigation of human moral powers created a problem for ethical action in social relationships because Luther negated the soul's capacity to move the body in moral action. Yet, Luther perennially insisted that moral action, or good works, must result from the God-human relation established in justification. To compensate, Luther glossed over the topic of the soul's moral powers, stating ambiguously in *The Freedom of the Christian* that any good works after justification resulted from Christ's love springing spontaneously from the soul.[9] The result was a further depletion of human moral agency. Not only was the human person totally passive in justification, she also lacked the capacity to move her own body. The body required Christ to somehow move it in good action. Therefore, it seems to be the case that Luther's theological focus on God in Christ usurped any theological, philosophical, or ethical questions related to human agency. This conclusion was the majority scholarly consensus throughout much of the twentieth century.[10]

Recent scholarship on Luther's indebtedness to the Renaissance, medieval philosophy, and mysticism has raised doubts about this previous consensus and created opportunities for locating human moral agency in Luther's thought.[11] Specifically, the *Antinomian Disputations* from 1537–1540 reveal a Luther who is concerned with the question of the ongoing utility of the law for supporting the Christian moral life, meaning

7. WA 1:225.37.
8. WA 1:224.15–19.
9. WA 7:60.28.
10. Althaus, *Gebot und Gesetz*; Ebeling, "Luthers Wirklichkeitsverständnis"; Elert, "Gesetz und Evangelium"; Hägglund, "Luthers Anthropologie"; Holl, "Der Neubau der Sittlichkeit"; Joest, *Ontologie der Person bei Luther*.
11. Helmer, "Introduction"; Holm, *Gabe und Geben*; Leppin, *Fremde Reformation*; White, *Luther as Nominalist*.

the significance of human agency after justification. This text consists of a series of theses framed according to the rules of medieval logic and academic oral debates known as disputations covering a four-year span. It has long been regarded with both curious fascination for the potential insights it contains and, simultaneously, suspicion as an anomaly in Luther's works because his views of human subjectivity seem to contradict his earlier positions on the topic. In this study, I investigate these disputations in order to examine how Luther understood human subjectivity and moral agency in relation to his doctrine of justification.

The *Antinomian Disputations* reflect a Luther who was revisiting the question of law in light of a controversy with his former student Johann Agricola (1494-1566) over the question of *poenitentia* (penitence). Penitence refers to a human act of sorrow for sin and a good intention not to sin in the future. Not only did Luther correct Agricola's conflation of law into gospel for justification, but he also used the opportunity to discuss Christian moral action *after* justification in relation to law. Thus, Luther theorized the significance of law in guiding the Christian's moral life. Furthermore, the notion of human subjectivity that Luther utilized to build his case against Agricola involved revisiting moral and anthropological resources in medieval philosophical theologies. These earlier discussions had to do with philosophical-theological questions about human agency, specifically the notion of how the human will and reason are habituated to the moral life and to God.

Luther's new appropriation of medieval ideas takes place in view of a new emphasis in his theology during the 1530s: the role of the Holy Spirit in stimulating the Christian's moral action, i.e., the doctrine of sanctification.[12] Pneumatology helped Luther to carve out new space for human agency between the anthropological and moral philosophical extremes of the medieval Scholastics and the Antinomians. He thought the Scholastics gave too much moral credit to the human subject *before* justification, placing her salvation at risk and driving despair. The Antinomians, by contrast, gave too much moral credit to the human *after* justification, similarly risking salvation and despair by spurring moral complacency. By increasing the connections between his pneumatology, concept of law, and the human subject, Luther found a new foundation for talking about the temporal effects of the God-human relationship in justification in reviving the human

---

12. WA 30/1:187-92; 45:465-733; 50:599.18-600.2.

person's moral subjectivity. He found a way to better explain how Christ's love springs spontaneously from the soul.

Luther's defense of law contra Agricola hints at the importance of the Holy Spirit for the creation of human moral capacity in relation to the law. In the chapters that follow, I explore the relationship between law, the Holy Spirit, and the human person in Luther's theology. In particular, I examine Luther's specification of the Holy Spirit as the divine agent of both the law and of human vivification and sanctification in the *Antinomian Disputations*. The dual pneumatological function presented in these texts offers possibilities for drawing together law and human agency in Luther's late theology.

This requires the investigation of three interrelated questions. First, how did Luther separate law from gospel contra Agricola while aligning the law to the Spirit and the human person? Luther was particularly interested in how the Christian relates to the law after justification. Therefore, answering this question will require that we reconstruct Luther's understanding of the changing human relationship with and experience of law vis-à-vis the Spirit across distinct moments within Luther's doctrine of justification. The second question moves out of Luther's interest in the human relation to law after gospel: how did Luther conceptualize human action on the law *after* justification in relation to the Spirit? To answer this question, it is necessary to develop greater clarity around Luther's understanding of human sin and righteousness, on the one hand, and how the law supports particular processes for purging sin and developing righteousness in the human person, on the other. The change from sin to righteousness suggests a notion of moral progress or improvement in the human person after justification in relation to the Spirit, i.e., a robust notion of sanctification. Therefore, the third question asks: how did Luther develop his theological anthropology to account for the Spirit's vivifying and sanctifying effects on the human soul in support of the Christian's changing moral status before the law? This inquiry will see us to more closely examine the soul's moral processes in the intellect and will in relation to the indwelling Spirit after justification. By answering these questions, this study contributes to scholarly conversations in Luther research about the anthropological grounds for the moral life.

Questions and Stakes in Modern Luther Scholarship

Questions about the relation between human agency, the Spirit, and the law in Luther's late theology are rooted in a century-long interpretive challenge introduced into scholarship at the start of the *Lutherrenaissance*. In a 1917 lecture at the University of Berlin commemorating the 400th anniversary of the Protestant Reformation, Karl Holl used a Kantian interpretive framework and anti-Catholic polemical stance to determine Luther's unique contribution to the history of Christianity. Holl's lecture was noteworthy because it used newly available primary sources from Luther and the Reformation made available in the recent publication of a critical edition of Luther's works, the *Weimar Ausgabe* (WA). Early volumes of the WA had only recently been released. Work began in 1883 to commemorate another 400th anniversary related to Luther, this time, of his birth.[13] Holl applied the historical-critical method to these original sources to analyze Luther's theological development and found that Luther established a "religion of conscience" (*Gewissensreligion*). Holl used a Kantian framework to identify the epistemological grounds of Luther's *Gewissensreligion*. It was rooted in the direct experience of God in the conscience—not in reason, as Scholasticism had done.[14] Holl concluded that Luther and the religious tradition he initiated were a stark break from the medieval Catholic past.

For Holl, the contrast between a religion of conscience and a religion of reason turned on the doctrine of justification. At stake was whether Luther utilized a merit-based or a grace-based logic. "Reason must maintain the principle that God is pleased with one who strives for a 'blameless' way of life," Holl claimed, linking reason and Scholasticism pejoratively to "works righteousness."[15] For Holl, reason's orientation toward "works righ-

---

13. Initiated in 1883 to commemorate the 400th anniversary of Luther's birth, the *Weimar Ausgabe* (WA), officially titled the *D. Martin Luthers Werke: kritische Gesammtausgabe*, was a by-product of the emerging historical-critical method in German biblical scholarship. The WA provided both historical and text-critical content that allowed (and still allows) Luther scholars to interpret Luther's writings in their historical context while comparing multiple versions of both written and verbal content to assess authenticity. Prior to the publication of the WA, the story of Luther and Lutheranism centered on the Lutheran confessional writings and the tradition received from Lutheran orthodoxy. Work on the WA lasted 126 years, reflecting the vastness of Luther's theological corpus and complexity of the text critical challenges it presents. The most recent volume was published in 2009.

14. Holl, *Was Verstand Luther unter Religion?*, 48–49.

15. Holl, *Was Verstand Luther unter Religion?*, 37.

teousness" made God's concern for the sinner incomprehensible. When Holl explicitly connected the works righteousness of a religion of reason to the theology and rituals of Roman Catholicism, he determined that Luther "differed decisively" in his emphasis on the transcendental concepts of personal freedom and conviction.[16] In this evaluation, Holl's anti-Catholic polemic combined with his Kantian idealism. He concluded that Luther's psychological understanding of religion was at odds with the moral underpinnings of the medieval Catholic theology Luther had rejected.

Holl located Luther's radical discontinuity from medieval Catholicism in his rediscovery of the absolute divine command and human incapacity to fulfill it.[17] This led Luther, per Holl, to theorize ways to reestablish the God-human relationship that resolved the human incapacity to satisfy the divine command. Holl determined that Luther solved this problem by grounding the God-human relationship in God's action toward the believer alone. In Luther's "religion of conscience," God's commands in the law operated at a psychological level to create the "psychological pre-conditions" for faith. The law made the sinner *aware* of her sins. The resulting psychological suffering and despair could then bring the sinner to God in faith.[18]

On the human person's part, Holl interpreted faith paradoxically as an "extremely active" passivity.[19] He described active passivity in faith as a total inwardness, as absolute trust (*unbedingtes Vertrauen*) in divine goodness despite the appearance and experience of God's actions as unintelligible and terrifying.[20] In Holl's reading, this made Luther's God unceasingly creative. God was working in human hearts even though divine activity was undiscernible to the senses and known only in the conscience through faith.[21] As Graham White has shown, this interpretation had to do with

16. Holl, *Was Verstand Luther unter Religion?*, 50.
17. Holl, *Was Verstand Luther unter Religion?*, 57.
18. Holl, *Was Verstand Luther unter Religion?*, 15, 35, 85.
19. Holl, *Was Verstand Luther unter Religion?*, 95n2.
20. Marit Trelstad has called attention to the resemblance of Luther's law/gospel structure to incident-reconciliation cycles in domestic violence. Holl's portrayal of faith echoes another form of domestic abuse known as gaslighting. According to the American Psychological Association's *Dictionary of Psychology*, gaslighting is a colloquial term referring to a form of extreme psychological manipulation that causes a victim to doubt their own thoughts, perceptions, and experiences. Gaslighting is a tactic associated with antisocial personality disorder and one which builds a victim's dependence on an abuser and thereby reinforces the abuser's power and control over a victim. See Trelstad, "Charity Terror Begins at Home"; "Gaslight."
21. "Luther sah nun Gott tätig nich bloss im Mummenschanz der äuseren Kratur,

a radical reorientation of Luther's religious language. Luther's medieval scholastic semantic theory was realist, meaning terms referred to real things. However, the idealist turn in Holl's reading saw terms to refer to mental concepts in Luther's religious language.[22] Thus, faith came to represent the *cognitive* overcoming of human experiential understanding of God as terror in favor of an equally psychological trust in divine goodness the human person could not otherwise experience. By framing Luther's theology in these cognitive-psychological terms, Holl reduced the human moral agent to a total dependence on God in the mind.

Holl's groundbreaking introduction of a historical methodology into Luther research propelled the use of historical questions and Kantian, anti-Catholic interpretations in Luther scholarship during much of the twentieth century.[23] The methodological questions became: "When did Luther make his Reformation discovery?"; "How do we identify it?"; and "How does it distinguish Protestantism from Catholicism?" The impact of these questions on scholarship translated into a bias toward the interpretive authority of the early Luther over the late Luther, a de-emphasis on the embodied, empirical subject over a psychological one, and a hermeneutic of discontinuity that approaches Luther's thought as a "breakthrough."

Just prior to the start of World War II, Werner Elert took Holl's Kantian conscience-motif to its logical conclusion in his concept of the "transcendental I." Elert understood the "transcendental I" as the "pure I," the Self that "cannot be further qualified in an empirico-psychological manner."[24] Elert separated the transcendental self from a person's empirical, embodied existence in the world. In fact, the gulf between the transcendental I and the empirical person was so great that Elert depicted embodiment as a threat: the empirical self could invalidate the benefits of faith in the transcendental I, which constitute its very being. In this regard, Elert claimed that

---

sondern im Innern der Menschenherzen. Wohl war hier sein Wirken ebenso sinnenfällig, wie das in der sichtbaren Welt. Nur der Glaube vermochte etwas davon zu schauen. Aber es war doch dasjenige Werk, das Gott als sein eigentlichstes trieb. Und es fehlte nicht an Spuren, wo man das Walten seines Zorns wie seiner Gnade in den Geschicken der Menschheit warnehmen konnte" (Holl, *Was Verstand Luther unter Religion?*, 100).

22. White, *Luther as Nominalist*, 145.

23. A number of recent studies have clarified Holl's impact on contemporary interpretations of Luther. See Assel, *Karl Holl*; Helmer and Holm, *Lutherrenaissance*; Helmer, *How Luther Became the Reformer*.

24. Elert, *Structure of Lutheranism*, 412.

> Christ's righteousness is my righteousness because the Word pertains to me. *But it pertains to me only if this righteousness remains unentangled with my empirical existence.* Faith, which hears this Word, has no other function than this hearing *and exists only by hearing.*[25]

By setting the transcendental self in radical antithesis to the empirical self, Elert perpetuated and escalated the separation between faith and good works in the body in Luther's thought. The separation of the transcendent and empirical self became a key structuring principle to be found in Luther's theology.

After the Second World War, Paul Althaus more explicitly connected the Kantian conscious subject to the interplay of faith and works.[26] In both his *Die Theologie Martin Luthers* (1962) and *Die Ethik Martin Luthers* (1965), Althaus took seriously a "new obedience" that results from faith.[27] After the experience of justification, Althaus claimed that the "certainty of salvation" leads to an "inner necessity to 'works.'"[28] Yet, Althaus took the locus of this activity as psychological, resulting from a change in the conscious subject—in her self-understanding as justified and a resulting "joyful service" to God. When Althaus considered this service as a moral-ethical activity, new obedience was separate from faith, neither "causing nor preserving" salvation for us.[29] Instead, new obedience operated again at an epistemological register to confirm and validate the existence of faith in and to the conscience. While Althaus took seriously the prospect of behavioral changes in the Christian's moral-ethical activity, he restricted these to the temporal realm as service to the neighbor across the three estates of social relations Luther identified, *ecclesia-oeconomia-politia.*[30]

Like Elert and Ebeling, Althaus also denied association between new obedience and moral improvement in the Christian moral subject. The real purpose of new obedience for Althaus was self-awareness as voluntary self-annihilation. New obedience does not create an "ethical high point" in the Christian life. Instead, new obedience reflects the depths of the total emptying of the self. It is a total loss of trust in oneself and the total desire

---

25. Elert, *Structure of Lutheranism*, 412 (emphasis added).
26. Althaus, *Gebot und Gesetz*, 32.
27. Althaus, *Theologie Martin Luthers*, 213–17; Althaus, *Ethik Martin Luthers*, 18–25.
28. Althaus, *Theologie Martin Luthers*, 214.
29. Althaus, *Theologie Martin Luthers*, 213.
30. Althaus, *Ethik Martin Luthers*, 43–48.

to drive out the sinful self. As Althaus understood it, justification does not produce moral change in the subject but rather a desire to be free of sin so strong that one is "ready and willing to die."[31] The partial opening to moral action in Althaus's interpretation does not correspond to a biblical notion of renewal of the self in the Spirit that one might anticipate in Luther. Instead, Althaus extended the denial and destruction of the moral self in Christ. New obedience came to connote the total dependence of the conscious subject, not her moral capacity.

In the 1970s and 1980s, Gerhard Ebeling's analysis of Luther's theological anthropology in his expansive four-volume tome, *Lutherstudien*, solidified the Kantian understanding of the human subject. Building on Holl's interest in Luther's so-called "reformation breakthrough," Ebeling sought a hermeneutical framework for understanding Luther and isolated scriptural principles in Luther's biblical exegesis in the early lectures on the Psalms (1513–1515).[32] Ebeling's discovery led him to elevate the *early* Luther as interpretively normative for all of Luther's theology and perpetuated the *Lutherrenaissance's* implicit anti-Catholic polemic that valued Luther's *theological* insights over his philosophical ones.[33]

---

31. The immediate context demonstrates Althaus's understanding of this claim in light of the transcendent self, not an elevation to corporeal self-harm. However, Althaus's interpretation has dangerous implications in light of contemporary understanding of mental health risks, theologically authorizing and valorizing an ethos of (psychological) self-harm. In relation to the Christian life as *simul iustus et peccator*, Althaus regulated the Christian life through the daily enactment of this ethos, stating that "the constant renewal of my surrender to God's working in me results in the progressive death of the old man and the resurrection of the new man." This led Althaus to a theory of self-annihilation, that "Luther, however, did not understand perfection as an ethical high point but as the depths in which a man loses all trust in himself and purely and strongly desires to be completely free from sin and to be completely one with God's will, that is, he is ready and willing to die" (Althaus, *Theology of Martin Luther*, 245). The German states: "Luther aber nicht al seine sittliche Höhe versteht, sondern als die Tiefe, in der alles Vertrauen des Menschen auf sich selbst gestorben ist, als das gereifte starke Verlangen, ganz von der Sünde frei zu werden, ganz eins mit Gottes Willen—daher die Bereitschaft und das Begehren zu sterben" (Althaus, *Theologie Martin Luthers*, 213). In this regard, Althaus follows Holl, who also began his study of Luther's ethics with the claim that self-judgment is at the heart of Luther's moral-ethical teaching. See Holl, "Der Neubau der Sittlichkeit," 155.

32. Ebeling, *Lutherstudien*, 1:3.

33. In his treatment of philosophy, Ebeling extends Holl's association between the "religion of reason" and medieval Scholastic theology, taking the position of a hermeneutic of discontinuity.

In his most important contribution to current understandings of Luther's anthropology, Ebeling applied Elert's Kantian interpretation of the "transcendent I" to Luther's theological and philosophical analysis of the human subject. Working from the interpretive finality of Luther's early theological insights about the human person, Ebeling analyzed the theses for Luther's 1536 *Disputatio de homine*. He determined Luther's views in this "late" work were predicated upon an absolute dialectic between theology and philosophy.[34] In an explicitly Kantian framework, Ebeling argued that theology in Luther's thought has to do with *cognition* of God.[35] This means that, while philosophy can speak of the temporal person and her moral action, theology takes the heavenly, eschatological person as its object.[36] In the way Ebeling applied Elert's framework of the transcendent and empirical selves to theology and philosophy, he ruptured theology from human moral subjectivity altogether.

Ebeling interpreted Luther to say that theology can only speak of the human person in her temporal, empirical existence as sinner.[37] In fact, as Ebeling read Luther, the only thing theology can say about the temporal human person or the soul's moral powers is to name sin and to describe incapacity. This conclusion extended methodologically to restrict Luther's theological anthropology to a set of external relations to God and Christ as those relations were established by faith.[38] This put theology and philosophy fundamentally at odds in Luther's thought. Either one spoke philosophically of the human person and thus kept the soul's moral powers and subjectivity in view, or one spoke biblically and theologically about the human person as sinner in herself or justified in relation to God in Christ.[39] Thus, Ebeling presented Luther as shutting down the question of human moral subjectivity on disciplinary grounds. Reason and volition were philosophical categories and pertained only to the human person's temporal, empirical existence in the world.

Ebeling also applied a Kantian framework to ontological questions about the effect of justification on the human subject. He was interested in clarifying the effect of the exchange of Christ's and human natures in

---

34. Ebeling, *Lutherstudien*, 1:33–34.
35. Ebeling, *Lutherstudien*, 1:35.
36. Ebeling, *Lutherstudien*, 1:36.
37. Ebeling, *Lutherstudien*, 1:37.
38. Ebeling, *Lutherstudien*, 1:185–86.
39. Ebeling, *Lutherstudien*, 1:186–87.

Luther's doctrine of justification. Ebeling tested "conventional ontology" as a way of "establishing the general conditions of being as the basis for movement and change."[40] But here, Ebeling's modern reliance on Kantian notions of being as consciousness conflicted with Luther's medieval understandings of being and change through Aristotelian categories. Ebeling denied the exchange of natures created any substantial change in the human person because he prioritized the conscious subject.[41] Ebeling isolated the preposition "*coram*" (before) as the key distinction between "traditional ontologies" and Luther's "ontological intention."[42] Building on Elert's dialectic between the transcendent and empirical self, Ebeling used this notion of *coram* to isolate *relational* categories that determined the human subject's temporal and eschatological conscious existence.

Ebeling understood these *coram* relations as ontologically constitutive of human subjectivity. He determined that Luther's usage of *coram* had to do with forums of intersubjective relations in human life—the person before God (*coram Deo*), before others (*coram mundo*), and before oneself (*coram meipso*). "The preposition *coram* ensures that even in ontology the human person does not evade one's own being-in-relation and therefore does not ignore the circumstances and relationships in which he lives."[43] This meant the exchange of natures had to do with a change in relations *coram Deo* but not in Aristotelian terms as a change in the person's substance. God came to relate to the human person as though she were righteous. The subject also underwent a change in relation to herself, *coram meipso*. As a conscious subject, she came to *understand herself* as sinner even while she remained empirically unchanged as herself.

Although Luther supposedly rejected the philosophical underpinnings of his own day, Ebeling followed Elert to locate a distinctly modern philosophical method in Luther's "relational ontology": a Kantian one. Luther's "relational ontology" grounded being in intersubjective consciousness. How I look at others, how they look at me, thus impacts how I look at myself, forming a "highly complex process for consciousness constitutive of being."[44] Determined *a priori* by scripture, Ebeling posited

---

40. Ebeling, "Luthers Wirklichkeitsverständnis," 416.
41. Ebeling, "Luthers Wirklichkeitsverständnis," 411.
42. Ebeling, "Luthers Wirklichkeitsverständnis," 416.
43. Ebeling, "Luthers Wirklichkeitsverständnis," 416–17 (translation mine).
44. Ebeling, "Luthers Wirklichkeitsverständnis," 417. Ebeling's conceptualization of a "relational ontology" has to do with the reinterpretation of Luther's realist semantics in

the human's passive relation to God "*coram Deo*" as a special theological extension of ontology into the eschatological realm. Here, the relation is determined by divine pronouncements. Either the human person is sinner or is righteous.[45] In *Lutherstudien*, Ebeling articulated this idea in existential terms; either the person is *Sein* (redeemed by external relation to God) or *Nichtsein* (nonexistent apart from the relation to God).[46] In Ebeling's relational ontology, neo-Kantian interest in consciousness and the eschaton won out over more medieval questions about substantial effects of the God-human relation on the human person's moral faculties—her intellect, volition, and affections. Thus, Ebeling's analysis sidelined the question of sanctification, or works after justification, in Luther because the only aspect of the human that mattered was the human's eschatological relation to God as the basis for being.

On the topic of law, Werner Elert used Hegelian notions of dialectic popularized by the Tübingen School to locate a strong opposition between law and gospel in Luther's thought. This dialectic worked alongside the neo-Kantian conscience-motif introduced through Holl's *Gewissensreligion* concept. The binary view of law and gospel supplied mechanisms in the form of divine speech acts by which the conscious subject could come to know herself. Elert, responding to Karl Barth, asserted that before a person can understand the gospel, she must know about law as an operative reality permeating all of human life.[47] In this reality, she stands condemned as a sinner. This self-knowledge as condemned sinner before the law creates the preconditions necessary for a person to know and accept by faith the divine grace offered in the gospel.

Barth advocated a view of law as an act of grace, a divine self-disclosure that preempted and undercut human action in the form of openness to God. In the context of widespread acceptance of Nazism among German Lutherans, Barth took this gracious act of divine self-disclosure to reveal an order of gospel-then-law.[48] However, Elert parted ways with

---

idealist terms that White has identified. See White, *Luther as Nominalist*, 19–20.

45. Ebeling, "Luthers Wirklichkeitsverständnis," 418–19.

46. Ebeling, *Lutherstudien*, 2:267. Joest utilized similar existential language in Joest, *Ontologie der Person bei Luther*, 273.

47. Elert, "Gesetz und Evangelium," 138–39.

48. Recent scholarship has examined the impact of Nazi-aligned theologians on the shape of modern Luther research. See Heschel, *Aryan Jesus*; Probst, *Demonizing the Jews*.

Barth and determined that life after the gospel is free from law as a life of spontaneity and freedom.[49]

Barth's question about the order of gospel then law spurred more debates after World War II. This time, however, the question was a more targeted debate over a third use of law, or whether there was a use of law after gospel.[50] Operating on the Hegelian dialectic and a Kantian repudiation of the empirical self, Elert refuted Barth's positive proposal for a third use by framing the law/gospel dialectic as essential to a Pauline-Lutheran understanding.[51] The *Antinomian Disputations* emerged as a critical text at the center of this increasingly caustic debate.[52] At question were several sentences at the end of the second disputation in which Luther appeared to define three uses of law.[53] Following Holl's historical critical method, Elert turned to text criticism. He concluded these sentences represented a textual anomaly present in only two of the nine manuscripts of the disputation. Reminiscent of the historical controversies between the Gnesio-Lutherans and the Philippists that questioned the authenticity of Melanchthon's reformation theology, Elert declared these sentences to be a later editorial addition by one of Melanchthon's students extracted from Melanchthon's 1535 *Loci*.[54] Luther's possible positive articulation of a role for law after gospel was deemed a forgery, aligning the topic of law more closely to the cognitive subject and her self-awareness than the empirical subject and her moral action.

In 1960, Gerhard Ebeling repeated the forgery thesis on the basis that law was restricted in Luther's thought to divine agency. When Ebeling sought Luther's hermeneutical principle for the concept of law, he prioritized the interpretive authority of the early Luther. He discovered a normative use of

---

49. Barth, *Evangelium und Gesetz*; Elert, "Gesetz und Evangelium," 157.

50. Lund recapitulates this century-long debate in detail in Lund, "Luther's 'Third Use of Law,'" 9–62.

51. Elert, "Gesetz und Evangelium," 168.

52. Althaus, *Gebot und Gesetz*; Ebeling, *Wort und Glaube*, 1:50–68; Elert, "Gesetz und Evangelium"; Joest, *Gesetz und Freiheit*.

53. Cf. WA 39/1:485.16–24.

54. Elert, "Eine Theologische Fälschung," 168–70; "Gesetz und Evangelium," 161–62. Elert's forgery thesis continues to be repeated by several scholars as a means of disqualifying Luther's approach to law in the *Antinomian Disputations*. Lund has convincingly challenged Elert's claim, demonstrating greater evidence for a deletion thesis—that the text was edited down from its original. However, Lund's view has not received broad recognition. See Lund, "Luther's 'Third Use of the Law,'" 223–42.

a *duplex usus* in Luther's 1522 *Church Postilles*, a series of sample sermons Luther wrote for Protestant ministers to use in their preaching.⁵⁵ In this "early Luther" source, Ebeling found only two uses of law. He applied this hermeneutical principle of the young Luther to the question of a third use of law in the *Antinomian Disputations* and affirmed Elert's conclusion. Like Elert, Ebeling also echoed the Gnesio-Lutheran appeal to "true" Lutheranism and rejected Melanchthon's potential influence on Luther's later thought. He used Luther's earlier 1522 text to explain away similarities between Melanchthon's *triplex usus legis* in the 1535 Loci and Luther's new formulation of the law across five *Antinomian Disputations*. Ebeling did admit, however, that Luther's distinction between the pious and impious relation to law in the *Disputations* warranted further research.⁵⁶

In more contemporary scholarship on Luther's concept of law, Timothy Wengert transmitted the Elert-Ebeling Hegelian dialectic and the acerbic tenor of their debate. In his 1997 monograph *Law and Gospel*, Wengert repeated the forgery thesis, noting antagonistically that "the modern debate over whether Luther in fact (if not in name) taught a third use of the law reflects later Lutheran controversies and historians' inability to understand the center of his theology."⁵⁷ Whether or not historians have the intellectual capacity to understand theology (though one should suppose they do), a number of well-regarded theologians and Luther scholars have challenged the Elert-Ebeling-Wengert interpretation. Wilfried Joest and Paul Althaus both drew out elements in Luther's theology that deconstruct the dialectical view of law/gospel.⁵⁸ Similarly, Jeffrey Silcock concluded that despite the

55. Ebeling, *Wort und Glaube*, 1:50; cf. Elert, "Gesetz und Evangelium," 167–69.

56. Ebeling, *Wort und Glaube*, 1:67; cf. Lund, "Luther's 'Third Use of the Law,'" 12.

57. Wengert, *Law and Gospel*, 192. Based on Lund's reconstruction, the abusive tone appears to have been set by Ebeling, who during the Fifth International Congress for Luther Research held in Lund, Sweden (1977), reportedly stonewalled a consensus among other scholars that Luther operated with an implicit third use of the law. See Lund, "Luther's 'Third Use of the Law,'" 44. The fervor with which some scholars are committed to rejecting a third use of the law in Luther, whether implicit or explicit, appears to legitimize appeals to counterfactuals. Even in the peer review of this study, a colleague with highly technical knowledge of the subject rejected the view of law presented here based on a claim that Luther did not have a third use of the law when he supposedly wrote the Formula of Concord in 1577. Luther died in 1546, making this peer reviewer's claim historically improbable.

58. See Althaus, *Theology of Martin Luther*, 261–66; Joest, *Gesetz und Freiheit*, 74. Both Althaus and Joest called for a full study of the series of disputations that makes up the *Antinomian Disputations*, noting the significance of these texts in clarifying Luther's understanding of law and gospel as theological constellations.

terminological absence of "tertius usus legis" in Luther's thought, the Reformer nevertheless possessed a concept of law consistent with a third use as used by Melanchthon and later the Formula of Concord.[59] Nevertheless, the Elert-Ebeling-Wengert trajectory represents the widely accepted view of law in Luther scholarship today.

The *Lutherrenaissance* spurred a transcendental and polemical interpretive narrative in modern Luther scholarship that perpetuates an incomplete, distorted picture of Luther's understanding of the human moral subject. The result has been an interpretive ethos in modern scholarship that restricts Luther's concept of law to a notion of divine accusation and its corresponding rejection of good works. In this model, faith under the rubric of gospel remains as the only viable anthropological category to speak of the human subject in theological terms.[60]

Faith was always a central topic in Luther's theology.[61] Yet, Luther's concept of faith never led him to understand the human self in faith as blank, vacuous, or disembodied. This is a distinctly modern, post-enlightenment understanding of the human person that is ahistorically read back onto Luther. A transcendent, disembodied self would have been foreign ideas to Luther, particularly in light of the *medieval* philosophical and theological underpinnings of his worldview. Rather, in conversation with Scholastic theologians going back to Lombard, Luther located a robust and dynamic human subject in faith vis-à-vis her relation to the Holy Spirit. This study helps to correct the interpretive framework by drawing attention to these additional aspects of Luther's understanding of human moral subjectivity.

Opportunities

Current scholarly discussions in Luther research aim at moving past these historical, methodological, and interpretive challenges. My analysis of Luther's theological anthropology in the *Antinomian Disputations* contributes another source of insight for resolving these issues. The *Antinomian Disputations* are crucial for this conversation in several ways. First, the

---

59. Silcock, "Luther and the Third Use of the Law," 126–27.

60. For example, Bayer wrote, "The pinnacle anthropological definition [is]: 'Humans are consequently human in that they need justification by faith.' Faith is not something *in* the human in addition to it but rather is its being itself" (Bayer, "Being in the Image of God," 77).

61. Hamm, *Reformation of Faith*, 172.

Disputations contribute to efforts to move past interpretive difficulties for human subjectivity in Luther's anthropology because Luther thematized the Holy Spirit. The Spirit is traditionally associated with human sanctification after justification. Thus, Luther's attention to this doctrine in the *Disputations* has significance for reconsidering works after justification in ways that reintegrate the human psychological and embodied subject and look for her regeneration via the Spirit rather than her self-destruction.

After Regin Prenter's 1953 publication of *Spiritus Creator*, several works in the past two decades have attended more carefully to Luther's trinitarian theology of the Holy Spirit. Pekka Kärkkäinen's monograph, *Luthers trinitarische Theologie des Heiligen Geistes*, represents the most substantial contribution to this effort. Kärkkäinen shed light on the ways Luther developed a picture of the Spirit through trinitarian themes drawn from late-medieval thought. In the outer Trinity, Kärkkäinen saw Luther to emphasize the Spirit's indwelling presence as a gift of love, pointing to the Spirit's regenerative possibilities for human affective capacity.[62] Theodor Dieter also explored a similar late-medieval background of the Spirit as divine love based on Luther's marginalia on Lombard's *Sentences*. Dieter examined Luther's questions about the need for a created structure (*etwas Geschaffenes*) in the soul that makes possible the Spirit's indwelling in the human person as love.[63] In this way, both studies bring greater attention to Luther's pneumatology as a source for greater insight into Luther's anthropology of the regenerate soul and for doing so in light of Luther's engagement with pressing theological questions in medieval Scholasticism.

This study builds on Kärkkäinen and Dieter, showing that Luther carefully detailed the Spirit's relation to the human soul's affective dimensions in the *Antinomian Disputations* vis-à-vis the *effects* and consequences of justification by faith. Moreover, Luther did so using concepts from medieval mysticism, which Volker Leppin and Jonathan Reinert have shown to fundamentally shape Luther's understanding of the God-human relationship and human spirituality.[64] Therefore, these texts offer a new way of understanding the Spirit's relation to and impact on the human soul after justification in Luther's thought.

Second, Luther's formulation of the Spirit in relation to the law in the *Antinomian Disputations* permits different questions than those of the

---

62. Kärkkäinen, *Luthers trinitarische Theologie*, 111.
63. Dieter, "Du mußt den Geist haben!," 69.
64. Leppin, *Fremde Reformation*; Reinert, *Passionspredigt*.

third use of the law that have kept scholarship on these critical texts at loggerheads for nearly a century. In the *Disputations*, Luther depicted the Spirit as granting anthropological efficacy to the law and did so within the temporal realm—the very region of human existence dismissed and denigrated in the Kantian discourse of German Luther research related to the transcendent self in faith. In drawing out this connection, the current study participates in efforts by Norman Lund and Phil Anderas to move past unproductive and antagonistic debates to set the *Antinomian Disputations* within accepted conceptual frameworks across Luther's writings during this period. Lund's unpublished dissertation established that Luther came at the question of the law in the Christian life from different angles in each of the *Antinomian Disputations*. Taken together, Lund found a coherent and consistent argument about the law's positive role in the Christian life built across the four disputations.[65] More recently, Anderas has shown how a notion of sin, grace, and an "Augustinian simul" provide an internal structure across the *Disputations* that hold Luther's logic about the law and human action together.[66] Both authors set the *Disputations* into conversation with Luther's other writings from the same period, showing how he worked out aspects of his arguments for the *Disputations* in other settings and also applied conclusions drawn during the debates with Agricola in his teachings for other audiences. The broader reading of law in these contextualized studies aligns with Sun Young Kim's suggestion that Luther's ideas about the law were already expanding at the time of his 1531 *Lectures on Galatians*.[67]

Third, Luther's adoption of medieval theological metaphors and categories from philosophical-theological anthropology in the *Antinomian Disputations* places him back into his late-medieval context. This contextualization helps to resolve Holl's interpretive legacy that emphasizes Luther's sharp discontinuity with the Middle Ages and the Catholic theology indicted therein.[68] In order to explain the Spirit's presence in and relation to the human soul after justification, Luther adopted and revised medieval moral psychologies. These psychologies described human moral action through the interplay of the will, intellect, and their powers. Luther used these categories to specify the Spirit's effect on and in the human soul. Careful

---

65. Lund, "Luther's 'Third Use of the Law,'" 355.
66. Anderas, *Renovatio*, 82.
67. Kim, *Luther on Faith and Love*, 161.
68. See Helmer, "Introduction," 4.

examination of the ways Luther redeployed these concepts offers insight into his life-long conversation with medieval Scholastic theology. It also adds nuance to our understanding of his contributions in the shift toward modern subjectivities, dispelling the narrative of radical discontinuity. This adds an anthropological and pneumatological angle to the work of Graham White, Risto Saarinen, Pekka Kärkkäinen, Theodor Dieter, and Aaron Moldenhauer who have shown Luther's continuity with late-medieval theology in the areas of disputational logic, philosophical anthropology, Aristotelian philosophy, and Christology.[69]

Furthermore, careful examination of these disputations helps to resolve a problematic methodological emphasis on the young Luther. This emphasis has led to corresponding interpretive commitments that grant the young Luther canonical status over the experience-informed insights of Luther's later writings. The *Antinomian Disputations* represent a four-year span in Luther's late theology, which makes them a fruitful test case for assessing conceptual development, consistency, and coherence in this late period.

Several studies have shown this was a time of significant development in other areas of Luther's thought as the University of Wittenberg theology faculty revived the practice of *disputatio* and reinvigorated the use of logic and philosophy for theological argumentation.[70] In his book *Luther as Nominalist*, Graham White analyzed Ebeling's understanding of the role of logic and semantic relations in Luther's disputations. He found that Ebeling got the format of disputations wrong because he assumed incorrectly that theses proposed for a disputation linked together to form an overall argument.[71] According to White, however, the rules of the late-medieval gameplay held that theses are only expositions of positions to be defended. Because the goal was to trick an opponent into logical error, theses were written with this goal in mind and not to outline a coherent argument or position.[72] This insight is paradigm-shifting when it comes to scholarly understanding of Luther's anthropology. The significance lies in the fact that Ebeling's analysis of Luther's *Disputatio de homine* is taken as the definitive interpretation, but Ebeling worked only with the

---

69. White, *Luther as Nominalist*; Saarinen, *Weakness of Will*, 119–30; "Ipsa Dilectio Deus Est," 199–202; Kärkkäinen, "Luther's Theological Psychology"; Dieter, *Der junge Luther und Aristotles*; Moldenhauer, "Analyzing the Verba Christi," 47–64.

70. Helmer, *Trinity and Martin Luther*; White, *Luther as Nominalist*.

71. White, *Luther as Nominalist*, 24.

72. White, *Luther as Nominalist*, 26.

theses for the disputation and assumed those theses represented Luther's overarching position. The pairing of theses and arguments together in the *Antinomian Disputations* means they provide a more complete picture of the semantic and causal relations Luther understood vis-à-vis the human subject. The genre of *disputatio* also means that Luther employed philosophy, specifically Aristotelian causality, in order to articulate and develop his theological understanding of the Spirit's relation to the human soul. This is significant because of the way Ebeling interpreted theology to supersede philosophical notions of human personhood using causal categories. The *Antinomian Disputations* sees the mature Luther to bring these regions of human inquiry back into conversation.

By carefully examining the connections between the Spirit, law, and human soul in Luther's thought, this study participates in larger efforts within Luther research to rehabilitate dimensions of human agency in Luther's thought and Lutheran theology more broadly. Volker Leppin, Gustaf Wingren, Kirsi Stjerna, and Deanna Thompson have located agency in other areas such as human experience in mystical union, in political/social relationships through vocation, and as a development of Augustine's definition of the self.[73] Bo Kristian Holm's research in particular has sought out agency in Luther's reception of Renaissance concepts, gift and reciprocity. Holm locates human agency in a socially articulated reciprocity by which the human gives God honor.[74] His approach is particularly relevant to the current study because in the *Antinomian Disputations* Luther envisions the Christian's moral action using these kinds of social relations via the gift concept.

Beyond Luther research, the study of religion more generally offers vital theoretical resources for approaching this problem of human subjectivity in Luther's theology in light of Luther's theological-philosophical position in late-medieval Nominalism and the *via Moderna*. Martha Nussbaum and John Corrigan have shown that the emotions play a vital role in motivating moral action and religious experience.[75] Birgit Stolt has applied emotions research to her linguistic analysis of Luther and shown that affective language is a significant force in Luther's theological

---

73. Leppin, "Transformationen"; Wingren, *Luther on Vocation*; Stjerna and Thompson, *On the Apocalyptic*.

74. Holm, *Gabe und Geben bei Luther*, 238.

75. Nussbaum, *Political Emotions*; Corrigan, "Introduction," 3–31.

thought.⁷⁶ This study draws from these theoretical perspectives to determine how Luther's theological-philosophical thinking on the human affect can be seen to spur human activity by connecting human emotions to Luther's concept of law and the Spirit.

Methodology

A comprehensive study of the scope of Luther's work would make an ideal method for analyzing human moral agency in his thought. The reality of Luther research, however, is that such a methodology has been the downfall of more than a few scholarly investigations. The scope of primary and secondary literature is simply too expansive. Luther was one of the most prolific theologians in Western history and left behind between 60,000 and 80,000 pages of text.⁷⁷ A comprehensive and careful theological analysis of such copious material is simply not feasible in a single study. The primary material must be limited in some way. A second factor is that Luther utilized a variety of literary forms in his writings that ranged from the pastoral (sermons, catechisms, prayer books), to academic (lectures, commentaries, treatises, disputations), to personal (letters, table talks). Each genre necessitates a unique methodology that further implicates the need to limit the scope of study.

Complicating matters, Luther is one of the most widely researched figures in Western history. The secondary literature is expansive and much of it is deeply flawed. For example, the topic of law/gospel, which is relevant to this project, is well-worn terrain that scholars continue to debate without many new insights. For these reasons, I chose to limit both primary and secondary sources to only the most critical texts. Secondary sources cited in footnotes were selected using two parameters: first, the paradigmatic texts, typically German, that orient the ongoing conversation; and second, more recent sources who have new or important insights for this topic. In the latter group, I seek to give voice to a more international, diverse, and gender-inclusive class of scholars. A more robust bibliography is included at the end of this volume.

---

76. Stolt, *Laßt uns fröhlich springen!*

77. Based on estimates for the critical edition of Luther's work, known as the *Weimar Ausgabe*, which includes 121 volumes with most volumes exceeding 500 pages and many with well over 600 pages.

The primary text for investigating Luther's notion of human agency in this study is Luther's *Antinomian Disputations* from 1537 to 1540. This text is important for this topic because Luther revisited the topic of *poenitentia* as human action on the law—the very topic he used to problematize human agency in his early polemics against Scholastic theology in the 1510s. However, in 1537 he did so with new theological resource: a robust pneumatology. His expanded pneumatology allowed him to approach the subject in new ways. Shifts and developments in Luther's thinking about the human person and moral action after justification emerge out of Luther's historical circumstances. Therefore, I connect these *Disputations* to several of Luther's other writings from the 1530s and the so-called "Reformation breakthrough" period (1517–20), building points of comparison and coherence that lend context and clarity to my argument. Luther discussed good works in the Christian life in multiple texts after 1530. However, the *Antinomian Disputations* occurred over a four-year period, meaning these texts offer the most sustained and expansive development of this topic in Luther's late theology.

Moreover, Luther developed his arguments about human moral action in proximity to the topic of law. This means that the *Antinomian Disputations* reflect a situation in which Luther revisited one of the most important topics from his early controversies with Rome. Between 1515 and 1520, Luther used the topic of human moral action on the law to critique and then differentiate himself from late-Scholastic theology and medieval piety, but he framed these early critiques in relation to Christ. When Luther returned to this topic in the *Antinomian Disputations*, he positioned the conversation in relation to the Holy Spirit, which allowed him to resolve his earlier points of critique in new ways. Thus, the *Antinomian Disputations* offer insights into an underlying structure available in Luther's theology for constructing a notion of human moral agency *after* justification, and for doing so in light of Luther's relation to Catholicism.

This study also references a number of Luther's other writings to provide both historical and conceptual context. Two critical texts for positioning the *Antinomian Disputations* historically are Luther's *Lectures on Galatians* (1531/35) and Luther's expositions for his *Sermons on John* (1537). The *Lectures on Galatians* are considered the *locus classicus* for Luther's law/gospel paradigm. They set the conceptual stage for drawing out the elements in Luther's own theology that influenced Agricola's antinomianism. These *Lectures* also inflect the developments in Luther's thinking on the topic of human agency in relation to law and gospel. The scriptural expositions Luther prepared in 1537 for his *Sermons on John* are pivotal for historically contextualizing Luther's position on law and the Spirit in the *Antinomian Disputations*. Luther began more fully discussing the role of the Spirit after the 1527 Church Visitations and in light of his 1530 sermon strike spurred by moral laxity among his parishioners.[78] However, his 1537 sermon expositions during the liturgical season of Pentecost reveal new developments in Luther's understanding of the Spirit's connection to the law on the basis of scripture. Given in the months when the antinomian controversy with Agricola was brewing, these sermons provide critical contextual insights for understanding Luther's new anthropological claims in the disputations.

Several texts from Luther's early controversies are also important for illustrating the embryonic stages of the anthropological concepts Luther used in 1537. The *Disputation against Scholastic Theology* (1517) and the *Bondage of the Will* (1525) are two paradigmatic texts in which Luther critiqued and distinguished himself from the medieval Scholastic position on the human person's moral powers. These texts reveal Luther's focus on the human capacity to both correctly judge and then will what is morally good. Yet, in both texts, Luther left openings for the possibility of good works resulting from justification, but his framing of good works in proximity to Christ meant he lacked the right theological tools to find fitting answers. In 1517 and 1525, Luther did not yet have a robust doctrine of the Holy Spirit to help make sense of good works after justification. In 1537, when his pneumatology was more robust, he also returned to other moral concepts: original and actual sin as well as alien (relative) and proper (formal) righteousness. He had engaged these concepts significantly during his early debates but had largely abandoned them by the mid-1520s. The "Sermon on Two Kinds of Righteousness" (1519) lays out these categories for inflecting types of sin and righteousness mapped according to Christ and the life after Christ. Luther reintroduced these moral determinations in 1537 along with anthropological categories to clarify new processes by which the Christian gains agency for good works after justification.

Luther's pastoral responsibilities played an important part in Luther's life and theology. Pastoral concerns pulse throughout the *Antinomian*

---

78. Cf. Brecht, *Martin Luther*, 2:259–72, 288–92. The 1530 sermon strike initiated a period in Luther's pastoral development in which he began to seriously reflect on the role and importance of moral improvement in the Christian life. The *Antinomian Disputations* should be interpreted within this trajectory.

Disputations. Luther expressed his concern that participants in the disputations, students in the doctorate of theology and, thus, pastors in training,[79] understand the correct way to teach laypersons about the delicate tensions between law and gospel, faith and works. To this end, Luther coupled theological argumentation using the rules of logic with practical and pastoral theology through topics like prayer. To draw out the pastoral nuances in Luther's arguments, I examine some of Luther's pastoral writings from the 1530s. Luther's *Small* and *Large Catechisms* (1529) and "A Brief Instruction on How to Pray for Peter Barber" (1535) reflect the development of a practical theology Luther would deploy in the *Disputations* a few years later.

By combining the *Antinomian Disputations* with earlier texts and the historical *Sitz im Leben*, I adopt a dynamic historical and systematic approach to Luther's thought on the topic of human agency vis-à-vis law and the Spirit. As Bernhard Lohse described it, Luther scholars primarily utilize two main methodological approaches in the analysis of Luther's theology. The historical-genetic approach views Luther within the context of his time and debates, granting precise contours to the historical starting points of Luther's thinking as they develop over the Reformer's lifetime. By contrast, a systematic-structural approach reconstructs the links between doctrinal loci and the inner conceptual structure of Luther's theology.[80] The systematic-structural logic to Luther's thinking is vital for understanding Luther's theological commitments and innovations. However, to do so abstracted from the driving tensions of his historical, sometimes literally life and death, circumstances is to miss the contextual impulse that drove Luther's thought.

If we seek to understand Luther's theological positionality, the pressing concerns of a historical moment cannot be separated from the intellectual resources of a conceptual logic. Theological concepts and structures provided Luther with tools to address the challenges of a given moment. That given moment, in turn, informed the way Luther applied theological concepts and what aspects of a concept he chose to stress and when. I blend the historical and systematic-structural approaches in this study. I approach Luther as a figure who had mastered the logical rules of

---

79. On the format and protocol of medieval academic disputations, see White, *Luther as Nominalist*, 21–23. On the relationship between human reason and theology in Luther's use of disputation, see Helmer, *Trinity and Martin Luther*, 42, 92.

80. Lohse, *Martin Luther's Theology*, 7.

medieval Scholastic theology. I hold this theological mastery in tension with the reality that Luther was thrust into earth-quaking circumstances for which there was no precedent. I hold as true that Luther maintained a certain baseline systematic theological structure, as is evident, for example, in his doctrine of justification. However, the convulsive nature of Luther's circumstances mean that he also pulled dynamically from his robust theological knowledge and skills to address emerging problems, to revise past positions, and to erect and police boundaries around his Reformation theology. Thus, the approach in this study is to first determine the problem or question Luther sought to resolve in light of historical circumstances; second, to isolate systematic concepts Luther used to resolve his question or problem; and finally, to analyze how Luther applied those concepts within the precise historical context. When I examine the conceptual resources Luther drew together, I work to clarify the inner logic of those concepts in connection with Luther's previous uses and the medieval discussions from which he drew them.

Argument and Chapter Summaries

In this study, I argue that Luther narrated a more robust theological anthropology in the *Antinomian Disputations* that saw the recreation of human moral agency to result *from* the benefits of justification, namely, a new relation to the Holy Spirit and to the law. Luther's doctrine of justification guaranteed the God-human relationship by escalating total divine agency in Christ, which also required total human passivity. In the face of antinomian readings of his Reformation theology that threatened moral laxity and false security, Luther now worked to revive and renew human agency for moral action *after* justification. This time, however, he emphasized an aspect of divine agency that was not in opposition with human agency: the Holy Spirit. As a divine agent, the Spirit actually sustains human moral agency after justification by recreating and then elevating the human person's moral powers. In presenting human agency in this way, Luther showed that divine grace has a real, temporal effect on the human person and her moral capacity, which reinstates the moral life. God does everything in justification, but God and the human person work together for moral action in sanctification as a result.

The following chapters develop this argument by examining Luther's notion of the human person in relation to the Spirit and the law. Chapter

2 begins by describing the medieval roots of Luther's challenge to human agency for good works and the law in the 1510s. The chapter then presents the reemergence of this problem in the Antinomian controversy with Agricola in 1537. Following this sketch, each successive chapter narrows the focus toward the human agent by more carefully nuancing one particular category from the previous chapter.

Chapter 3 begins this task by mapping a human experiential dimension in Luther's law/gospel schema. At the outset, the chapter dwells on the historical backdrop of Luther's controversy with Agricola as this debate emerged out of Luther's teaching on the law in his *Lectures on Galatians* (1531) and expository reflections on the Spirit in his *Sermons on John* (1537). Rather than rehearsing and taking a position on methodologically flawed and irresolvable debates over Luther's views on the third use of the law, the chapter begins by establishing an interpretive framework for Luther's law/gospel paradigm and pointing toward important developments in Luther's thought that posit a relation between the Spirit and the law. Having established these new developments in Luther's pneumatology, the marrow of Luther's problem with Agricola crystallizes. He must keep the Spirit connected to the gospel while simultaneously clarifying the Spirit's connection to the law and do so without conflating law into gospel.

This problem leads Luther to clarify two points: first, the Spirit's relation to law, and second, a change in the human person's affective relation to the Spirit and to law that tracks across his law/gospel structure. As a result of Luther's expanded pneumatology, he identified the Spirit as the "Author of the law." This insight percolated the view that the Spirit animates the law's accusing power prior to the gospel. Luther maintained this causal relation between the Spirit and the law even when the Spirit is given as Christ's gift in justification. Because the move from law to gospel meant a change in the human person's relation to Spirit and to law as it was mediated through Christ, Luther created a new function of law, which I am calling the sanctifying use. When the Spirit as Author of the law gets mediated through Christ in the gospel, the Spirit speaks the law to the Christian in a sanctifying way in order to admonish and exhort to the good. The chapter then explores how Luther plotted the persons' evolving affective response to law in light of these changes using penitential language. I isolate and then expand on an order Luther introduced to describe the human experience of law "before Christ" (law), "under Christ" (gospel), and "in the Spirit" (after justification). At each of these stages, the Spirit enlivens the law to elicit the appropriate human emotional response in terms of sorrow for sin and a good intention for future action.

Chapter 4 sharpens the focus on the human relation to law and the Spirit in the final stage of the order pinpointed in chapter 3, "in the Spirit" or the stage after justification in Christ. The primary question is how this stage, "in the Spirit," opens up the Christian life for good behavior in relation to the sanctifying law. To make sense of this, the chapter first examines Luther's reintroduction of hamartiological categories he utilized and then abandoned in the 1510s, namely a moral distinction between original and actual sin. Luther reinvigorated these categories in order to isolate two distinct ways that law reveals moral problems in the human condition. Accusing law exposes original sin and its effects; sanctifying law admonishes and exhorts the sinful inclination that drives ongoing actual sin.

Luther aligned these problems of original and actual sin with corresponding processes for their resolution. The process of imputation hides sin from the accusing law by attributing the moral result of "relative righteousness"—a justice conferred by a relation to Christ—to the human person. However, relative righteousness does not actually change the individual human person in her temporal life; she commits "actual sin" after justification. Luther found a remedy for "actual sins" through the process of purgation in the stage of a person's being "in the Spirit." In purgation, the Spirit brings the sanctifying law to the Christian to help her resist and purge her ongoing sin. The result, Luther claimed, is that the Christian begins to fulfill the law with the Spirit's help and she begins to become righteous in herself, or "formally righteous." The chapter connects this language of "form" with the Aristotelian causal language Luther used to describe the human soul as the person's formal cause in his *Disputation on Man*. Luther built his polemical position against Agricola by showing the law's ongoing utility for transforming the form or shape of the soul from sin to righteousness with the divine agency of the Spirit.

At this point Luther's arguments become interesting for the question of moral agency because Luther set purgation into the terms of practical theology. He depicted the Christian as an active agent in restraining sin and developing righteousness. Chapter 4, therefore, turns to examine how the human person purges her sin through an encounter with the Holy Spirit and the sanctifying law in prayer. Evidence from Luther's pastoral writings on the topic of prayer in the 1530s reveals his reliance on medieval mysticism as he depicts meditative prayer centered on the Lord's Prayer, the Ten Commandments, and the Creed to speak law as a moral directive specified to the individual. But these prayers also concentrate an intensified encounter with the Holy Spirit who, Luther claimed, takes over the person's thoughts in prayer and elucidates the law within the Christian's mind. These explanations specify the law to a particular temptation the Christian is facing, showing her what God wills her to do or not to do. The effects of this intensified pneumatological relationship affect more than just the mind's understanding of the law. In prayer, the Spirit also elevates the Christian's willpower to resist a sinful affection by loving God and to obey God's will specified in the law and now the Christian's own thoughts. The Christian's choice to run to the Spirit in prayer is at the heart of her capacity to purge sin and become formally righteous.

Chapter 5 dives deeper into the Christian's formal righteousness to give prominence to Luther's anthropological language for moral progress. This chapter complicates the scholarly emphasis on a dialectical anthropological construct Luther used to describe the condition of the justified Christian, *simul iustus et peccator* (simultaneously righteous and sinner). Although the construct appears in the *Antinomian Disputations*, Luther did not accentuate the righteous dimension of the person in relation to God as scholars assume. Rather, Luther distinguished between this *simul* construct as seen from a total aspect (*totus-totus*) or a partial aspect (*partim-partim*). Luther used the *partim-partim* distinction to magnify the sinful *peccator* dimension in conjunction with the formal causal language he introduced in relation to purging sin in the Christian's temporal life. As it turns out, Luther connected the Christian's righteous, *iustus* condition to relative righteousness and her sinful, *peccator* dimension to formal righteousness. By linking Luther back to his Nominalist background, we discover that there was a medieval precedent for using the language of formal cause in relation to the soul's moral powers of intellect and will. The form of the *peccator* pertains to her moral capacities as they struggle to overcome sin and build formal righteousness. Because Luther established early on that sin blinds the intellect and binds the will, he reintroduced the Spirit and the sanctifying law in relation to the anthropological forms to reestablish and elevate the soul's moral powers. With the law guiding the intellect and the Spirit boosting the will's love of God and God's law, Luther depicted the *peccator* to march slowly but progressively toward the shape of righteousness in her soul, her formal cause.

This chapter then puts forward another anthropological construct that Luther used to describe the *peccator* as an agent in her quest for formal righteousness, the Christian soldier. Drawing on Crusader imagery and new reflections on Christian responses to the threat of Ottoman invasion, Luther depicted the relative righteousness imputed to the Christian in justification to push her into a spiritual battle against sin and evil. Protected by Christ, she incites and arms herself for this spiritual battle using the law and the Spirit as her battle cry and weapons. Though a view of her internal moral processes sees her subjectivity blurred with the Spirit, this outward perspective construes the Christian as an uncompromising agent in her moral battles. She takes sin captive by judging her affections with the law, cutting away sinful inclinations, and choosing to obey God so that she becomes more and more righteous in herself every day.

The conclusion of this study recapitulates the major arguments of each chapter. It also contains reflections on Luther's use of moral categories in this theological anthropology and on the question of the third use of the law, which is relevant for discerning Luther's contributions to modern discussions of human moral agency and subjectivity in theology and religious studies.

Chapter 2

Medieval Roots

Luther's controversy with Agricola in 1537 centers on the question of human action in relation to the law. However, this was not the first time Luther discussed this topic. In the early years between 1515 and 1525, Luther took up the topic of human action and the law in response to medieval Scholastic and Nominalist conversations about human merit. Luther problematized the medieval reliance on merit for grounding the human relationship with God. In light of human sin, Luther questioned how we are to trust that we have merited divine grace. In 1517, Luther resolved this challenge by escalating human passivity in the God-human relation. These early solutions reemerged in inner conflicts between the Wittenberg reformers beginning in 1527 and led to Luther's controversy with Agricola in 1537. Therefore, we must begin by asking what drove Luther's human agency problem and the solutions he developed. To answer this question in the context of the *Antinomian Disputations* in 1537, we must first clarify the stakes in Luther's early polemics against Scholasticism in 1517–1520. In doing so, Luther's ongoing problems and resources for resolving the debate with Agricola will become clear.

Luther's Nominalist Backdrop

To understand Luther's early challenge to human agency, we must begin by sketching the medieval problem for human agency and divine grace that Luther inherited through his early theological education in Erfurt. In the twelfth century, Peter Lombard (1100–1160 CE) laid the groundwork for this complex picture when he investigated the effect of original sin on human moral powers in book II, distinction 24 of his *Sentences*. Lombard defined human natural powers as "free choice." Free choice is "a faculty of reason and will by which the good is chosen with the assistance of grace, or evil without its assistance."[1] Lombard investigated human moral powers under each term, freedom and choice. Freedom required that the human will possess the capacity to turn itself to either good or evil. Choice likewise denoted a power of human reason to discern between good and evil and thereby to judge the moral value of possible actions and guide the will's desires. The highest aim of free choice was to judge God as the highest good in the human intellect and then to turn the will toward love of God for God's own sake.[2]

Human volitional capacity to love God turned on the presence or absence of divine grace for Lombard. He maintained that sin made the will impotent. It "is not able to raise itself to will the good efficaciously or to fulfill it in action unless it is freed and aided by grace: freed in order to will, and aided in order to achieve."[3] He determined that "operating grace" helps the human will the good—to free the will by making it good. "Co-operating grace" aids the will to achieve its volition in action—to help the will put volition into deed.[4] At the start of this medieval conversation so important for Luther's theological challenges, human agency, generated through the interaction of the human reason and will, required the help of divine grace.

One century later, John Duns Scotus (1265/66–1308 CE) and William of Ockham (1285–1347 CE) escalated the voluntarist dimension of Lombard's moral picture. Their innovations would erode the possibility of moral agency for Luther. Scotus, responding to Thomas Aquinas (1225–1274 CE), determined that freedom required *contingency*. Contingency had to do with Scotus's insight that the human will possessed affections for both justice and pleasure. These affections sometimes conflicted. So long as both

---

1. Lombard, *Sentences* II, d.24, c.3.

2. Luther wrote marginalia on Lombard's *Sentences* in 1509 as part of his theological education. On this particular passage about turning from evil, he commented, "That is in a privitive sense, but only as a contrary" (*scilicet privative, sed tantum contrarie*) (WA 9:70.5).

3. Lombard, *Sentences* II, d.25, c.9.

4. Lombard, *Sentences* II, d.26, c.1–3.

were judged good by human reason, the affections for justice and pleasure created multiple possibilities or potencies for action.

Scotus's younger contemporary, William of Ockham, adopted and revised Scotus's insight about contingency, calling it the "liberty of indifference." The liberty of indifference expanded contingency beyond the ability to choose between multiple affections. Instead, Ockham reasoned that the human will could actually will for or against any possible actions determined by reason.[5] This indifference introduced the possibility of dysfunction into the interaction between the human will and reason. The human will was no longer controlled by human reason and could will against the dictates of reason.

Ockham also applied the liberty of indifference to God. However, he did so through his Nominalist lens, which denied the existence of universals and looked to terms and predicates as the metaphysical structures of reality. Ockham brought this nominalist philosophy to bear on moral values of goodness and evil. Goodness and evil were not universals existing in an object or action. Rather, an object only becomes morally good because God declares it so. This meant that God could command either love of God or hatred of God as the highest good.[6] Goodness in the love or hatred stemmed from the divine command alone, not a universal inhering in the act itself. In these terms, hatred of God could be good simply because God declared it as such. Although Ockham maintained God would not command hatred of God, in theory, God could. For Luther, Ockham's theory eroded the reliability of both the human will and reason's ability to judge the highest good because that good was now located in a potentially arbitrary divine command.

Ockham's interpreter, Pierre d'Ailly (1350–1420 CE), further destabilized human moral agency for Luther by undermining the normativity of the moral law. Like Ockham, d'Ailly was a nominalist and escalated divine omnipotence through the divine command. He parsed the divine liberty of indifference according to divine power in creation and eternity.[7] In creation, God limited God's own power (*potentia Dei ordinata*) through the conditions of creation itself. These conditions supplied evidence to human reason about the way God wills things to be done, a

---

5. Adams, "Ockham on Will, Nature, and Morality," 253.
6. Adams, "Ockham on Will, Nature, and Morality," 266–67.
7. d'Ailly, *Quaestiones* I, q.9, a.2.

concept known as natural law.[8] Furthermore, God ordains certain things be done through precepts and prohibitions revealed in the Decalogue and Christ's double love command, which together constitute positive law.[9] In eternity, however, God's power is absolute (*potentia Dei absoluta*) and is restrained only by the law of noncontradiction.

When d'Ailly applied Ockham's divine liberty of indifference to God's absolute power, he determined that God could will something new at any moment or decide not to accept obedience to God's prior dictates. Because these changes occurred in eternity, the moral law located in creation was unreliable. Human reason had no direct access to God's changing will. D'Ailly's nominalist God was capricious: God could change God's mind. Not only were human faculties of reason and will suspicious, but now Luther had to contend with the possibility that a person could produce all kinds of works in obedience to God's will just for God to will the opposite. The pressing question became, how was one to know and satisfy God's will?

This was the question Luther's fellow Erfurt Augustinian Gabriel Biel (1420–1495 CE) took up in the generation prior to Luther. Biel decided that the solution to this troubling picture of divine capriciousness was divine acceptance of human effort. For Biel, all of the available evidence suggested the requirement for the infusion of justifying divine grace was love of God for God's own sake.[10] If the Christian did her best to love God, Biel posited, God would accept the effort and by grace transform the person's imperfect love into perfect *meritorious* love.

Biel was also optimistic about human affections. As a pilgrim (*viator*) journeying toward love of God, the human person had to "do what is in one" (*facere quod in se est*)—to muster all of one's available moral resources to do one's best to love God for God's own sake.[11] Though the person may initially turn toward God out of self-love and fear of punishment, he thought that the evidence of God's goodness in Scripture or the church would eventually lead the Christian pilgrim to transcend fear of punishment. The pilgrim would begin to love God for God's own sake.[12] God would accept this effort and by grace transform it into *meritorious* love. Thus, God and the person would become friends. The only problem was mortal sin, a sin which

8. d'Ailly, *Quaestiones* I, pro. 3, 4.
9. d'Ailly, *Quaestiones* I, q.14 b.
10. Biel, *Collectorium* II, d.35, q.1, a.1, D–E.
11. Biel, *Collectorium* II, d.27, q.1, a.3, DUB 5.
12. Biel, *Collectorium* III, d.26, q.1, a.3, DUB 3.

threatened to separate the pilgrim from God if she died before repentance and absolution. If the Christian fell back into mortal sin, doing one's best also became more difficult.[13] Thus, human effort supplied risky prospects for assuring divine grace through human merit.

Luther inherited this Nominalist picture through his education in Erfurt. He quickly experienced the spiritual, psychological, and philosophical challenges it created for human agency in justification. If God can change God's mind, how do you know if your effort to love God and obey God's commands are enough? And what if you will against what you know to be God's will? What if you muster the will to love God, but you actually just fear punishment? What if you died in a moment of despair and did not love God? To overcome the agony of these questions, Luther needed something other than human agency to guarantee the divine-human relationship.

Luther's Human Agency Problem in Justification

Luther's human agency problems were birthed in nominalist conceptions of God and moral action. Nominalism and the Bible would supply his solution. Like Ockham, d'Ailly, and Biel, Luther maximized divine omnipotence and applied this principle to justification itself. God must do everything in justification. The human can do nothing.

This insight began to percolate during Luther's early years lecturing on the Bible as a professor of theology in Wittenberg. In 1515-1516, Luther lectured on Romans and the Psalms. He discovered a view of human sin in Paul and the Psalmist that called into question the human capacity to act meritoriously.[14] In 1517, Luther articulated these biblical insights as philosophical syllogisms in his *Disputation against Scholastic Theology*. He posited that human reason is unable to infer correctly about God's will. Even if it could, the human will is only able to will love of the self and cannot love of God for God's own sake.[15] Every intellectual and volitional act that a person does without divine grace amounts to an act against God.[16] On this basis, Luther agreed with Biel; to become God's friend, God must do all the work. Where they disagreed was how.

---

13. Biel, *Collectorium* II, d.27, q.1, a.2, concl. 4.
14. WA 56:171.26—173.18.
15. WA 1:224.15-16, 30-31.
16. WA 1:225, 9-10.

Luther devised an alternative to Biel's theory of divine acceptance that saw total divine agency as the only mechanism for justifying grace. He articulated this solution as a dialectic: law and gospel.[17] Luther's notion of law retained the contours of divine commands as moral precepts and prohibitions that communicated human moral obligations to God. Luther saw a problem with Biel's formulation, however. God in God's omnipotence could not accept imperfect human effort as though it were perfect. God required that God's commands be kept scrupulously, a task the person could not complete. Rather than guiding the person's ascent to God through meritorious action, divine commands in the law actually exposed the human incapacity to meet God's demands. Thus, law accused the human as sinner and condemned her. Law fulfillment was a task that God alone could satisfy.

Gospel followed law in Luther's new dialectic to convey God's declarative promise to fulfill the law on the sinner's behalf through a gift of Christ's righteousness in faith.[18] In 1520, Luther articulated this notion using bridal mysticism in his treatise, *The Freedom of a Christian* (*De libertate christiana*). In a "happy exchange" (*fröhliche Wechseln*) between Christ and the soul, Christ's righteousness is communicated to the human soul in faith. Christ, the bridegroom and heir to divine kingship, gives all that is his to the human soul, his bride. She gets his righteousness, life, inheritance, and salvation. He gets her sin, death, and damnation.[19] Friendship with God, sealed by faith, was guaranteed through a fully divine work, which was done on behalf of the human as a passive, receptive subject.

Luther's law/gospel solution to the nominalist human agency problem excluded human action in justification. Justifying works were dead. However, the way he formulated this solution also introduced problems for parsing human agency for good works *after* justification, or *resulting from* it as sanctification. He obfuscated the effect of divine grace on human moral powers in the mind and will. Where his medieval teachers enumerated the interplay between divine grace and human faculties, Luther seemed to describe the effects of justification largely in relational terms.[20] He compared

17. WA 40/1:207.3–4.

18. Bayer elevated the framework of *promissio* as the definitive shape of Luther's early theological discovery. Reflecting on the sacrament of penance, Luther came to realize that the declaration of forgiveness spoken in the absolution is Christ's performative speech. The declaration creates the reality of which it speaks. See Bayer, *Promissio*, 172.

19. WA 7:45.33–37; 55.1–4.

20. The exact nature of the effect of justification in Luther's thought is a matter of significant disagreement. German Luther research, and with it much of the American

the effects of Christ's righteousness on the human to a mother hen who covers and protects her chicks under her wings.[21] In doing so, he implied that the justifying grace conveyed in the gospel is external to the human; she, as she is in herself, seemingly remains unchanged.

Luther also blunted the medieval system for categorizing different types of grace according to the effect on the human person. Lombard, Biel, and Luther's other medieval conversation partners differentiated various modes of God's gracious activity in human life, including justifying grace (*gratia gratum faciens*), gratuitous grace (*gratia gratis data*), healing grace (*gratia sanans*), and elevating grace (*gratia elevans*). Each type worked on the human in distinct ways to justify her, sanctify her, bring her charismata, and even to assist her intellect and will as she aimed toward good works. By contrast, Luther consolidated these descriptive notions of divine activity into a single type: *sola gratia*. Grace alone meant *justifying* grace alone. He deprived himself of the ability to carefully parse the impact of divine grace and outcomes of justification on human moral functioning in the temporal life. As a result, Christ remained the only theologically and philosophically viable moral subject.

Revisiting Human Agency

Twenty years later, Luther had seemingly put these controversies behind him. His new focus was on building the emerging Reformation movement, training pastors and theologians, and on political developments within the Schmalkaldic League. He was also facing serious health issues with his heart and kidneys.[22] His letters from the time reflect renewed urgency in articulating and clarifying his Reformation theology for posterity before his feared demise.[23] As Martin Brecht has shown, this process of clarification intro-

---

scholarship, interprets Luther's doctrine of justification in forensic, relational terms. Finnish scholarship in the Mannermaa school, however, has highlighted themes in Luther's theology such as theosis and deification that suggest there may also be ontological effects of justification in his thought.

21. WA 8:124.20–21.

22. For a discussion of Luther's evolving health concerns in this period, see Brecht, *Martin Luther*, 3:185–88.

23. WA BR 7:568–70.

duced new conflicts as differences between Luther, Melanchthon, Cruciger, and the other Wittenberg theologians bubbled to the surface.[24]

In this context, Luther's early teachings on human agency vis-à-vis law and gospel reemerged amid new challenges. Now, however, Luther approached the topic with consolidated insights and the fresh perspectives that twenty years of experience and problem-solving can bring. At stake was not *whether* the Christian performs good works, but *when* and *how*. The 1536 Cordatus controversy, as it is known, revived the question of human works *in* justification. Caspar Cruciger (1504–1548), the German humanist and Hebraist who assisted Luther on his Bible translations, sought to clarify the process of justification. Using Melanchthon's notes, he taught that human repentance was a necessary partial cause in justification along with Christ's work insofar as justification does not occur without it. Conrad Cordatus, an Austrian humanist who had come to Wittenberg in 1524, understood Cruciger's clarification to threaten justification by faith alone.[25] Cruciger appealed to Melanchthon as his defense, exposing possible disagreement between Melanchthon and Luther on this most central Reformation teaching.[26]

Consensus was reached, however, through a series of academic disputations in 1536–1537.[27] All agreed; Christ's work alone is necessary for justification. The human work of repentance, though involved in justification, was neither philosophically necessary nor a partial cause of justification by faith alone through grace alone. There was no human agency *in* justification itself. However, these discussions also opened up another insight. Good works were nevertheless an essential part of the Christian life after justification. A new obedience *in the Christian life* was clarified as an essential validation of justification. The consensus reached during

---

24. Brecht, *Martin Luther*, 3:147. The topic of law and human agency was clarified across a series of internal controversies between the Wittenberg theologians beginning with Melanchthon's 1527 conflict with Agricola on the topic of law and human agency in *poenitentia*, again in 1536 during the Cordatus controversy on the role of repentance in justification, and culminating in 1537–1540 during the antinomian controversy. Jeffrey Silcock's introduction to the *Antinomian Disputations* in the recently published volume 73 of the American Edition of Luther's Works (*Disputations II*) provides a helpful, albeit brief, summary of the building controversies. See Silcock, "Introduction," 5–13.

25. Brecht, *Martin Luther*, 3:148.

26. Silcock, "Introduction," 7.

27. Luther, *Disputation Concerning Justification* (1536), WA 39/1:104–5; *Disputation on the Works of Law and of Grace* (1537), WA 39/1:227–29; *Circular Disputation on the Wedding Garment* (1537), WA 39/1:264–65, cited in Silcock, "Introduction," 7.

the Cordatus controversy answered when good works occur, but "how" a human agent produces them remained unresolved.

Building on the new clarity that good works occur after justification, 1537 would prove to be a watershed moment in the development and resolution of human agency for moral action after justification in Luther's thought. The more mature Luther, battle-scarred by the Peasants' War and internal battles with other Protestants over the real presence, entered into a new discussion about human agency that differed from his previous engagements with the topic. Now, Luther was provoked to revisit the question of law in relation to moral agency *after* justification through the circulation of Antinomian theses in Wittenberg. He insisted that law was not only necessary for bringing the sinner to Christ in justification but also relevant to the Christian life. But on what terms? On the terms of his earlier theology that had negated the use of the law for moral agency? Or on new terms?

The Antinomian Challenge to Law and Gospel

The antinomian controversy arose in the spring of 1537. In February and March, Luther was away for a meeting with the Lutheran princes of the Schmalkaldic League. His former student Johann Agricola had recently returned to Wittenberg at Luther's invitation and took over Luther's preaching and teaching responsibilities while the Reformer was away. One such duty involved preaching at the assembly of the league of princes in Zeitz.[28] Upon his return to Wittenberg in March, Luther received complaints that while there Agricola had used "new terminology" that appeared to reject the preaching of the law.

Instead, Agricola asserted that the revelation of God's wrath is revealed in the gospel. While Agricola's sermon at Zeitz has been lost, three of his contemporaneous sermons were published in Wittenberg in July of 1537.[29] In one sermon preached on February 25 of that year, Agricola argued for a similar "double revelation" of the gospel that negates law. Per Agricola, the gospel reveals two things: (1) God's righteousness and how one becomes righteous before God; and (2) the wrath of God that befalls anyone who rejects the righteousness of God revealed in the gospel.[30] Agricola's "new terminology" appeared to invert Luther's theological order of law then gospel.

---

28. Brecht, *Martin Luther*, 3:158.
29. See Agricola, *Die Sprichwörtersammlungen*.
30. Agricola, *Drey Sermon und Predigen*, cited in Silcock, "Introduction," 8.

Around the same time, during the spring and summer of 1537, a set of anonymous antinomian theses began to circulate around Wittenberg. Melanchthon, Luther, and others soon recognized them as theses Agricola had composed and circulated some years earlier.[31] Agricola's antinomian sermons published in July made it further possible to attribute the anonymous theses to him.

At first, the controversy smoldered behind closed doors as Luther sought to reform his friend and former student's errant views. The increasingly caustic debate became public on September 30, 1537, however, when Luther preached a sermon subtlety titled *"Evangelium"* ("Gospel") in which he publicly reaffirmed the necessary distinction between law and gospel.[32] He preached a second sermon on the topic the following week on October 2.[33] By November, animosity had taken root between the two friends and efforts to privately handle the matter were abandoned. Luther decided to elevate the public nature of the disagreement, raising the stakes for his formerly beloved student. Luther leveraged the power of the printing press[34] to expose Agricola and published:

- eighteen anonymous antinomian theses Luther understood to be Agricola's;
- a set of "pure" and "impure" statements about justification the antinomians attributed to Luther; and
- eight conclusions Luther drew from views on law espoused in Agricola's published sermons.

Accompanying the antinomian theses was a set of Luther's own "Theses against the Antinomians" for public dispute, the first of which occurred on December 18, 1537.

The antinomian theses quoted Luther's early sermons, written in the midst of the Reformer's Scholastic critiques, to support the abrogation of

31. Letter from Jonas Melanchthon et al. to Elector John Frederick, April 5, 1540, in Förstemann, *Neues Urkundenbuch*, 326, cited in Silcock, "Introduction," 8n32. On Luther's attribution of the theses to Agricola, see Brecht, *Martin Luther*, 3:158.

32. WA 45:145–56.

33. WA 45:157–60.

34. Pettegree has argued that Luther's intentional use of the Wittenberg printing press to advance a "more aggressive and confrontational intellectual agenda" at the newly founded University of Wittenberg both revived the town's failing business venture in printing and elevated the obscure professor-monk subsequent celebrity. See Pettegree, *Brand Luther*, 39–52.

the law. Among these early sources were Luther's "Sermon on the Suffering of Christ" (1519),[35] his early Prefaces to the Bible (1522),[36] and Melanchthon's *Commentary on Paul's Epistle to the Romans* (1532).[37] Among other points, the theses used these texts to assert that:

1. "Penitence is not taught by the Decalogue or the law of Moses, but by the suffering of the Son in the gospel";[38]
2. "It was necessary for Christ to die and in this way to enter his glory, so that in his name both penitence and remission of sins would be preached";[39]
3. "For law accuses of sin and this without the Holy Spirit, therefore it accuses unto damnation";[40]
4. "For Christ's gospel teaches the wrath of God from heaven, and at the same time God's justice (Rom 1). Therefore, it is preaching penitence in conjunction with the promise, which reason does not deduce from nature, but by divine revelation."[41]

On these premises, the theses reflected the conclusion that:

5. "The law of Moses need not be taught as the beginning, middle, or end of justification."[42]

The antinomian theses used Luther's own teachings to conflate the essential theological dialectic between law and gospel that structured his theology. The theses revealed Agricola's view that gospel not only consoled the

---

35. "Sermon von der Betrachtung des heiligen Leiden Christi" (WA 2:131–42).
36. See WA DB 1—6.
37. Melanchthon, *Commentarii in epist. Pauli ad Romanos*. Agricola's decision to cite Melanchthon's writing in his anonymous theses demonstrates the acerbic nature of the controversy between old friends. Melanchthon developed his notion of the "third use of the law" (*tertius usus legis*) to clarify the law's function in guiding the Christian's conscience toward good works after justification following his own 1527 conflict with Agricola. By citing Melanchthon's 1532 text, Agricola was reviving that older conflict. For Wengert's in-depth analysis of Melanchthon's developments in light of his conflict with Agricola, see Wengert, *Law and Gospel*, 191–206.
38. WA 39/1:342.9–10.
39. WA 39/1:342.11–13.
40. WA 39/1:343.16–17.
41. WA 39/1:343.21–23.
42. WA 39/1:342.29–30.

terrified conscience but also prepared the human for Christ by exposing God's wrath against sin—a function Luther strictly ascribed to law. As such, Agricola asserted the second, theological use of the law in the church was abrogated, having no place before, during, or after justification.[43] The law's first, civil use remained strictly to control the sins of unbelievers.[44] Agricola's confusion of law and gospel required that Luther and the Wittenberg theologians now clarify the exact role and functions of law across the span of the Christian life before, during, and after justification.

The Antinomian Challenge to Luther's Pneumatology

The way Agricola formulated his theses also provoked another region of Luther's theology, one overlooked in earlier analyses of this controversy.[45] Agricola misconstrued Luther's pneumatology. For most of Luther's career, his view of the Holy Spirit went largely undeveloped, carrying forward common positions in medieval pneumatologies.[46] Luther regurgitated views from Lombard that the Holy Spirit is the gift of divine love and a love by which the Christian loves God and neighbor.[47] Luther's church-building phase, beginning in the late 1520s, saw the Reformer to engage with the subject more actively as he began expositing the Creed and addressing issues of moral laxity in Wittenberg and other Saxon churches.

Notably, Luther's pneumatology saw significant development in the spring of 1537, when he began preparing Pentecost sermons on John 14-16 after returning from Schmalkald. This passage in John recounts Christ's final speech to his disciples. In line with the liturgical calendar, Luther

---

43. WA 39/1:342.29-30.

44. WA 39/1:344.30.

45. Scholarship on the *Antinomian Disputations* focuses largely on Luther's treatment of law but does not give serious consideration to the pneumatological developments surrounding his views. Similarly, Regin Prenter's investigation of sanctification in *Spiritus Creator* separated the Spirit's work in sanctification from a third use of the law.

46. See Kärkkäinen, *Luthers trinitarische Theologie*; Dieter, "Du mußt den Geist haben!" By contrast, Helmer has suggested that an association between the Spirit and divine judgment is present in Luther's preaching as early as 1523. See Helmer, *Trinity and Martin Luther*, 154.

47. See Lombard, *Sentences* d.17, c.4. Lombard's formulation of the Spirit as gift proved problematic for separating out parameters for divine and human agency in justification, a problem which will also haunt Luther. On this difficulty in Lombard, see Adams, "Genuine Agency," 23-60.

attended to Christ's teachings on the Holy Spirit. When Luther came to John 16:8, however, he encountered a different perspective on the Holy Spirit in Christ's words than he had previously understood. In the published expositions adapted from his sermons, Luther commented that Christ taught that "the Holy Spirit will convict the world of sin and of righteousness."[48] If the Spirit convicts the world of sins, Luther reasoned, the Spirit must have another function alongside its office as gift of infused divine love conceptualized in medieval pneumatologies. In connection with John 16:8, Luther began to connect the Holy Spirit to the law.

Escalating the vindictive grandstanding between the former friends, Agricola cited Luther's new insight about the Spirit's connection to law to validate his errant view of law and gospel. In thesis three, Agricola named the Spirit's conviction of sins in John 16:8.[49] He then asserted on this basis that the gospel must both convict of sins and console with the promise about Christ's righteousness because the Holy Spirit is only given in the gospel, not by the law.[50] Luther took the bait and engaged John 16:8 at length across the resulting disputations. Thus, this passage in John 16:8 plays a key role in Luther's view of law in the *Antinomian Disputations*.

Agricola's use of John 16:8 presented Luther with a new challenge for clarifying law and gospel. Per John 16:8, Luther needed to find a way to keep the Spirit connected to the conviction of sins, a function of law, while also keeping the Spirit under gospel as a gift of justification. He could have simply reiterated his early formulations of law and gospel as a corrective to Agricola's antinomianism. However, the addition of the Holy Spirit and the Spirit's conviction of sins complicated matters because the conviction of sins is a shared function of law. He had to somehow connect the Spirit to both law and gospel without conflating them.

The problem was, for the Spirit to convict the world of sins, the Spirit had to be the divine agent of law. But how could the Spirit be the agent of the condemning law and also comfort the soul under gospel as the gift of divine love? To keep the Spirit connected to gospel, Luther had to find a

---

48. WA 46:34.21. Casper Cruciger edited Luther's 1537 sermons on John 14–16 for publication in 1538, removing indications of where individual sermons began or ended and working the sermons into a continuous commentary. A similar approach was taken with Luther's sermons on the Sermon on the Mount published a few years earlier. This work was undertaken most certainly with Luther's approval, evidenced by Luther's declaration in 1540 that "this is the best book I have written" (LW 24:ix–x).

49. WA 39/1:342.14–15.

50. WA 39/1:342.27–28.

new way to bring law as a function of the Spirit back into the Christian life after justification. This required that he revise his earlier formulation of "law, *then* gospel" as "law, then gospel, *then* law under gospel." However, Luther's passive anthropology from the 1510s and 1520s did not support such a formulation. He would also have to revisit and expand his anthropology in relation to the Spirit to make room for the moral agency that he had thrown out in 1517.

New Challenges, New Opportunities

1517 and 1537 were different times, different places, and different interlocutors in Luther's life and career. The antinomian controversy with Agricola forced Luther to reflect on the role of the law in the Christian life and to do so in relation to the Holy Spirit. On Luther's own terms, the gospel did not simply abrogate the law nor did human passivity *in* justification negate human moral action *after* justification. Luther's challenge was to clarify the role of the law *after* gospel with respect to the human agent without problematically implying that obedience to the law *before* the gospel somehow justifies. He had to finally resolve the "how" question of human moral action.

The setting for taking up this "how" question in 1537 was different in another way. Luther's Wittenberg colleagues had already been working on the question of human agency and law. Thus, Luther's collegial setting provided both new insights to consider and a larger conversation to engage. In 1527, Luther's colleague and friend, Philipp Melanchthon had his own Antinomian controversy with Agricola while Agricola was a pastor in Eisleben. In response, Melanchthon introduced a concept of the third use of the law (*tertius usus legis*) into the discussion in his 1534 *Scholia* on Paul's letter to the Colossians.[51] The third use of the law was meant to clarify the ongoing relevance of law in the Christian life. Like Melanchthon's conflict with Agricola, Luther's *Antinomian Disputations* historically contextualize an emerging problem on the topic of law with new innovations in the topics of human subjectivity and pneumatology. They provide a new text to consider in the question of human agency in Luther's thought that shows a human relation to law beyond simply its first and second uses (civil and theological). In his own response to Agricola, Luther took a similar trajectory to Melanchthon

---

51. Wengert, *Law and Gospel*, 195–200.

and enumerated a variety of pedagogical functions for law that support the Christian's moral life and sanctification.[52]

The problem, however, was Luther's weak anthropology was incompatible with a more robust notion of law. He thought the human capable only of morally evil acts, namely love of self and fear of God. This means that Luther's defense of the law after gospel contains the seeds for articulating a more robust concept of human subjectivity because Luther's new understanding of law and the Spirit spurred revisions to his earlier anthropology. What Luther needed was a view of the person with powers of the soul to act well *after* justification.

Luther's challenge was to construct an anthropology open to the possibility of human moral agency *after* justification, but without any possibility for a human contribution to meritorious action *prior* to justification. In other words, Luther needed to deflate Agricola's antinomianism without succumbing to the reliance on human moral efforts that he had refuted in nominalist theology in 1517. To do this, Luther looked to the Holy Spirit in conjunction with the medieval anthropological categories that he had supposedly thrown out. A robust pneumatology became the theological resource for a more dynamic moral picture of the justified person. In the next chapter, we will begin to excavate the way Luther newly brought the Spirit, law, and human person together in the *Antinomian Disputations* in relation to the law/gospel paradigm he first developed during the early polemics against Scholasticism.

---

52. Luther never used the terminology of the *tertius usus legis*. Lund argued that Luther nevertheless "recognized a third use of the law and was in agreement with Melanchthon in his understanding of its use." See Lund, "Luther's 'Third Use of the Law,'" 1, 5.

Chapter 3

Law/Gospel and Human Experience

LUTHER SCHOLARS FOR MUCH of the twentieth century have understood Luther's law/gospel paradigm to define the two primary aspects of Luther's understanding of the God-human relationship.[1] The "*Gesetz und Evangelium*" entry of the encyclopedic publication to Luther and his works, *Das Luther-Lexikon*, summarizes the scholarly consensus of law and gospel in this way:

> Moving out of the medieval meaning, Luther defined . . . the law as God's expectations or demands for the human's disposition and actions and the gospel as God's own agency in Jesus Christ to save the sinner through Christ and in which the Holy Spirit through his Word in oral, written, or sacramental form moves the human to faith in God. Every pronouncement that accuses or humbles the human functions as law and every pronouncement that causes comfort and trust on the basis of Christ's death and resurrection functions as gospel.[2]

This definition reveals the way law and gospel ascribes a moral determination to the human person in relation to God in Luther's thought.

---

1. In *Zwischen Gnade und Ungnade* (1948), Werner Elert elevated the law/gospel principle as a key interpretive paradigm for Luther's theology in his famous response to Karl Barth's dialectical theology. Law/gospel has since become the great "dialectic" of Lutheran theology in the twentieth century, connoting the radical mismatch between human sin and divine grace.

2. Kolb, "Gesetz und Evangelium," 252.

Scholars agree, Luther understands "law" to both place God's demands on the human and to expose her failure to meet them. Law articulates God's determination of the human vis-à-vis God as sinner, lawbreaker, and condemned. Gospel functions as the divine foil to law. Gospel is God's Word of promise that God has fulfilled God's own demands on the person's behalf. Thus, while the human person may remain a sinner and lawbreaker in herself, her status as condemned changes in the move from law to gospel. She is sinner and condemned under law, but she becomes sinner and justified under gospel.

This *Luther-Lexicon* definition of law/gospel also demonstrates the scholarly interpretive emphasis on divine agency alone. Law/gospel is construed in terms of divine action on a purely passive human recipient. God articulates demands and expectations as law. Gospel has to do with God's action alone to fulfill those demands through Christ's agency. When it comes to faith, it is not the human person who produces faith but rather the Spirit's agency working it within her. Human action is absent. This scholarly emphasis on divine agency introduces a binary into the God-human relationship: God does everything; the human does nothing. The result is to render the human person and her capacity for moral action as impotent in Luther's thought. Under law/gospel, she is acted upon; she is not a self-efficacious agent for the change of her status from condemned to justified or change in her moral condition as sinner. Does this binary really represent Luther's thinking?

New evidence shows there may be reasons for trying to excavate a human agent out of this God-human relation articulated in law/gospel. Scholars have tried to open up interpretive space here by investigating the human *response* to law and gospel as a site of human agency.[3] Mapping Luther's understanding of the human person's noetic powers vis-à-vis his medieval interlocutors has built a critical framework for viewing human response as a type of agency.[4] Emotional responses to God and, on this basis, to the world and other persons is a primary mode of this agential response.[5] These approaches have clarified Luther's understanding of the human soul as well as types and locations of agency the human expresses.

---

3. Cf. Bayer, *Freedom in Response*; Holm, *Gabe Und Geben*.

4. Kärkkäinen, "Interpretations of the Psychological," 256–79; "Jodocus Trutfetters"; Saarinen, "Ipsa Dilectio Deus Est," 185–204.

5. Stolt, *Martin Luthers Rhetorik des Herzens*; *Laßt uns fröhlich springen!*; Raunio, "Martin Luther and Love."

Yet, it remains unclear how Luther conceived of the human to act with intentionality and initiation vis-à-vis law and gospel. How did Luther understand the human person *as an agent* who was capable of particular responses under law and gospel?

Luther's polemical stance toward medieval theology has encumbered scholarly efforts to parse the human dimension of law and gospel. Luther's escalation of divine agency is posited as a repudiation of medieval doctrines of justification that granted too much agency to human action. To say anything about the human as agent appears to undermine the theological house of cards of divine agency upon which Luther's doctrine of justification was built. Yet, careful attention to the dynamic ways Luther engaged medieval theological concepts and methods can open interpretive space to better understand Luther's law/gospel paradigm vis-à-vis human experience and action. We must distinguish between critique in Luther's engagement with medieval sources and his active participation in those theological conversations and constructive appropriation of the ideas they contained. We must also attend to Luther's own theological development, evolving questions, and shifting historical contexts as a key factor in his engagement with these ideas.

The *Antinomian Disputations* provide an important opportunity for this kind of careful attention. The reasons are twofold. First, Luther discussed human agency for the law vis-à-vis medieval theories in these disputations to refute Agricola's antinomianism. Second, Luther did so by revisiting and clarifying some of his early critiques of Rome and medieval theology, which Agricola had used to ground his antinomian positions. Because these early debates are the basis of scholarly interpretation of Luther's core theological commitments related to human and divine agency, the *Antinomian Disputations* are critical for understanding Luther's mature thought in this area.

The *Antinomian Disputations* play a critical role in clarifying the interplay between divine and human agency in Luther's thought for another reason. Luther revisited the question of human agency and the law in light of divine action. By 1537, Melanchthon had been parsing distinct ways human persons encounter and engage law, leading to his notion of the *tertius usus legis* in 1535. In 1537, the antinomian controversy also forced Luther to nuance his concept of law, which seems more positive than in Luther's earlier periods. This more positive approach to law has spurred intractable disagreement between Luther scholars.[6] Divorced from Luther's historical and theological context in the late 1530s, Luther's more positive approach to the law in the *Antinomian Disputations* seems irreconcilable with the law/gospel paradigm found in his earlier writings. Therefore, this chapter aims at two goals. The first is to make sense of the *Antinomian Disputations* within Luther's historical and theological context of the 1530s. In doing so, the second aim is to clarify how the disputations reveal Luther's mature views on the human dimension of the God-human relationship articulated in the law/gospel paradigm. By opening up this human dimension, we will be positioned to parse anthropological categories for moral action vis-à-vis the Spirit in the coming chapters.

This chapter examines how Luther articulated a more nuanced notion of the human person in relation to law from the perspective of the human under gospel. The first step in this study is to work out the specific theological challenges Luther faced in his controversy with the Antinomians. These challenges emerge as a new theological question: how is the Spirit connected to both the law and the human person under law and gospel? Then, I examine how Luther resolved this question. First, he introduced medieval penitential language to articulate human experience of law under law and gospel. Second, he utilized a particular theological ordering of the human life in relation to law and the Spirit within the law/gospel paradigm. As a result, Luther can be seen to develop an increased role of the Spirit in relation to law and gospel in the *Antinomian Disputations*. This pneumatological expansion clarifies the human's changing relation to law while maintaining Christ's total agency in justification.

The Antinomian Challenge to the Law and the Spirit in the Christian Life

Luther's theology was radically contextual. His theological insights grew out of biblical study for sermons and lectures. They were sharpened in conversation with colleagues whose biblical and theological ideas stimulated Luther's own ongoing reflections. Luther's positions evolved in response to pastoral challenges, letters, and questions from colleagues, political authorities, and followers. Through the fires of controversies that revealed ambiguities in his Reformation theology, Luther refined a theology that would shape western civilizations for half a millennium. The situational nature of

---

6. See Lund, "Luther's 'Third Use of the Law,'" 44.

Luther's theology makes historical context indispensable for understanding his thought process, evolving insights, and conclusions.

In the middle of the twentieth century when much of the existing research on the *Antinomian Disputations* was done, the immediate historical context of Luther's intellectual and personal life and its impact on shifts in Luther's thought in the late 1530s was left unexplored. Instead, scholars emphasized a developmental hermeneutic in Luther's thought based on conceptual terminology. Early texts like the 1522 *Kirchenpostille* or 1525's *Wider die himmlischen Propheten* served as interpretive guardrails for understanding Luther's later writings.[7] A linguistic-terminological approach based on Luther's early thought won out over a descriptive-analytical one that permitted shifts and developments in his thought over time and experience.[8]

This pattern is evident in Gerhard Ebeling's analysis of Luther's concept of law. Ebeling isolated an early example of a distinction between three "needs" (*Gebrauch*) and three "uses" (*usus*) of law in Luther's early work. Yet because the phrase "*tertius usus legis*" could not be located in Luther's writings, Ebeling concluded that a third use of law was "only a secondary thought" for Luther. This thought was abandoned without becoming an "ultimate conceptual impression."[9] Luther's descriptive frameworks were downplayed in favor of theological terms. The historical events, controversies, and theological disputations of the 1530s were not considered as contextual or explanatory resources that could lend insight into Luther's descriptive conceptual evolutions.

To make sense of Luther's views of law in the *Antinomian Disputations*, we must contextualize Luther's understanding of law and gospel within his academic and pastoral activities from the 1530s. Jeffrey Silcock recently contributed to this effort by setting the conflict with Agricola in context with the 1536 Cordatus Controversy.[10] Luther's *Lectures on Galatians* (1531/1535) and his *Sermons on John* in the spring of 1537, less than six months before the first *Antinomian Disputation*, shed additional light on important developments in Luther's thought vis-à-vis Agricola's

---

7. Elert, "Eine theologische Fälschung," 168.

8. A consequence of this emphasis on the early Luther was the sidelining of Luther's philosophical thinking and disputational logic, which became an important aspect of his later work when academic disputations were reintroduced into the Wittenberg theological faculty in 1533. See White, *Luther as Nominalist*, 22.

9. Ebeling, *Wort und Glaube*, 1:53.

10. Silcock, "Introduction," 7.

antinomianism. These developments underlie questions that Luther aimed to resolve in the disputations.

Luther's Law/Gospel Paradigm in the Lectures on Galatians (1531/1535)

Luther developed his law/gospel paradigm while lecturing on the Psalms, Romans, and Galatians as a young professor and monk in Wittenberg, sometime between 1510 and 1520.[11] In 1531, Luther delivered a second set of lectures on Galatians, which were sent to press in 1535. Current scholarly consensus holds these 1531/1535 *Lectures on Galatians* (*Galaterbriefvorlesungen*) as the *locus classicus* for Luther's articulation of the law/gospel paradigm.[12]

In the 1531 *Lectures on Galatians*, Luther identified two uses of law, a civil use that bridles sin in society and a theological use specific to God's justifying work.[13] In Luther's law/gospel paradigm, the theological use of law is in view. Here, law functions as part of the law/gospel paradigm to make demands and to expose one's failure to meet those demands. Luther wrote, "Law wants something to be done, [it] wants something to be done on account of God."[14] In the earlier 1517 *Disputation against Scholastic Theology* and the 1518 *Heidelberg Disputation*, Luther had understood the law's primary demand in the terms of medieval Scholastic theology as love of God above all else.[15] He recognized the problem that no one is able to fulfill this demand because no one is able to conform her will to love God. Instead, the soul is guilty of hatred of God. These insights led Luther to ask, "Who is without sin?" to which he concluded, "There is no one who

---

11. Kolb, "Gesetz und Evangelium," 252.

12. See Bornkamm, *Luthers Auslegungen des Galaterbriefs*; Elert, "Eine theologische Falschung," 167; Ebeling, *Wort und Glaube*, 1:58. Two more recent studies show Luther's concept of law in the Galatians Lectures may be more complex than typically understood: Kim, *Luther on Faith and Love*, 56; Lund, "Luther's 'Third Use of the Law,'" 5.

13. WA 40/1:487–88.

14. WA 40/1:425.12.

15. Theodor Dieter contrasts divine and human love in thesis 28 of the *Heidelberg Disputation*. Divine love is able to satisfy the law's love demand because it creates goodness in its object, but human love is acquisitive. The human will is only activated by objects it seeks to acquire for self-enhancement. See Dieter, *Der junge Luther und Aristotles*, 136–42.

loves God with his whole heart."[16] To be under the law, Luther then said, is to be "under a curse" because the law does not give what is needed to obey, namely, the Holy Spirit, who is itself divine Love.[17] Instead, the law is an "exactor, demanding what we owe."[18] Therefore, Luther determined that the law works to "demand something of us" and to "reveal sin and kill" when we fail to fulfill it.[19] Law exposes the human person as sinner and accuses the guilty conscience.

Luther conceptualized gospel as the foil to law because gospel gives to the human person what the law demands. Luther defined gospel as "a gift [that] offers a gift."[20] The first gift is Christ and his righteousness, and the second gift is the Holy Spirit. These gifts work together to remove sin and console the terrified conscience. He stated, "We are justified solely by faith in Christ, without works, and the Holy Spirit is granted solely by hearing the message of the gospel with faith."[21] Through faith in Christ, the human's sins are remitted. The person is also given what Luther called the "righteousness of faith" (*iustitia fidei*).[22] Luther deemed the righteousness of faith a "passive righteousness" because the righteousness of faith is imputed from without. Unlike other types of righteousness he identified (ceremonial, political, or righteousness of the law), faith does not require human action. Instead, "nothing is worked by us, but we are born by the works of another, [which] God certainly permits in us."[23] Thus, gospel foils law by removing sin through the imputation of Christ's righteousness to the human being.

The secondary gift of the Holy Spirit is central to the gospel's justifying effect in contrast to the law. Luther isolated the Holy Spirit as the key element of Christ's proclamation of faith. This proclamation justifies, he said, specifically because "it brings with it the Holy Spirit."[24] The reason is

---

16. WA 40/1:428.2–3.

17. WA 40/1:428.3; 336.8–9. Kim argues that Luther only opposes a human use of law in the *Lectures on Galatians* when it is used to usurp Christ's righteousness. She indicates that in 1531 Luther's concept of the accusing law (second use) was already becoming more complex. See Kim, *Luther on Faith and Love*, 232.

18. WA 40/1:337.1.

19. WA 40/1:337.2.

20. WA 40/1:337.5.

21. WA 40/1:336–37.

22. WA 40/1:64.4.

23. WA 40/1:41.4–5.

24. WA 40/1:336.7–8.

the Spirit constitutes a type of shared agency between Christ and the Spirit in the justified soul: "Christ rules with his Holy Spirit, who now sees, hears, speaks, works, endures, and does everything in me."[25] In other words, the gift of the Spirit is effective for justification because it begins working all that the law requires in the person. By contrast, Luther says, the law "never brings the Holy Spirit," neither by its message nor its effect, "therefore it does not justify."[26] The gift of the Spirit—not just Christ's righteousness—is the essential distinction between law and gospel.

Luther separated law and gospel as two functions of God's word. Both law and gospel teach something, but only gospel gives or creates something to justify the sinner. The law teaches what we ought to do because law is a divine word of demand.[27] Gospel teaches what we ought to receive, namely, Christ's righteousness and the Holy Spirit.[28] In contrast to law, gospel is a divine word of promise spoken about Christ.[29] Discussing Christ's relation to law and gospel, Luther depicted Christ to announce: "The law is horrible and wrathful, but be not terrified nor flee, but remain. I myself fulfill what you owe and satisfy the law on your behalf."[30] Because Christ fulfills the law on behalf of the sinner, Luther determined that the gospel is an efficacious word. It actually creates what the law demands. The law remains an inefficacious word. It makes demands without giving anything to fulfill them.

---

25. WA 40/1:290.10–11. Luther echoed medieval philosophical theologies from Lombard to Ockham that sought to resolve how God and creatures should share genuine agency in counting creatures and their actions as worthy of eternal life. Adams has shown that a special presence of the Spirit through divinely infused habits was one of two identified possibilities. See Adams, "Genuine Agency," 23–60.

26. WA 40/1:336.5, 8–9.

27. WA 40/1:337.1–2. The German theologian Oswald Bayer is largely responsible for the understanding of law and gospel as functions of divine words. Bayer argues that "law" is an "ineffective" word because it does not create what it demands, while gospel is an "effective" word because it declares the sinner to be just and, thus, the sinner becomes so. See Bayer, *Promissio*, 280, 283. Schulken used Bayer's Word theology to distinguish between the law as indicative and imperative divine words in his study of law in the *Antinomian Disputations*. Schulken admits an "effective" use of the law in the Disputations, however, he construes this across the law/gospel schema such that the effective nature of law has to do with accusing the conscience alone. See Schulken, *Lex efficax*, 134–36, 392. Closer examination of the Spirit as divine agent behind the law can open up the law category as an effective divine word.

28. WA 40/1:336.2–3.

29. WA 40/1:45.7–8.

30. WA 40/1:503.22–24.

The contrast between the law's demanding/accusing words and the gospel's promising/creative words led Luther to fully separate law from gospel. He said law and gospel are "separated as opposites."[31] "Demanding and granting, receiving and offering" are oppositional functions. Thus, law and gospel "cannot coexist."[32]

As a result, in the *Lectures on Galatians*, Luther seemed to hold the view that gospel overtakes law. God's promise in Christ speaks the final word against the law's accusations. The principal theological purpose of law is to reveal sin and drive one to gospel by revealing to the person that she is God's enemy. But, once that has been accomplished, Luther asserted that the law "has done its office and its time is complete."[33] The gospel alone remains as a divine pronouncement into the Christian life. In 1531, Luther appeared to maintain the strict law/gospel dialectic highlighted in twentieth-century Luther scholarship.

Summer of 1537: Luther's Discovery of the Spirit's "Punitive Office"

Six years later, between Easter and Pentecost of 1537 (roughly March to June), Luther preached on Jesus's final speech to his disciples before the crucifixion. We have the sermons based on his favorite New Testament book, the Gospel of John, in edited form.[34] Luther set Cruciger on the task of preparing the sermons for publication. For this, Cruciger edited out dates and the transitions between individual sermons, leaving the sermons in the form of a biblical commentary. Cruciger's edits won Luther's approval. Luther later delighted that his *Sermons on John* were his most important work.[35]

Luther's exegetical emphases aligned with the liturgical themes; he highlighted the shift from the end of Jesus's earthly life to the coming of the Spirit and the Spirit's work. Therefore, Luther theorized about the office and work of the Spirit throughout the sermons. In John 15:26, he identified and commented on the Spirit's office "to bear witness to Christ." This witness comes in the form of a sermon, in which the Holy Spirit makes Christians

31. WA 40/1:337.3.
32. WA 40/1:337.3.
33. WA 40/1:509.12–14.
34. LW 24:ix.
35. LW 24:x.

into witnesses and confessors of Christ.[36] While he does not overtly reference law/gospel, this type of paracletic activity falls squarely under the rubric of gospel. The Spirit is bringing people to faith and the divine promise.

When Luther came to John 16:8–11, he made a discovery. Christ identified not one, but two offices for the Spirit—to convict the world of sin and of righteousness. The former did not fit with the Spirit's typical paracletic work, which positioned the Spirit as Christ's gift under gospel. As such, Luther expounded on this alternative office. In John 16:8, he discovered Christ to "clearly define" the Spirit's office and work "to convict the world of sins."[37] This particular office involved "attacking all of [the world's] deeds and being, and to tell [everyone in the world] that, as they are found, they are entirely guilty and unjust before God and must believe this word about Christ or be eternally damned and lost."[38] Luther began to characterize the Spirit's work to convict of sins as an *accusing* office. The Spirit accuses the human being of sin[39] and "pronounces judgment" that sinners, those without belief in Christ, "are and must remain under God's wrath and damnation."[40] He renamed this accusing function the Spirit's "punitive office" (*das Straf Ampt*) and named the Spirit as the "eternal judge."[41] The Spirit's punitive office shared surprising contours with Luther's theological notion of law.

36. WA 45:730.3–11.
37. WA 46:34.21–23.
38. WA 46:34.31–34.
39. Kim also identified a similar punitive and salutary function of the "righteousness of God" in Luther's *Lectures on Galatians*. In contrast to a punitive righteousness of God, the salutary function of divine righteousness communicates that God wants to bless, not sentence sinners with death. See Kim, *Luther on Faith and Love*, 124.
40. WA 46:38.24. In his analysis of Luther's concept of the Holy Spirit in the *Antinomian Disputations*, Kärkkäinen shows that Luther understood the Spirit as God to be the giver of the law, without whom the law cannot reveal sin. The power of the law to expose sin is, for Luther, a divine attribute, which the law cannot accomplish apart from God. Luther seems to go further here than what Kärkkäinen finds in the *Antinomian Disputations*, identifying the Spirit itself as the one who accuses and condemns using the law as a mediate cause. See Kärkkäinen, *Luthers trinitarische Theologie*, 136.
41. WA 46:47.2. Kärkkäinen touches on Luther's understanding of the Spirit's relation to law. However, Kärkkäinen claims that Luther's understanding of the Spirit is shaped primarily according to the Spirit's paracletic activities to (1) bring the person to faith, and (2) initiate sanctification. In this regard, Kärkkäinen shows Luther's deep indebtedness to medieval pneumatologies after Lombard in which the Holy Spirit was understood as the divine *caritas* that is given to the Christian in infused grace for love of God and neighbor. This objective leads Kärkkäinen to identify the Spirit's "*Eigentumlichkeit*" as

Alongside this accusing, punitive work, Luther also saw a version of the Spirit's traditional paracletic office, which answers the condemnation delivered in the Spirit's punitive office. The Spirit "bears witness" to Christ, announcing to sinners "that they must either obey the message about Christ or be eternally damned."[42] The Spirit also announces that Christ is the only deliverance from God's wrath.[43] In John 16, Luther found a biblical warrant that positions the Spirit on both sides of justification, as both accuser and consoler.

In this context, Luther observed functions for the Spirit that bear a remarkable resemblance to law/gospel. First, the Spirit tells people they are under God's wrath and requires acknowledgement of this condition. This punitive office aligns with law. Then, the Spirit shows how to be delivered from this condition by faith in Christ.[44] This paracletic office resembles gospel. Interestingly, Luther himself never overtly made this connection between the Spirit's punitive office with the accusing function of law in his *Sermons on John*. What is clear is that, in light of John 16:8, Luther was thinking about the person and work of the Spirit in new ways leading into the fall of 1537. These new ideas about the Spirit gave fodder to Agricola and laid the groundwork for Luther to connect the Spirit's punitive office to the law in the *Antinomian Disputations*. The Spirit is not just the comforter or advocate sent by Christ, as traditional paracletic imagery inferred. The Spirit also speaks divine judgment over sin just like the law.

Fall of 1537: Agricola's Escalation of the Galatians Law/Gospel Schema

In the late winter and early spring of 1537, Johann Agricola was filling in for Luther's preaching duties while Luther was away for a meeting of the

---

the *Liebe Gottes*. Kärkkäinen, *Luthers trinitarische Theologie*, 50–52, 57. A similar view is presented in Dieter, "Du mußt den Geist haben!," 66–69. Dieter shows Luther to "follow the medieval consensus" that "the Holy Spirit is love, through which the Spirit itself works together with the human will as an act of love" (66). These recent works build on Regin Prenter's 1953 book, *Spiritus Creator*. Prenter limited his analysis of Luther's pneumatology to the rubric of Gospel. The Spirit's relation to law or accusation via the *Straf Amt* was not considered.

42. WA 46:34.34.
43. WA 46:38.25.
44. WA 46:40.28-33.

Schmalkaldic League.⁴⁵ Agricola and Luther were close. During the early days of the Reformation, Luther had been Agricola's professor and pastor (*Seelsorger*).⁴⁶ Agricola had been Luther's closest student and his disciple in promulgating the new Reformation theology.⁴⁷ Kjeldgaard-Pedersen reports that Agricola also held a position of trust in the most tumultuous period of Luther's professional and personal life. Agricola was Luther's secretary at the 1519 Leipzig Disputation and the notary for Luther's November 1520 appeal for a general council. When Luther infamously had Leo X's 1520 bull, *Exsurge domini*, burned at Wittenberg's Elster Gate, Agricola was charged with burning the bull and all other papal books in Wittenberg.⁴⁸

As Martin Brecht has suggested, Agricola's antinomianism seems to have originated from a static interpretation of Luther's early theology. Agricola often cited Luther's early sermons on law and gospel.⁴⁹ Agricola "believed the law's demands belonged in the past; a believer is converted, justified, and instructed through the proclamation of the gospel in Christ. The continuing divine demand of the law . . . was no longer of interest in this context."⁵⁰ Agricola's affinity for Luther's early, unmatured theology had caused earlier issues with Melanchthon. During a 1527 supervisory visit to Eisleben where Agricola was then teaching, Melanchthon noticed an omission in Agricola's preaching of law. He quickly demanded an increase in the law's teaching in Eisleben.⁵¹ A heated controversy ensued and prompted Melanchthon to flesh out his own ideas on the precise functions of law in the Christian life.⁵² The result was Melanchthon's concept of the third use of the law (*tertius usus legis*).

45. The Schmalkaldic League (*Schmalkaldischer Bund*) was a political alliance between Lutheran princes within the Holy Roman Empire during the 1530s and 1540s. The alliance was meant to guard against the Holy Roman Emperor Charles V's attempts to extinguish the Reformation movement. As such, participating princes agreed to ascribe to the Augsburg Confession and to share military power.

46. Kawerau, *Johann Agricola von Eisleben*, 14.

47. Brecht, *Martin Luther*, 3:157.

48. Kjeldgaard-Pedersen, *Gesetz, Evangelium, und Busse*, 15–18.

49. Rogge, *Johann Agricolas Lutherverständnis*, 118.

50. Brecht, *Martin Luther*, 3:156; cf. Kjeldgaard-Pedersen, *Gesetz, Evangelium, und Busse*, 380.

51. On the Church Visitations, see Brecht, *Martin Luther*, 2:259–79.

52. According to Wengert, Melanchthon's controversy with Agricola had actually led him to conceptualize the ongoing role of law in the Christian life on the basis of a forensic notion of justification in Wengert, *Law and Gospel*, 201–2. Lund has shown that this development in Melanchthon became an important influence in Luther's thinking in the *Antinomian Disputations* (Lund, "Luther's 'Third Use of the Law,'" 8).

By 1537 Agricola was back in Wittenberg. By the summer, Agricola's theological positions began circulating in the form of anonymous theses around Wittenberg. Though Agricola would not claim the theses, his authorship was an open secret. Many of the theses were verbatim quotes from his published writings.[53] The theses were suffused with references to John 16:8.[54] One thesis asserted that "Christ says in John (16:8) that the Spirit will convict the world of sin, not the law."[55] Framed in this way, John 16:8 seemed to support an antinomian conflation of law into gospel for the conviction of sin.[56] Agricola concluded the law is unnecessary because the Spirit, who is given in the gospel, convicts of sins—not the law.

Luther relocated the Holy Spirit under gospel in the *Lectures on Galatians*. This move reinforced Agricola's view that the law is useless in relation to God. Echoing the Galatians letters, the eighth thesis proposed: "However, the Spirit was given formerly, and is given continually, and men are justified, without law, solely by the gospel about Christ."[57] Luther and Agricola agreed: the Spirit is given in the gospel. For Agricola, however, this meant that the gospel convicts of sins precisely because it brings the Spirit as the divine agent of law. The law was arbitrary in this interpretation because the gospel supplied the divine causes to both convict of sin—the Spirit—and to give righteousness—Christ.

John 16:8 seems to have validated Agricola's view that one teaching, the gospel, works both the conviction and the remission of sins.[58] Alluding

53. Silcock, "Introduction," 11–13. Silcock relies on the historical account in Edwards, *Luther and the False Brethren*, 156–79.

54. Whether Luther's sermons on John reinforced Agricola's antinomianism or Agricola's use of John 16:8 motivated Luther's attention to this biblical passage in his sermons cannot be known because Cruciger edited out the exact dates of Luther's sermons on John in the spring and summer of 1537.

55. WA 39/1:342.14–15.

56. Wengert indicated that Agricola rejected any positive function of law—not even to drive the sinner to Christ. This "theological use" was embedded within the gospel, which functioned to "condemn whatever is exalted and stands against the worship and faith in God" (Wengert, *Law and Gospel*, 29). Kjeldgaard-Pedersen clarified Wengert's analysis, suggesting that Agricola actually misunderstood Luther's law/gospel principle as a supercessionist denigration of the Old Testament in favor of the New (Kjeldgaard-Pedersen, *Gesetz, Evangelium, und Busse*, 380).

57. WA 39/1:342.27–28.

58. Wengert shows this was Agricola's position by 1525 in Wengert, *Law and Gospel*, 27–29; Kjeldgaard-Pedersen suggests this was a "peculiarity" of Agricola's "Wittenberg theology" from the beginning (1516 onwards), in Kjeldgaard-Pedersen, *Gesetz, Evangelium, und Busse*, 379.

to this biblical warrant, one of the antinomian theses stated, "Yet [a] doctrine is necessary that with great efficaciousness not only condemns, but also saves at the same time. This is, however, the gospel that simultaneously teaches repentance and the remission of sins."[59] Another of Agricola's theses used this warrant to redefine gospel. "Gospel" had to do with "God's wrath from heaven and, at the same time, God's righteousness."[60] Agricola understood both of these to be communicated in Christ's suffering on the cross. Agricola bolstered his collapse of law into gospel using Luther's association of the Spirit with the gospel in the *Lectures on Galatians* and the Spirit's office to convict of sins in John 16:8.

Agricola disassociated law from the accusing function within Luther's law/gospel paradigm. Instead, Agricola relocated the accusing function to the Spirit as the Spirit is given by Christ in the gospel. He concluded on this basis that law is nullified for the Christian in relation to God because it was inefficacious for justification; it only led to condemnation. "The law only convicts of sin and is certainly without the Holy Spirit; therefore it convicts to damnation."[61] Agricola reaffirmed the law's capacity to accuse of sin, but he rejected the possibility that its accusations could lead to justification because it reveals sin apart from the Spirit.[62] Agricola understood John 16:8 to support this position. Thus, Agricola asserted, "By whatever the Holy Spirit is not given, and by whatever men are not justified, this need not be taught, neither as the beginning, nor the middle, nor the end of justification."[63] Agricola removed law in the way Luther understood it as an independent precursor to gospel.[64] Instead, Agricola moved the accusing function typically associated with law to the Spirit in light of the Spirit's punitive office. He also understood this accusing Spirit to be given over through the gospel as Luther's *Lectures on Galatians* had also suggested.

Agricola challenged Luther to clarify his law/gospel paradigm in relation to the work of a particular trinitarian person. Luther's law/gospel schema as he developed it in the *Lectures on Galatians* hinged entirely

---

59. WA 39/1:343.18–20.
60. WA 39/1:343.21–23.
61. WA 39/1:343.16–17.
62. Cf. Wengert, *Law and Gospel*, 28–29.
63. WA 39/1:342.24–25.
64. This conclusion aligns with Kjeldgaard-Pedersen's opinion that Agricola fundamentally misunderstood the theological shape of Luther's law/gospel principle, confusing "law" and "gospel" with scriptural determinations in the Old and New Testament. See Kjeldgaard-Pedersen, *Gesetz, Evangelium, und Busse*, 379–80.

on the person of Christ. Christ answered the law's accusations with the imputation of his own law obedience to the human in gospel. Luther presented the law/gospel paradigm in this way without specifying the trinitarian person who animates the law and its accusations. When Agricola conflated the law's accusing function with the Spirit under gospel, Luther was pushed to rearticulate the law/gospel paradigm in light of his new view of the Spirit's punitive office.

Luther's New Challenge

Agricola's antinomianism challenged Luther to reconcile the law/gospel paradigm he set up in the *Lectures on Galatians* with the new Spirit-law association he discovered in John 16:8. As Luther understood law and gospel, the law was required to drive people to Christ.

By conflating law into gospel, Agricola threatened the theological calculus of Luther's logic. No theological mechanism remained to bring people to God. Agricola also ruptured Luther's notion of gospel as a divine word of promise, of good news, of consolation when he located the conviction of sins under gospel. Morally and ethically, Agricola's teaching on law also threatened to elide the moral character and behaviors that Luther thought befitting of the Christian life. Given the moral laxity rampant in Wittenberg in the 1530s, this threat imposed practical problems for social norms and behaviors in Luther's immediate context.

After the Cordatus Controversy, Melanchthon's increasingly nuanced concept of law, and Luther's new insights about the Spirit, the antinomian controversy provided Luther with an opportunity. He would now clarify the law-Spirit connection implied by John 16:8. In doing so, he would expand his pneumatology to explain how the Spirit could be both punitive and consoling. This more robust pneumatology would also provide resources for discussing his lifelong interest in the moral dimensions of the Christian life. Thus, the *Antinomian Disputations* go beyond debates about a third use of law. They also thematize the law's relation to the Spirit and the implications of this relation for the Christian moral life.

Spirit as Author of the Law

The first and second disputations, held twenty-six days apart in December 1537 and January 1538, saw the development of the Spirit's relation to law.

Luther interrogated this relation in arguments parsing the correct order of law then gospel and human penitential responses to that order. Luther provided a biblical logic to build a theology in which the Spirit could be connected to the law apart from gospel. He connected the giving of the law at Mt. Sinai to the coming of the Spirit at Pentecost.

Luther approached the Spirit's relation to the law by investigating how the law convicts of sins, or how the law gains this type of agency. In other words, what enlivens the otherwise inanimate law to accuse of sin and evoke a human response? Luther harkened back to the Spirit's punitive office in John 16:8 for the answer: "The law does not accuse of sin without the Holy Spirit."[65] But why? Luther developed his response across three distinct arguments in which he connected the Spirit to the giving of the law at Mt. Sinai. While the biblical narrative itself does not specify a particular divine person at Sinai, Luther decided that the Spirit reached out of eternity and "writes [the law] on tablets of stone."[66] On this basis, he determined that the Spirit is the "author of the law" (*autor legis*).[67] The Spirit is the divine agent who enlivens the law, revealing it at Sinai and animating it for the accusation of sin.

Following an interpretive tradition that aligned the Hebrew Bible and New Testament themes, Luther correlated the giving of the law at Sinai with the coming of the Spirit at Pentecost. Exodus 19 and 20 narrate God's giving of the law to Moses and Aaron at Sinai. Exodus 20:1 introduces the pronouncement of the Decalogue, saying: "God spoke all these words, saying . . ." The term for God used here is Elohim (אֱלֹהִים), a general word for deity and divinity that is often used as a proper name for Israel's God. In context, the plural form of the word is used in conjunction with a singular verb. This led Luther to interpret the passage in a trinitarian sense, but he took creative license when he identified the Spirit as the divine Person referenced in the text.[68]

---

65. WA 39/1:371.1–2; cf. 389.3–3; 391.18–19; 484.14. Christine Helmer has shown that Luther understood the Spirit "as the person who, in its outer-trinitarian role, reveals the inner-Trinity to Christians." See Helmer, *Trinity and Martin Luther*, 215.

66. WA 39/1:389.8–9; cf. 370.11; 371.2; 484.14.

67. WA 39/1:389.8–9.

68. My sincere thanks to Esther Menn, the Ralph W. and Marilyn R. Klein Professor of Old Testament/Hebrew Bible at the Lutheran School of Theology at Chicago, who provided valuable consultation on Luther's biblical interpretation.

This creative reading allowed Luther to build a pneumatology structured by the *deus absconditus*.[69] The Spirit comes as a "terrifying tempest"[70]—an allusion to the violent storm and wind that tie Exodus 19–20 and Acts 2 together in the literary tradition. This law-giving Spirit at Sinai, Luther said, was the Spirit in its "divine majesty."[71] The Spirit's "incomprehensible," "dreadful," "crushing glory" had to be veiled and caused the people of God to flee. This was an encounter with the Spirit as "bare divinity"[72] and the Spirit in its divine "nature, substance, and majesty."[73] This Spirit was—and is—terrifying.

The law accuses of sin because it is animated as a divine word of the Spirit in this unmediated divine majesty. When the Spirit comes to the human person in this way, the Spirit comes as the divine agent of law.[74] Unmediated, the so-called "crushing glory" of the Spirit's divinity causes the law to crush, condemn, and destroy sin. Thus, Luther made sense of the claim in John 16:8 that the Spirit convicts of sin because he thought the Spirit comes to the human person in its bare, unmediated divinity as law.

This view of the Spirit stands disturbingly alongside the more traditional paracletic conceptions of the Spirit as consoler, sanctifier, and vivifier in Luther's analysis.[75] Mediation is central to Luther's understanding here. When the Spirit comes to the human person in these positive ways in the gospel, the Spirit's divinity is mediated and masked. This occurs in two specific ways: through Christ's gift and through external signs. Luther asserted that "Christ the mediator" sends the Spirit as a gift in faith.[76] When the Spirit is sent as gift, then the human person experiences the Spirit as consoler and Spirit of truth.[77]

---

69. Anderas observes the duplication of the hidden and revealed God framework in movement from Luther's theology of the cross to his understanding of the Spirit. See Anderas, *Renovatio*, 78; cf. WA 1:362.1–19.

70. WA 39/1:484.5–7; 390.15.

71. WA 39/1:370.19; 484.6–7, 13.

72. WA 39/1:391.3.

73. WA 39/1:370.12–13; cf. 391.17–18.

74. Cf. Kärkkäinen, *Luthers trinitarische Theologie*, 134–40, 145–50.

75. Marit Trelstad has described Luther's understanding of the terrorizing Spirit in the *Antinomian Disputations* as a "theology of abuse," drawing out the troubling implications of the Spirit's terrorizing and paracletic aspects for victims of domestic violence. See Trelstad, "Terror Begins at Home."

76. WA 39/1:389.6, 10–11.

77. WA 39/1:389.8–9.

The Spirit as gift, veiled and enveloped in signs, transforms the way the Spirit comes to human persons. As gift, the Spirit is "enveloped" in signs such as the dove who descended at Christ's baptism and the tongues of fire at Pentecost.[78] Luther juxtaposed the Spirit's presence in its majesty with its presence "veiled in signs." The former is incomprehensible, kills, and crushes; the latter becomes "bearable and easy."[79] There is a protective quality to these signs, which moderate the Spirit's majesty so that it no longer crushes, terrifies, or kills. This transformation in the way the Spirit comes to the human is key to Luther's thinking about the ongoing role of law in the Christian life. We will return to this theme below.

As we have seen, Luther clarified the Spirit's relation to law by reading Exodus 19–20 together with Acts 2. He understood the two offices identified in John 16:8 to summarize a biblical theme. The Spirit appears in two moments as a terrifying storm where it speaks to God's people. In the first instance, the Spirit's divine majesty is uncovered and unmediated. Here the Spirit speaks law. In the second instance, the Spirit's divinity is veiled, making it bearable for the divine-human encounter. Interestingly, in the arguments where Luther developed this Spirit-law connection, he did not address the second part of the Spirit's office identified in John 16:8—the Spirit convicts of righteousness. Nor did he associate this second office with the giving of justifying faith in the Gospel. To better understand the Spirit's two offices, we must now return to the human person to explore how the Spirit's relation to law aligns with human penitential responses to law and gospel.

"Penitence" and the Human Dimension of Law/Gospel

We are working to understand how Luther constructed a theological logic that preserved the law in the Christian life contra Agricola. We have just looked briefly at the pneumatological dimension. Luther expanded his understanding of the Spirit's two offices in John 16:8 to identify the Spirit as the author and agent of the law. The Spirit is now connected to both law and to gospel. Now, we are going to look at the human dimension. To preserve the law in the Christian life after gospel, Luther introduced the concept of penitence (*poenitentia*)[80] as two moments of human experience correlated

---

78. WA 39/1:370.20–21; 484.15.
79. WA 39/1:484.5–7.
80. Christine Helmer documented the "distinctly anti-Catholic inflection" of Luther

to law and gospel. Luther defined penitence in the first thesis proposed for debate against the Antinomians on December 18, 1537. The thesis asserts: "According to the testimony of all, and in fact, penitence is sorrow because of sin with the added intention of a better life."[81] Penitence names two human *affective* experiences, sorrow and a good intention.

In the medieval theology of Luther's day, penitence referred to three interrelated sacramental activities—contrition, confession, and satisfaction. It was thought that these three activities were necessary for the absolution of sin, which was spoken by a priest in the words "*te absolvo*," I absolve you.[82] The medieval discussions of penitence familiar to Luther saw heightened interest in one of these activities in particular, contrition. Contrition was understood as an inner affective process of sorrow and a renewed intention not to sin again. This process occurred in the human conscience. Luther's elevation of the human conscience in law and gospel was not new but rather was situated as a part of this theological shift and should be understood within that trajectory.

---

interpretation during the *Lutherrenaissance*. Protestant theologians elevated certain texts and translated medieval (Catholic) terms into more palatable Protestant ones to highlight difference and discontinuity—emphasizing Luther's "radical innovation rather than connection to the medieval Catholic tradition." See Helmer, *How Luther Became the Reformer*, 69. Translation of poenitentia into "repentance" is one example of this legacy. Rather than translating the Latin *poenitentia* into its modern English equivalent, penitence, English-language Luther scholarship perpetuates the anti-Catholic agenda of the *Lutherrenaissance* in translating this concept as "repentance" without clarification. *Poenitentia* is constructed in Protestant terms as a confession of faith (as repentance), abstracting the term from its medieval sacramental context Luther would have understood. This sacramental activity aimed at supporting the sanctified life over the span of the Christian life. Translated as "repentance," this context is lost to a psychological awareness of the self as sinner that constantly renews the individual's confession of faith in Christ. By contrast, Jared Wicks's lifelong work on Luther's *sacramentii fides* includes a view of lifelong penitence, which ascribed a role to good works in the Christian life. See Wicks, *Luther's Reform*, 15–42. Although Luther eliminated the distinctly sacramental view of *poenitentia*, I use the translated term "penitence" to retain the ritualized reference that would have been apparent to Luther's medieval audience. By preserving this conceptual context, penitence also maintains the conceptual integrity between justification and sanctification in Luther's thought.

81. WA 39/1:345.16–17.

82. Andreas Stegmann shows how by 1519, Luther was already revising the structures of high medieval sacramental practice of penitence by shifting the gift of divine grace prior to satisfaction and priestly absolution. The result was that absolution became a distinct outward communication of the grace already internally received while satisfaction was relocated to the day-to-day activity of the Christian life after the justification experience. See Stegmann, *Luthers Auffasung vom christlichen Leben*, 249.

Eleventh-century Gregorian reforms ignited interest in contrition by stressing the role of the conscience in questions of virtue. Peter Lombard transmitted this interest in contrition into the Middle Ages in book IV of his *Sentences*, which Luther commented on in 1509.[83] Quoting Ambrose the bishop of Milan (fourth century CE), Lombard repeated the historical understanding that "penance is to decry past evils, and not to commit again things which are to be decried."[84] In his own definition, Lombard highlighted the emotional and volitional dimensions of penance: penance is a virtue by which we *bewail* and *hate* evils we have committed.[85] This disposition, however, anticipated the future; it included an intention. Sorrow and hatred of sin has the "purpose of amendment" so "we will not commit again the things we have bewailed."[86] Lombard then determined that this inner contrition is accompanied by outer penitential acts performed at two other anthropological sites. Confession is penance in speech. Satisfaction is penance in the physical body expressed through deeds and behaviors.[87] Luther largely took over this understanding of penitence as inner contrition. As the following chapters will show, however, he also maintained important roles for speech and the body in the performance of lifelong penitence as prayer and moral action.

In the second half of the fifteenth century, the Augustinian cloister in Erfurt became home to complex discussions about the nature of contrition. Luther would take his own monastic vows in this very Erfurt cloister just a few decades later. Of interest was the relation of human and divine action in contrition and how contrition relates to the infusion of justifying divine grace. Gabriel Biel (d. ca. 1495 CE) understood contrition via the principle of doing one's best (*facere quod in se est*). He thought God rewarded human effort in attrition, which the medieval understood as self-love in fear of punishment. Per Biel, God rewarded human effort by transforming one's fear of punishment into contrition out of true love of God for God's own sake. Sorrow for sin, then, resulted from a desire

---

83. Cf. WA 9:28–94.

84. Ambrose, *Sermo* 25n1, cited in Lombard, *Sentences* IV, d.14, c.2. Note: Silano opted to translate *poenitentia* in Lombard as penance.

85. Lombard, *Sentences* IV, d.14, c.3.

86. Lombard, *Sentences* IV, d.14, c.3. Lombard and Luther both cite the Christ's command in Luke 10:37 as the basis of the good intention. See WA 39/1:465.1.

87. Lombard, *Sentences* IV, d.16, c.1. Lombard divided penitence into three "performances" acted out at various anthropological sites: contrition is penance in the *heart*, confession is penance in *words*, and satisfaction is penance in *actions*.

to please and be united with God as the good intention even if this desire originated in fear.[88] In Biel's formulation, both divine and human agents had a hand in forming contrition in the human affect.

Biel's interlocutor and colleague in Erfurt, Johannes von Dorsten (d. ca. 1481 CE) parsed contrition somewhat differently. He distinguished what he called "true contrition" (*vera contritio*), as contrition by grace (*contritio per gratiam*), from contrition by punishment (*contritio per poena*), which he saw to result in sorrow for sin out of fear of punishment, i.e., attrition. Dorsten thought that the love upon which sorrow for sin and the good intention occurred in true contrition required a divine cause.[89] Thus, Dorsten advocated a divine cause of inner contrition that preceded outer penitential acts in confession or satisfaction. Though Luther's familiarity with Dorsten is not known for certain, Luther's position on contrition resembles Dorsten's, even evoking Dorsten's language of "true contrition."[90]

In 1517, Luther infamously nailed this medieval discussion to the Castle Church doors in Wittenberg.[91] But what he said was not necessarily new. His theses against indulgences asserted that inner contrition brings the Christian remission of guilt and punishment in absolution, apart from any outer acts of confession and satisfaction.[92] Inner contrition brings justifying divine grace apart from further action. But in 1537, Luther picked back up what we thought he left on the Castle Church door. He returned to penitence for resources to describe the human dimension of law and gospel. What he found was a conceptual resource for articulating human affective responses to law and gospel: penitence is the "entire life" of the Christian.[93] As we will see, the Spirit's relation to law and gospel would

---

88. Oberman, *Harvest of Medieval Theology*, 132–35. Similar contours emerge in Scotus's conception of contrition. See Wawrykow, "Sacraments in Thirteenth-Century Theology," 8.

89. Zumkeller, *Erbsünde, Gnade, Rechtfertigung und Verdienst*, 357–58.

90. Cf. WA 39/1:569.5.

91. The first mention that Luther posted the theses on the Castle Church door can be tracked back to Melanchthon's preface to the second volume of Luther's Latin works, published after Luther's death in June 1546. Historical record shows Luther sent the theses as part of a letter to Archbishop Albrecht on October 31, 1517. Whether he also posted the theses on the church doors cannot be known for certain. See Wengert, "[95 Theses or] Disputation," 22–23.

92. WA 1:233.12–14; 235.3–8. Stegmann described Luther's understanding of *poenitentia* here as an "evangelical penitence" (Stegmann, *Luthers Auffassung*, 251).

93. WA 39/1:350.20–21. We will see Luther conceptualize penitence across the entire life of the Christian as both a move from law to gospel in justification and a cyclical

be critical to Luther's understanding of these affective responses. To begin, however, we will explore these affective responses vis-à-vis Luther's traditional categories of law and gospel.

Sorrow Is Emotional Suffering under the Law

Sorrow is the first component in the logical order of law/gospel and contrition. Sorrow (*dolor*) is the inner response to the accusing law. For example, Luther wrote, "The first part of penitence, sorrow, is caused solely by the law . . ."[94] The law causes sorrow by working specifically in the human's affective center, the heart.[95] To this, Luther suggested: "Properly speaking, sorrow is nothing else—and cannot be anything else—than the touch or feeling of the law in the heart or the conscience."[96] Luther described human experience by bringing together his typical notion of the accusing and terrifying law with the linguistic framework of medieval sacramental theology. Law produces a particular feeling in the heart; that feeling is the first part of contrition, sorrow.

Sorrow specifies a negative emotional register as the anthropological effect of law. As the "proper effect" of law,[97] Luther characterized sorrow in negative affective terms: "to suffer," to be "shook," and to be "stung in the

---

process of sorrow and the good intention in relation to the Spirit as sanctification. This position helped Luther to counter Agricola's understanding vis-à-vis Colossians 1:10 that penitence occurs in the Christian life as an increase in one's relation to the Word and a growth in self-knowledge. On this point, see Wengert, *Law and Gospel*, 36.

94. WA 39/1:345.22–23. Wengert shows Agricola to separate sorrow from contrition in his *Annotations* on 2 Corinthians. Highlighting the need Luther will encounter for defending the affective response in contrition, Wengert writes that "Agricola could not bring himself to mention this kind of feeling (after all Judas had felt bad, too)" (Wengert, *Law and Gospel*, 42).

95. Luther's understanding of the heart is typically understood in terms of his distinction between the inner and outer person, which implies Luther did away with nuanced understanding of human noetic powers. This view is challenged in Stolt's linguistic analysis, which shows that Luther's terminology, "heart," encompasses all the faculties of the rational soul: intellect, will, and affect. For example, when Luther discusses Psalm 51:12, Stolt shows him to use the language of *animam*, *intellectum*, *voluntatem*, and *affectum* to parse the meaning of the phrase, "Create in me a clean heart, O God." See Stolt, "Herzlich lieb habe ich dich," 407–8. Stolt's argument is critical for understanding the way Luther uses anthropological language in relation to "heart" in the *Antinomian Disputations*.

96. WA 39/1:345.18–19.

97. WA 39/1:415.17; cf. 445.5.

heart."⁹⁸ Law produces the emotional response of sorrow because it exposes the person's weakness—her sin and disobedience. Law, as Luther explained, "makes known and reveals true sin and, in this exposure, reduces man to nothing and condemns and impels [him] to seek help from Christ."⁹⁹ Law escalates this inner suffering by making demands that cannot be met: "The law requires its fulfillment, which no one at any time surpasses or will surpass."¹⁰⁰ Sorrow is the human person's experience of anguish and torment in response to the law's impossible demands and one's own ongoing inability to meet them. Thus, sorrow appears as inner emotional suffering.

The Good Intention Is the Emotional Response to Gospel

Sorrow leads into the good intention. Luther also defined the good intention in affective terms. Like sorrow, the good intention has to do with the heart's affective disposition toward God: "To hate sin out of love of God truly is a good intention."¹⁰¹ Love of God correlates inversely to hatred of what is offensive to God. In this sense, there is a repellent quality to this love. It deters the lover from things that God hates and simultaneously draws the lover toward God's self.

As one might expect, Luther grounded the good intention in faith as the first positive affective response to God. Faith constructed an affective foundation from which a multitude of good intentions would be produced over a lifetime.¹⁰² Luther took up this topic in the second disputation in January 1538. In an argument against the conflation of works and *poenitentia* in justification, Luther outlined the correct order of faith then works. He began with a classic faith-oriented statement: "Who believes in Christ has eternal life and is just."¹⁰³ Works and the good intention follow: "Then the righteous and pious person, where she accepts the remission of sins, does good works and has a good intention."¹⁰⁴ The good intention of faith is

---

98. WA 39/1:346.9-10; 408.9-10. Wengert shows Melanchthon, like Luther, to defend the necessity of contrition prior to grace contra Agricola. See Wengert, *Law and Gospel*, 144-45.
99. WA 39/1:371.14-16.
100. WA 39/1:393.5-6.
101. WA 39/1:346.28-29.
102. WA 39/1:472.9-10.
103. WA 39/1:472.6-7.
104. WA 39/1:472.7-8.

the necessary condition for subsequent good intentions and associated good works. As the first good intention, faith functions like a fountain for action across a lifetime. Luther continued, "For faith is the principal good intention from which afterwards the rest of the good works flow as fruits and endure for the entire life."[105] Faith grounds subsequent works because of the way faith orients the human affect expressed in the good intention. After belief (*credo*) in Christ, the human affect is organized around God. She "wants to believe and [wants] to love and magnify God's word."[106] These inner affective responses are correlated as intentions for outer action as well. She intends not to commit adultery, associate with harlots (i.e., fornicate), and not to succumb to drunkenness.[107] Thus, Luther constructs a complex view of the good intention, grounded in his traditional concept of faith, with lifelong positive affective responses to God in heart and action.

This God-ordered affective orientation in the good intention renews the epistemic need for law. Unlike sorrow, which operates strictly on a negative emotional register, the good intention has both negative and positive affective dimensions. There is a push and pull evident in Luther's description of the good intention in this argument. The Christian *loves* God and all that pleases God and correspondingly *hates* all that offends God. Yet, Luther was committed to the blindness of the intellect.[108] As such, the blind intellect requires a guide in knowing what is and is not good vis-à-vis God.

Luther developed the law's epistemic value for the good intention. He presented law as a guide and encouragement to the good. The justified (*pii*) "need the law as a kind of guide" in their daily struggle against sin, Luther said.[109] Before justification (*ante iusticationem*), the law accuses and terrifies, but Luther was clear that it serves a different purpose for the justified: "It encourages them to the good."[110] As the theological register

---

105. WA 39/1:472.9–11.

106. WA 39/1:472.11–12.

107. WA 39/1:472.13–14.

108. Cf. Luther's summary of human intellectual and volitional powers in thesis 34 of the *Disputation against Scholastic Theology*: "In brief, a person by nature has neither correct precept nor good will" (WA 1:225.37).

109. WA 39/1:432.11–15.

110. WA 39/1:474.21–22. Luther's comments here problematize the dogmatic rejection of a third use of the law in Luther scholarship. Complicating the entrenched position among Luther scholars, Lund identified 12 distinct positive uses of the "*salutarum usus legis*" for sanctification in the Christian life in Luther's arguments. One of those uses is pertinent here: "*lex hortetur ad bonum*." See Lund, "Luther's 'Third Use of the Law,'" 199.

under which the human responds with the good intention, the gospel allows the law to function in this way by freeing the Christian from the law's terror.[111] Gospel must be added to the law, Luther says, "so that the conscience can intend the good."[112] Law doesn't disappear under gospel in this picture. Rather, it is transformed in human experience through the move from law to gospel. Law no longer terrifies. Instead, it serves an epistemic purpose to reorient the good intention toward God.

Christ as Gift and Example Reinstates Law under Gospel for the Good Intention

Alongside Luther's new emphasis on the human dimension of law/gospel in penitence, there is another important dimension to the good intention that saw Luther resume his traditional emphasis on Christ's agency in justification. In justification, Christ elevates the human conscience to the good intention under gospel by liberating the conscience from the law's accusations. Christ also reintroduces a form of law under gospel that guides the good intention in the liberated conscience.[113] Luther articulated these two effects of Christ on the human person using a modification of an Augustinian trope: Christ as gift and example (*donum et exemplum Christi*). As gift, Christ liberates from the law. As example, Christ models obedience to the law.

Augustine developed his idea of Christ as sacrament and example (*sacramentum et exemplum Christi*) in book IV of *On the Trinity*. The trope explained how Christ functioned in two ways to effect salvation. Each way was "in harmony" with an effect of sin on humans. Humans are dead in "both soul and body," Augustine explained, in soul because of sin and in

---

111. WA 39/1:345.24–25.

112. WA 39/1:345.28–29.

113. In his 1534 *Scholia*, Melanchthon argued that forensic justification, the declaration of the Christian as righteous on account of Christ, actually made the human conscience good. On this basis, he understood the law to be reinstated in the Christian life as a guide for the justified conscience to please God. Wengert dismisses similarities in Luther's arguments in the *Antinomian Disputations*, suggesting Luther was merely defending his friend's position. See Wengert, *Law and Gospel*, 196–99, 210. Contra Wengert, the way Luther connected law to both the *exemplum Christi* and the Spirit suggests a development in Luther's understanding of law beyond even that of Melanchthon's position. This aligns with Lund's claim that "it appears that Luther's conflict with Agricola sharpened and strengthened his doctrine of the *donum spiritus*, of sanctification, and of the third use of the law. A line of development can be traced throughout the controversy" (Lund, "Luther's 'Third Use of the Law,'" 355).

the body because of the punishment of sin.[114] Christ as sacrament effects salvation on the repentant human soul by bringing the mystery of the crucifixion to the soul in the Eucharist. Christ as exemplum effects salvation of the body through Christ's own resurrection, supplying an example of the resurrected body to comfort the saints until the last days.[115] Luther studied this trope during his theological studies at Erfurt, where he wrote marginalia on Augustine's *De Trinitate* in 1509.[116] Luther appropriated and modified Augustine's sacramental and eschatological image to expand the temporal and ethical significance of these concepts.[117]

In Luther's terminology, Christ as gift liberates the sorrowful soul from the terrors of the law. Like Augustine's sacramental concept, Luther associated Christ as gift with remission of sins in the soul.[118] However, Luther incorporated overtones of Anselm's satisfaction theory into this otherwise Augustinian picture. The effect made more explicit the precise way remission of sins by the divine gift occurred. Christ as gift justifies by (1) satisfying the law's demands, and (2) giving that benefit over to the Christian in faith. Anselm's influence is evident in Luther's description of Christ as gift: "When [Christ] is present, the law loses its power. The law is satisfied. It cannot administer wrath because Christ has freed us from it."[119] Christ as gift works the remission of sins in this description by ameliorating the law, by giving what it demands.

The other side of the gift sees the imputation of this freedom from Christ to the soul. Here, Luther echoed his 1520 treatise the *Freedom of a Christian*, noting that Christ as gift "gives liberation from the terrors of the law, from sin and death . . . [because] whoever lays hold of this benefit of Christ by faith has by way of imputation fulfilled the law."[120] Because Christ as gift both satisfies the law and marks the justified as righteous, Christ negates the law's accusing capacity in the life of the Christian. The Christian no longer experiences the law's condemning accusations. We have here

---

114. Augustine, *On the Holy Trinity* 4.3.5 (NPNF 3:71).

115. Augustine, *On the Holy Trinity* 4.3.6 (NPNF 3:72).

116. Cf. WA 9:15-27.

117. Bo Holm discusses Luther's use and adaptations of the metaphor in Holm, *Gabe und Geben*, 193.

118. WA 39/1:462.16-22.

119. WA 39/1:372.20—373.1.

120. WA 39/1:387.2-4; 388.4-5.

Luther's classic law/gospel construct that sets human and divine agency in inverse relations in the fulfillment of the law and justification.

Luther's doctrine of justification occupied only one part of the trope. When Luther turned to the second part, Christ as example, he did something surprising. Where Augustine understood Christ as example in eschatological terms as resurrection of the body, Luther construed it in moral-ethical terms. Peter and Paul, he commented, "present to us Christ as example so it follows that we might become imitators of good works."[121] There is a correct order to the action here. Christ acts, then the human acts: "Christ fulfilled the law, and now it is certainly appropriate that we follow his footsteps by living piously and saintly, that you not be an adulterer, a thief, a robber."[122] Christ as example pertained to action in the temporal life, not the eschatological one.

Consistent with this temporal dimension, there is a clear shift in emphasis from human passivity in reception of Christ's gift to human activity in response to Christ's example. Luther introduced this shift by noting that "Christ is presented to us as gift or sacrament and example so that we might follow his footsteps."[123] When Luther specifies Christ as gift, the human is passive: "As sacrament and mystery . . . we cannot follow him." The reason is the disparity in human capacity. "Christ is sacrament because he redeemed me from sin, death, and devil, which my righteousness is unable to do."[124] Yet, when Luther described Christ as example, he elevated human capacity for a type of mimetic activity: "As example, we are able to follow and imitate [Christ]" and "to become imitators of good works."[125] This mimetic action is rooted in the effects of Christ as gift. Because Christ redeemed the sinner "from all impiety and death, so we preach and glorify him by imitating good works."[126] The move from gift to example was not simply about satisfaction of the law for justification but included an

---

121. WA 39/1:462.23—463.2.
122. WA 39/1:464.25—465.1.
123. WA 39/1:465.7-9.
124. WA 39/1:465.12-14.
125. WA 39/1:465.9. Luther emphasized the good intention as itself a dimension of law obedience. He also wanted to show that action in response to the good intention is possible. In doing so, he reflected the shift from intention and action as the locus for sin and righteousness in medieval theology after Abelard (cf. Abelard, *Scito te ipsum*, 12-16, 45-57).
126. WA 39/1:462.17-20.

outcome in the Christian's life.[127] Christ as gift makes possible human action in the temporal realm modeled after Christ as example.

In this way, Christ as example actually re-establishes law under gospel and models its fulfillment. Norman Lund argued that Luther understood Christ as example to actually "establish the law more powerfully" by creating an imperative for good works in the Christian life.[128] Lund's claim is validated by Luther's analysis of Christ as rabbi, or "teacher of the law." Luther claimed that in this role Christ "interprets the law ... so that we might understand what kind of work or fulfillment it is that the law requires of us."[129] It would be easy to weaken the role of human action here by casting Christ's interpretation of law exclusively as a call to faith. To be sure, Luther included that interpretation.[130] Yet, Luther also expanded this interpretation by grounding Christ's interpretation of law as actions and behaviors in the Christian life:

> Christ as example is nothing else than to show in what manner we ought to live in obedience to God, parents, and superiors, and to be a good follower of all works and virtue ... therefore the law has not been abolished by Christ but rather established. One ought to teach: Christ fulfilled the law and now it is surely fitting that we follow his steps in godly and holy living.[131]

Luther's reference to the three estates (*ecclesia, oeconomia,* and *politia*) demonstrates the temporal social dimension to the human mimetic activity in response to Christ's example.[132] After justification, human social life is the domain where law obedience occurs. Christ as example thus functions as another type of epistemological aid to clarify the moral contours outlined in law that should shape the temporal life.

---

127. Kim has shown that this theme was essential in Luther's unfolding understanding of a type of law under gospel throughout the 1530s. She notes that "Christ the example has nothing to do with the justification of sinners" (Kim, *Luther on Faith and Love,* 94).

128. Lund, "Luther's 'Third Use of the Law,'" 216.

129. WA 39/1:387.5–7. Lindbeck isolated what he called a "rabbinic mind" in Luther's *Catechisms*, noting that Luther devoted over half of the writings to the Decalogue as instruction or teaching (*doctrina*) as a guide to the Christian life. Lindbeck did not address the rabbinic nature of Christ himself as teacher of the law in Luther's thinking. See Lindbeck, "Martin Luther," 151–52.

130. Cf. WA 39/1:387.8—388.4.

131. WA 39/1:464.19—465.1.

132. Cf. WA 7:65.10–25.

The move from Christ as gift to Christ as example aligns with the shift from sorrow to the good intention under law/gospel. Sorrow, evoked as a response to the accusing law, is soothed by Christ as gift, who offers—and indeed is—the consoling Word that the law's demands stand fulfilled. Christ as gift moves the soul from law to gospel in justification and returns again and again as the Christian combats her sin. Under gospel, the human person's good intention is generated out of a new love of God and guided by the law toward the things pleasant to God. Christ as example works under gospel to reinstate and model law obedience, not for justification but a new obedience resulting from it. Christ's example shows in practical ways how to obey the law in action.[133] In this respect, Christ's example functions as another support to the human intellect, modeling in application how one can fulfill the law and live out their new love of God in social arenas.[134]

In summary, to counter Agricola, Luther clarified the anthropological dimension of his law/gospel paradigm. He described a human affective dimension into his law/gospel principle that pertains to the human experience of law. His conceptual apparatus was the medieval notion of penitence (*poenitentia*) situated across law and gospel. The human person responds to law in the heart with sorrow for sin. When Christ as gift liberates the person from the law's accusations, she can then respond with a new understanding of the law's requirements for the good intention to love God and neighbor. This new understanding finds a model in Christ as example. When Luther considered the divine dimension of law/gospel, he saw Christ as the agent of salvation. Christ's righteousness fulfills the law and gives this law fulfillment over to the Christian in the gospel. But the introduction of the human dimension to law/gospel allowed Luther to identify two distinct instantiations of law. The accusing law evokes sorrow for sin in the human heart before gospel. The law reinstated by Christ's example guides the good intention under gospel. Thus, "law" corresponds

---

133. Kim interprets the *exemplum Christi* as a "paradigm" of Christian love. "The prototype for imitation is found in how God handles human beings in and through Jesus Christ. That is, what is revealed in the vertical relation, which is actively initiated by God and passively responded to by human beings through faith in Christ, becomes the paradigm for Christians in their horizontal acts of love" to the neighbor (Kim, *Luther on Faith and Love*, 190–91). In this regard, Kim echoes Kitamori's concept of "service to the Pain of God" in Kitamori, *Theology of the Pain of God*. Steiger roots Luther's understanding of the *exemplum Christi* in Luther's reliance on Renaissance thought, foregrounding Marcus Terentius Varro (116–27 BCE) on this topic. See Steiger, *Fünf Zentralthemen der Theologie Luthers*, 257.

134. WA 39/1:464.19–22.

to two experiences the human undergoes in relation to law and gospel. The experiences of sorrow and the good intention in penitence reveal the human dimension of law and gospel.

Before Christ, under Christ, and in the Spirit: Categories for the Human Dimension of Law/Gospel

In the previous section, we established that Luther preserved the ongoing role of the law in the Christian life contra Agricola by using penitential language to sketch the human affective responses under the rubric of law and gospel. Luther demonstrated that Christ does not actually do away with law in justification. Rather, Christ as gift alters the human relation to law by ameliorating its accusations. This stance paved the way for Luther to preserve the law after justification in relation to the human's good intention. However, this meant Luther needed to clarify exactly how the law functions under gospel. This required that he reposition law in relation to its divine agents. To do this, he charted specific moments of justification correlated to law and gospel, Christ and the Spirit, and the new anthropological dimension of sorrow and the good intention. Out of this framework, a role for law in the Christian life under gospel emerged.

Law and gospel appear as a theological binary, but Luther was actually quite interested in distinguishing distinct moments in human experience across the trajectory of law and gospel. To parse these moments, he investigated what he called the "order of the thing" (*ordo rei*) as this order aligned with his law/gospel principle. Since Augustine, theologians have tracked changes in the human condition and relation to God in what is typically called an "order of salvation" (*ordo salutis*). Luther also used this idea and mapped the *ordo* to law and gospel.

For Luther, God's order of salvation was unbound by the rules of the natural order. This is evident in his reversal of life and death in theological matters: "The order of the thing itself is that death and sin are in nature before life and righteousness."[135] Luther aligned this order with his law/gospel principle to establish an anthropological shift from sin to righteousness, saying:

> For we know, deeply feel, sin is present, that death utterly terrifies us, etc. This first thing is taught by the law . . . so that we do

---
135. WA 39/1:347.1–2.

> not despair, that other doctrine is being preserved in the church, which teaches consolation against the accusation and terrors of the law, grace against God's wrath, remission of sins and righteousness against sin, life against death. That doctrine is the gospel.[136]

The theological order of law/gospel inverted the natural order of deterioration. According to the logic of the natural order, righteousness should devolve into sin and life into death. For Luther, the reverse was true in theological perspective. The *ordo rei* he developed in the *Antinomian Disputations* would clarify how these processes work at varying stages of human spiritual and temporal life.

This same inverted theological order is described with greater specificity in four categories that Luther deployed to define the changing relation of the law and the human person. He oriented this changing relation around particular divine persons, namely Christ and the Spirit. Luther introduced these categories in two theses for the second disputation where he posited that:

> 45. As the law was before Christ, it accused us. But under Christ, [law] is placated by the remission of sins. Then, [law] is to be fulfilled in the Spirit.
>
> 46. Thus after Christ in the coming life, there, [law] will remain as fulfilled when that new creature, what it meanwhile demands, is brought about.[137]

Four sequential categories in the human relation to law can be isolated in these theses: "before Christ" (*ante Christo*), "under Christ" (*sub Christo*), "in the Spirit" (*deinceps Spiritus*), and "after Christ" (*post Christum*).

What we see in the moments of this order is unprecedented. Luther used particular categories to sequence moments in the law-human relation that keep the law and the Spirit together in relation to the human. Before Christ, the law exposes the human sinful condition and accuses it. Under Christ, Christ's righteousness is imputed to the human, satisfying the law's demands and fulfilling it for justification. Thus, "before" and "under Christ" indicate a change in the human-law relation that sees the dissolution of the law's accusations on account of the human's imputed righteousness. This is Luther's traditional move from law to gospel.

---

136. WA 39/1:361.14–16; 362.5–9.
137. WA 39/1:349.39—350.2.

The categories "in the Spirit" and "after Christ" are striking. They reveal Luther doing something different as he delineated progressive stages of the human person's salvation. Of particular interest for our purposes is the category "in the Spirit." This stage sees a type of law fulfillment worked in the human herself *after* justification but *before* death and resurrection, i.e., in the temporal life.[138] Yet, this peculiar law fulfillment occurs only in relation to the third person of the Trinity, the Spirit. Below, we will work to determine what type of law fulfillment Luther has in mind here. By breaking the law/gospel order down into this particular sequence, Luther kept law/gospel together with Christ and the Spirit and, remarkably, did so with the additional perspective of anthropological experience.

These categories have antecedents in medieval theology. For example, Peter Lombard borrowed an Augustinian picture of the human relative to grace from the perspective of salvation history, the *ordo salutis*. Lombard sequenced the order of the human's progression through this history in four stages: (1) the original condition (prelapsarian); (2) after the fall/before regeneration (postlapsarian); (3) after regeneration/before eternal consummation (post-regeneration); and (4) in eternal life (eschatological/resurrected).[139] Stage two in Lombard's *ordo* describes the human sinner before justification and stage four reflects the resurrected life. But in the move from stage two to stage three, Lombard shows the addition of divine grace to justify the human person in the temporal life before death.

Luther's categories are largely consistent with the theological trajectory outlined in Lombard's order. However, the stage "in the Spirit" is new and allowed him to clarify the role of law under gospel. Luther's category "before Christ" aligns with Lombard's stage two. Both categories describe the postlapsarian human person, but apart from grace. Here, she is "sinner." This maps onto Luther's traditional category of law. Luther's category

---

138. It is noteworthy that Luther discussed the Christian relation to law "in the Spirit" in terms of fulfilling the law, not keeping the law. Typically used in conjunction with critiques of merit, the former term implies a certain justifying satisfaction of law. The latter, keeping the law, had rabbinic overtones for Luther and as such was chided with his anti-Jewish attitudes.

139. Lombard, *Sentences* II, d.25, c.6, 9; d.26, c.7. Lombard took his picture from Augustine, who defined the stages as (1) pre-sin (*ante peccatum*), (2) post-sin, pre-restoration by grace (*post peccatum ante reparationem gratiae*), (3) post–restoration by grace, pre-eternal life (*post repartionem ante confirmationem*), and (4) perfected in eternal life (*post confirmationem in gloria*). See Augustine, *De Correptione et Gratia* in PL 44:936–37; *City of God* 22.30. On Luther's use of Lombard, see Wieneke, *Luther und Petrus Lombardus*.

"under Christ" aligns with stage three of Lombard's *ordo* to denote the human in a justified state *after* the addition of divine grace in the cradle-to-grave life. This is the theological region Luther traditionally called gospel. "After Christ" similarly aligns with Lombard's fourth eschatological category, "in eternal life." Because our primary focus is the human temporal life, we will cover "after Christ" only peripherally.

Luther's addition "in the Spirit" finds no parallels in Lombard's system and appears to be a new addition to the sequence. Lombard had a robust concept of divine grace that allowed him to carefully parse the effect of divine grace on the human person. By differentiating between types of grace, he could distinguish God's gracious act to justify the human soul from God's gracious act to sanctify and regenerate it. Luther lacked this conceptual specificity. This new category that he added to the process enabled him to articulate temporal effects of justification in Christ on the human in the temporal life by talking specifically about the gift of the Spirit.[140]

The transition from stage two to stage three in Lombard's structure is of particular significance for Luther in describing the move from law to gospel. His choice to frame this move in christological terms—from "before Christ" to "under Christ"—reflects the clear position he had taken in 1517 regarding medieval doctrines of justification. The medieval conversations centered on the human's capability to perform meritorious works in the movement from the postlapsarian to regenerate life. The questions centered on the kind of divine grace and extent of its assistance. Most scholastic theologians from Lombard to Ockham decided primarily in favor of the role of divine grace, but Luther objected to Gabriel Biel's solution. Biel decided that the human by nature, without grace in stage two, *is able* to merit divine grace for stage three by obeying God's law to love God above all else. But, he thought, the human achieves this not by grace, but by hearing about God's goodness in Scripture and the church. This sort of "faith by

---

140. Though Lombard does not use this category in his *ordo*, he may still be the source of such a concept. As Theodor Dieter points out, Luther saw himself to side with Lombard over the later-Medievals on the nature of the Spirit's infusion as divine *caritas* into the soul, which is clarifying for the way Luther presents this stage in terms of the Spirit as Christ's gift. As Dieter formulates it, the question is not *if* Luther understood the Spirit to work through the mediation of something created in the soul, but *what* that created thing might be. In this section, we begin to formulate an answer to that question by probing the Spirit's creative activity in the human will. See Dieter, "Du mußt den Geist haben!," 72.

hearing," Biel surmised, led the sinner progressively from love of self and fear of punishment to eventual love of God for God's own sake.[141]

When Luther articulated the human relation to the law in christological and pneumatological terms, he both borrowed categories from this medieval discussion and positioned himself within the debate. Contra Biel, Luther asserted that Christ alone acts to move the human from "before Christ" (stage two) to "under Christ" (stage three). However, contra Agricola, Luther framed human moral action as a possibility "in the Spirit," the auxiliary stage Luther named after justification in Christ where the work of justification is complete.

To reiterate, Luther articulated the sequence of his version of the *ordo salutis*, or *ordo rei*, as "before Christ," "under Christ," "in the Spirit," and "after Christ." Each of these categories orients a distinct human relation to law. For the remainder of this section, I will examine the first three stages, which occur in the temporal domain. We will proceed in sequential order to show how Luther parsed the specific functions of law in relation to Christ and the Spirit and human penitential responses.

Before Christ, Law Accused Us

We are plotting distinct moments of the human-law relation in the transition from law to gospel and correlating those moments with Christ and the Spirit. Luther's first stage, "before Christ," describes the human as sinner in relation to law. It is the domain of accusation, condemnation, and terror, caused by the law and occurring in human experience. Across the five sets of theses prepared for the *Antinomian Disputations*, Luther developed this domain to define a function of law in human experience. In this domain, the human person is firmly separated from the life-giving dimensions of gospel, including Christ, faith, and salvation. Before Christ, Luther asserted, law accused us.[142] A similar construct is present in the fourth set of theses: the law is "present before justification."[143] By the fifth set of theses, Luther juxtaposed being "crucified and dead in Christ by faith" with being "outside of Christ under law, sin, and death."[144]

---

141. Biel, *Collectorium* II, d.23, q.2, a.2; III, d.27, q.1, art.2, con.4.
142. WA 39/1:349.39–40.
143. WA 39/1:353.37–38.
144. WA 39/1:354.31—355.1.

Luther's language deploys temporal and spatial imagery to connote separation of the human from Christ. This separation inflects the human experience of law. It comes to her in its "exacting" form, as "letter," unfulfilled and still quite demanding to be fulfilled by us.[145] Here in the domain before Christ, or outside of Christ, the human being stands in proximity to law in her own right, *qua* human. "Outside of Christ," she stands unprotected and unclothed, truly as she is. Unprotected by Christ, she encounters the law in its merciless precision as accusation.

"Before Christ" names the human-law relation prior to justification. This is Luther's classic formulation of "law" in the law/gospel framework. However, there is a notable distinction between law/gospel and "before Christ" in this *ordo rei*. Law/gospel describes a *theological* orientation. It categorizes the human relation to God across two distinct ways that God comes to the human in and through divine pronouncements. In this structure, "law" is the divine pronouncement that accuses the human as sinner. By contrast, Luther's *ordo* provides a more specific articulation of the human relation to law itself. "Before Christ" specifies the human encounter of law as unmediated and direct. She stands before the law as she really is in herself—exposed. Thus, the bilateral relation captures both divine and human acts: God's accusation in the law and the human response of terror.[146] Where law/gospel attends primarily to the divine action in pronouncements, the anthropological focus of "before Christ" specifies the human status—in herself and vis-à-vis a divine person—that causes the law to interact with her in quite particular ways.

The Spirit as author of the law lies in the background here. In argument two of the second disputation, Luther invoked the Spirit as author of the law to compare the Spirit and Satan's effect on the human person before faith and before Christ. The Spirit who "before had written in our hearts by his finger" used Moses's written laws to "shake up our mind and senses, so that, touched by the feeling and power of the law, we might finally

---

145. WA 39/1:354.27–28.

146. Christine Helmer has shown that Luther's logic of "before" and "after" is oriented around a specific temporal logic that plots the Spirit and Christ's relation to the human creature vis-à-vis one another. The Spirit's advent as judge is not metaphysically distinct from the Spirit's advent as summons to joy, but rather two distinct narrative moments under the Spirit's advent per se. Christ marks the shift in the narrative moments of the Spirit as judge (past) to the Spirit as joy (present). See Helmer, *Trinity and Martin Luther*, 153–56.

learn to beg for help."[147] The devil uses law to cause despair without hope for the forgiveness of sins in Luther's logic. Thus, the devil uses law to kill. By contrast, the Spirit as author of the law animates law so that the human has "terror beaten into him in an evangelical way."[148] By leading the human person to hell through the law, the Spirit "drives to despair for the sake of salvation."[149] A few arguments later, Luther returned to this theme to describe the law's proper effect of despair on the "corrupt nature." He connected this effect back to the Spirit. The Spirit makes this despair "useful" to drive the human person to Christ.[150] In this stage "before Christ," the human, separated as she is from Christ's life-giving goods, does not just experience an unmediated law. Luther paints a disturbing pneumatological picture. The Christian actually experiences the Spirit, apart from Christ as author of the law, to terrorize her through the law.

Thus, we can see that "before Christ" describes a stage in the human relation to law as that law is animated by the Spirit in its office as author of the law, vis-à-vis John 16:8. This Spirit, as we saw earlier, is bare divinity, crushing glory, terrifying. Thus, "before Christ" names an encounter between bare humanity and bare divinity as that encounter occurs in the human relation to law. Just as Luther does in his law/gospel framework, we will now see Luther move into "gospel" in the next stage but to do so in a way that maintains the focus on the human relation to law in that domain.

Under Christ, Law Is Placated by the Remission of Sins

"Under Christ" designates Luther's sequential category describing the Christian's relation to law after justification. As such, "under Christ" turns us from law to gospel. There is a clear christological orientation here as Luther maintained his traditional commitment to Christ's total agency in justifying the human person. This orientation to Christ, however, had important pneumatological implications as Luther clarified changes in the human-law relation after justification contra the Antinomians. As we will see, the Spirit's office as author of the law was consequential in light of Christ's satisfaction of the law. Christ's effect on the human relation to

---

147. WA 39/1:426.10–13.

148. WA 39/1:427.9. On the abusive overtones of this concept of God, see Trelstad, "Terror Begins at Home."

149. WA 39/1:426.19.

150. WA 39/1:446.11–12.

law also altered the human relation to the Spirit. Of interest here is Christ's relation to the law in two ways: (1) Christ fulfills the law on behalf of the human person and (2) Christ keeps but transforms the law. In the next section, we will see how the latter was critical for Luther's effort to maintain the Spirit's paracletic office under gospel in light of the Spirit's relation to law articulated in John 16:8. In this section, we will begin by looking at how Christ altered the human relation to law.

First, Christ fulfills the law and placates its punishments in the human's stead. Luther contrasted the status of law before and under Christ. Before Christ, the law and the prophets sound forth, but under Christ, the whole law stands fulfilled.[151] Satisfaction of the law's punishments was a vital component of this law fulfillment. Christ suffered the law's punishments despite his innocence, thus absorbing the law's condemnations.[152] In another argument, Luther framed this in the give-and-take language seen elsewhere in the happy exchange metaphor. He stated, "[Christ] died for us, bore the curses and punishments of the law, and gave us his innocent righteousness."[153] Thus, to remove the Christian's sin in her standing before the law, Luther understood Christ to both fulfill the law's demands and assuage the law's wrath and punishments. This is Luther's classic presentation of justification *sola gratia*.

Luther did not stop there contra Agricola, however. In this context, he argued that the combination of law fulfillment and satisfied punishment actually alters the human relation to law under Christ.[154] Luther understood Christ to give this changed relation through the remission of sins. He said, "Whoever lays hold of this benefit of Christ by faith has by way of imputation fulfilled the law."[155] What's more, the human person's

---

151. WA 39/1:454.19–20; 455.6–7.

152. WA 39/1:380.1.

153. WA 39/1:375.6–7.

154. In the *Scholia*, Melanchthon suggested that what actually happens when God declares the human sinner as righteous on account of Christ in justification is that the person's relation to law is altered. Christ's works alone justify, but the law becomes a moral guide and teacher for good works that please God. The law itself does not cease in justification for the Christian, only its accusing power. The justified person is freed to obey the moral law, to resist sin, and to develop a second kind of righteousness in her conscience. Thus, the law gains a new function to guide the Christian away from sin and toward good and righteous works. The passive justification in Christ opens up both the law and human agency for good works after justification while excluding good works before justification. Wengert, *Law and Gospel*, 189.

155. WA 39/1:388.3–5, 15–17. Kim also identifies a transformed law, which she calls

ongoing sin also does not count. Sin is removed by imputation, Luther claimed, such that any "ongoing sins do not get attributed" to the Christian.[156] Therefore, we have here a classic trope in Luther's thought: Christ justifies the human by fulfilling the law and suffering its punishments on her behalf and then by imputing this righteousness to her. Her relation to law is construed against this imputed righteousness. She now relates to law as though she were righteous.

"Before Christ" depicted the human's separation from Christ and full exposure to the law in temporal and spatial terms. "Under Christ," Luther deployed spatial and relational idioms to characterize the Christian's new relation to law as though she is righteous. Christ effects the human relation to law in the domain of gospel by repositioning her vis-à-vis Christ and law. Luther claimed that faith brings the Christian "under Christ" where she is "sheltered" from the law.[157] Elsewhere, Luther described the Christian as being protected under Christ's wings like a protective mother hen[158] and hidden under Christ's cloak.[159] These depictions all point to deflection as a primary way Luther understood the benefit of Christ's relation to the human in this stage "under Christ." As the law moves toward the human, Christ shields her from it, diverting the consequences of her sins "as if" her sin is nothing.[160]

These beneficial shifts in the human's relation to law all stem from Christ's "proper office" as Mediator.[161] Positioned between the law and the human, Christ rarefied each subject in the law-human relation, causing them to relate to each other in a new way. He marked the law as satisfied, ameliorating its demands, and the Christian as righteous, as one satisfying the law's demands. "Before Christ" depicted the human's separation from Christ in temporal and spatial terms. "Under Christ" Luther deployed spatial and relational idioms to characterize the protective quality of Christ's effect in the domain of gospel.

When we look at Luther's approach to the law side of this new relation, it is striking that Luther did not say that the law is abrogated under

---

the "Christ-given law of love" (Kim, *Luther on Faith and Love*, 155–65).

156. WA 39/1:431.10–12.
157. WA 39/1:482.16.
158. WA 39/1:506.6; 514.18; 521.14.
159. WA 39/1:514.17; 522.2.
160. WA 39/1:493.4–5.
161. WA 39/1:535.9–10; cf. 493.3.

Christ. Rather, he showed the law's relation to the human under Christ to be *transformed*. Christ "renders the law undefiled"[162] and restores the law's honor,[163] but the law does not go away. Instead, the law remains but not in an accusing way. As Norman Lund has shown, Luther's articulation of this view of law evolved across the disputations.[164] In the first, he seemed to still think of law in the Christian life under Christ in terms of the accusing law. This is evident in argument 18 of the first disputation. Describing the transformation of law after Christ's fulfillment of it, Luther concluded with the observation that "to the extent [Christians] have flesh, however, to that extent the law and sin rule in them."[165]

This argument nevertheless contains seeds for a more nuanced view of law that then developed over the remaining disputations; Luther noted that "through grace, which Christ brings and bestows freely, we die to the law *that accuses and condemns* us."[166] Notably, Luther does not say here that Christians die to the law itself only to the accusing and condemning relation to law. This is consistent with an earlier statement in the first disputation, where Luther commented that "when Christ is present, the law loses its power. It cannot administer wrath because Christ freed us from it."[167] Here, again, it is not the law that is removed but rather a change occurs in the human-law relation.

By the second and third disputations, Luther made a starker distinction overtly separating accusing from other non-accusing functions of law under Christ. In the second disputation, for example, Luther stated that we are not under the accusing law but a "different" one.[168] This evolved again in the third disputation, where he asserted that "under Christ" evangelical preachers were to "let Moses depart" when Christ appeared as a teacher of the law. He noted, "there is no Moses here," that is, there is no accusing,

---

162. WA 39/1:373.6–7.

163. Sasja Mathiasen Stopa shows honor to play an important role in Luther's relational anthropology. She notes that in the *Lectures on Galatians*, the only demand Luther sees God to place on the human person is to ascribe honor and divinity to God. Here, in that sense, Christ's activity to restore the law's honor could be seen as a means of restoring the human relation to law as a divine Word. It is no longer to be feared and instead to be honored and obeyed. See Stopa, *Soli Deo honor et gloria*, 175.

164. Lund, "Luther's 'Third Use of the Law,'" 355.

165. WA 39/1:392.15.

166. WA 39/1:392.2–3 (emphasis added).

167. WA 39/1:372.20—373.1.

168. WA 39/1:436.2–3.

condemning function of law here.[169] Thus, across the series of disputations, Luther seemed to come to the nuanced view that the accusing capacity of law alone is removed under Christ, not the law itself.

Instead, Luther claimed that under Christ the law is to be taught to admonish and exhort.[170] Luther's theological argument pragmatically addressed the reality that the saints "still have flesh and blood and sin battling against the law of God in their flesh."[171] Even after justification, Christians need the law, not to accuse them but rather to help them battle and purge this ongoing sin.[172] The Christian life, thus, becomes a kind of "military service" where the war against sin in the flesh is waged.[173] Faith is the key criterion for facilitating this shift. Faith ascertains Christ as gift and brings the human person under Christ. This new position initiates the new phase of the human's relation to God and law in which the law admonishes the Christian against remaining sin and helps her to fight against it.

The exhortation component comes through Christ as example. The reason is, Christ as example mediated the law to the Christian in this new, non-accusing way.[174] Christ preached the law, Luther claimed, by teaching how to live a chaste, godly life.[175] Christ's example "firmly established" the law to commend the human being to follow Christ's footsteps in leading a godly life.[176] In this phase under Christ, the Christian encounters a type of law in Christ's example which shows her how to live a life congruent with law.

Thus, Luther located two purposes for law in relation to the human person in the stage "under Christ." We will deepen the anthropological dimensions of this new twofold relation to law as admonishment and exhortation in subsequent chapters. For now, the point is that law keeps going *in a transformed way* in this new phase "under Christ," first to admonish ongoing sin, then to exhort to the good intention. Moreover, this occurs through faith vis-à-vis Christ as gift and example. Both purposes took seriously the lived reality that Christians retain sinful flesh after justification,

---

169. WA 39/1:504.10; 506.5–6.

170. Lund connects these to the *salutarem usus legis* among those who know the Spirit as *donum*. See Lund, "Luther's 'Third Use of the Law,'" 357.

171. WA 39/1:455.10–11.

172. WA 39/1:455.10–11.

173. WA 39/1:492.5–6.

174. WA 39/1:462.22–23; 483.3–4.

175. WA 39/1:534.18–19.

176. WA 39/1:463.1, 5–7.

which they needed to address. They needed law to show them where remaining sin remained, and to do so without accusation or condemnation. They also needed the law to show them what to do instead, how to live a better life. Luther's new question would become, how do Christians under Christ become able to relate to law in this way?

At the end of the 1530s, Luther now had a new resource for answering this question: the Holy Spirit as author of the law. Luther made use of this pneumatological insight in the next stage of his *ordo rei* to supply an answer to this "how" question in the human's relation to law. In summary, "under Christ" articulates Luther's classic position of justification by faith. Yet, there is also innovation present in Luther's deployment of Christ as gift and example. Christ as example allows him to keep the law going while Christ as gift makes it possible to present the law in a transformed way. In the next section, we will see how he reconnected these ideas to the Spirit as author of the law in the stage "in the Spirit" to continue his rebuttal of Agricola.

Under Christ, Law Is to Be Fulfilled in the Spirit

In the stage "under Christ," Christ transforms the law and opens it up to the Spirit and the justified Christian in a new register. Luther located the Spirit's new relation to law under gospel in an auxiliary stage after justification through faith (i.e., "under Christ") called "in the Spirit." In this auxiliary stage "in the Spirit" that Luther added "under Christ," the Spirit reorients the law to guide the Christian's good intention after justification.

In the shift from "before Christ" to "under Christ," Luther described how Christ comes to the Christian through faith as gift and as example. Faith is central to this process. Luther identified two distinct "benefits of faith" that the Christian receives from Christ. The first benefit, as we have seen above, is that "faith alone (for it alone can lay hold of Christ) gives to me Christ who is the fulfillment and the end of the law."[177] As gift, Christ conferred imputed righteousness and fulfillment of the law, thus ending the law which accuses and condemns. Luther has the second use of the law, the accusing law, in mind here. He then identified a second benefit of faith: "What else does faith give? It requests and brings with it the Holy Spirit."[178] This second gift of the Holy Spirit initiates an auxiliary

---

177. WA 39/1:482.14–16.
178. WA 39/1:482.17—483.1.

stage "under Christ" within the rubric of Gospel. Luther called this new, auxiliary stage "in the Spirit."

The position of this "in the Spirit" stage under Christ is critical for Luther's view of the Spirit as author of the law. Just as Christ mediated a new relation to law "under Christ," so too Christ mediates a new relation to the Spirit in this auxiliary stage. Luther's wording here suggests he understood Christ to convey not just his righteousness but also his own unique relationship to the Spirit: "Christ alone has done the will of God and fulfilled the law and received the Holy Spirit. Whoever lays hold of this benefit of Christ has fulfilled the law by way of imputation and receives the Holy Spirit."[179] Given Luther's view of the Spirit as author of the law, the sequence in his first sentence suggests Christ's fulfillment of the divine will and the law orient a particular type of relation to the Spirit, one characterized decidedly as something other than terrifying accuser. When Luther continued to name the transfer of the benefits of faith in the second sentence, Christ's gifts of law fulfillment and the Spirit no longer stand as two unrelated benefits of faith (e.g., a list). Rather, the gift of Christ's law fulfillment shapes the way the Spirit is given as gift. The second benefit of faith is the reception of *Christ's relation* to the Spirit as author of the law, which is premised upon Christ's law fulfillment and the Spirit's status as satisfied.

When Christ gives both law fulfillment and the Spirit in the benefits of faith, he transforms the Christian's relation to the Spirit. The Spirit, who came to the Christian "before Christ" as bare divinity and terrifying author of the law, now comes to the Christian "under Christ" as consoler, vivifier, and sanctifier.[180] These new ways of relating to the Spirit under Christ are inseparable from the Spirit's office as author of the law. When Christ gives his law fulfillment and the Spirit in justification, he gives the Spirit as one whose legal demands are satisfied, particularly the demand of the first commandment to be honored as God. However, as the cause and agent of the law, the Spirit brings the law under gospel for a new purpose: "Christ earns the Spirit for believers in order that they begin to fulfill the law."[181] Before Christ, the Spirit animated the law to accuse

---

179. WA 39/1:388.2–5.

180. WA 39/1:391.18–20; cf. 365.2–3.

181. WA 39/1:365.3–4. Kärkkäinen sees this as fulfilling the spiritual law. Because the Spirit is a gift of love, the Christian has the required love of God already in the heart in Kärkkäinen, *Luthers trinitarische Theologie*, 155. Lund links this to the moral law, claiming that "it becomes ever clearer in the *Antinomian Disputations* that Luther identifies this evangelical, moral use of the law with sanctification, even though he seldom employs

of sins. Now, under Christ, the Spirit's relation to law will commence a new type of incipient righteousness in the Christian after justification. The Spirit will use the law to work sanctification.

What do we call this new orientation of law for sanctification "in the Spirit"? For decades, scholars have been unproductively caught up in debating *whether* this is a "third use" of the law in the sense that Melanchthon deployed in his 1535 *Loci Communes*.[182] Unfortunately, Luther did not simplify the scholarly task by naming a new function of law. Nor did he use the language of "third use of law" that Melanchthon had introduced in 1535. To continue engaging this debate distracts from the reality that Luther described a variety of works and effects of "law" in the Christian life, regardless of what we call it. Thus, the more productive scholarly task is to map those functions of law across different stages in Luther's *ordo rei* in focus in this chapter. As Lund and others have shown, approaching Luther's understanding of law in this way reveals a significantly more complex view of law in Luther's thought than earlier scholarly debates permitted.[183] By attending to Luther's descriptions rather than his specific vocabulary and naming conventions, it is possible to elevate this question of the Spirit's use of law after justification out of the long-entrenched debate. The result is a better view of what Luther might have been doing when he discussed the Spirit and the law as Christ's gift to the Christian.

In the *Antinomian Disputations*, Luther employed three particular "uses," or works and effects, of law vis-à-vis the Spirit pertinent to this discussion. First, he named a salutary use (*usus salutaris*) of law. One aspect of the salutary use sees the law interpreted by the gospel. Luther explained

---

the term" (Lund, "Luther's 'Third Use of the Law,'" 288).

182. See Melanchthon, *Loci Communes* in CR 21:716-19. Why Luther did not utilize this language of the third use of the law is an open question.

183. Lund tracks the sharpening and strengthening of Luther's treatment of law across the series of *Antinomian Disputations*, showing that "a line of development can be traced throughout the controversy." The evolution begins with a recognition of the Christian's freedom from the *maledicto legis* (accusing law) on account of Christ, which opens up a new *delectatio* (love) of the law in the first disputation. In the second disputation, Lund shows how Luther identified new functions of law under this freedom from aspect, including for the purgation of sin, as an exhortation to formal and imputed righteousness, as an exhortation to the good, and that the law is softened for the believer. Building on this theological and textual analysis, Lund refutes the forgery thesis propagated by Elert and Ebeling. He shows a clear development of a "third use of the law" for two purposes by Luther's third disputation: as a guard against false security and as a guide in sanctification, where Lund sees Luther to affirm a moral use of the law in Christians. See Lund, "Luther's 'Third Use of the Law,'" 355, 174-77, 195-201, 223-29, 279-97.

that "the gospel comes [as a promise about Christ] and removes the sting of the law and makes out of it an instructor (*paedagogum*). The law ought to be interpreted in this way by the gospel and be reduced by the impossible to a salutary use, to Christ."[184] The Spirit, who Luther correlates as the efficient cause of the law, is critical to this salutary use. The law "by itself is able to produce only terrors and lead to hell."[185] Yet, the Spirit "makes an instructor" out of the law, causing it to "lead you to Christ by terrifying, afflicting, and killing you, and prepares you for Christ himself."[186] Thus, in one aspect, the salutary use is a retrospective view of law, interpreted by the Spirit and refracted through gospel, to show the law's accusations in a positive light as they bring the sinner to Christ.

The salutary use also includes another disciplinary function in the life of the Christian after justification. When the law

> is taken in a spiritual way, and before God . . . terrifying consciences—not in a diabolical, but in an evangelical way—then it is something different. There, instruction accomplishes something. For the expression, the instructor toward Christ, is a . . . very joyous definition of the law.[187]

Luther described an effect of the salutary use of law for "pious minds": "The law does not [administer despair] but shows sin to you."[188] Later in the second disputation, Luther reframed this pedagogical orientation to law more clearly in terms of lifelong repentance in the Christian life. "Even the saints who here have accepted Christ still have flesh, blood, and sin battling against the law of God in their flesh."[189] The law continued to work here to drive believers back to Christ: "To be sure, even the saints and the good like David, Jeremiah, and others were terrified. But this took place to exercise

---

184. WA 39/1:445.21—446.3. I part ways with Lund slightly on Luther's view of the salutary law. Lund associates the salutary use of law with the positive use of law by Christians for sanctification. While I initially also held this view, careful rereading has convinced me this "evangelical" use of law is more closely linked with justification. When Luther discusses functions of law more aimed at sanctifying processes in the Christian after justification, he talks about the law's admonishment (*admonenti*) against sinful inclinations and exhortations to the good (*lex hortetur ad bonum*). I call the tandem function of these works of law in the Christian the "sanctifying law."

185. WA 39/1:445.20–21.

186. WA 39/1:445.12–13; 442.14–15.

187. WA 39/1:441.8–12.

188. WA 39/1:443.2; 441.15–16.

189. WA 39/1:455.10–11.

faith, or at least to drive them to prayer, lest they become intoxicated with too much fortune and become obstinate against God."[190] This secondary aspect of the salutary use of law in the Christian life repeatedly brings the Christian back to Christ and faith by revealing the sin that continues even after justification. Thus, the salutary use sees Luther continuing his traditional view of law in the law/gospel construct to reveal sin for the purpose of lifelong repentance.

However, Luther also assigned additional functions to law under Christ and in the Spirit. These new functions of law grew out of Luther's commitment to different types of law fulfillment. There was law fulfillment that justified the soul before God. Having been completed in Christ, this was not the type of law fulfillment Luther had in view for the Christian life. Rather, this non-justifying type of law fulfillment had to do with preventing actual sin and developing active righteousness. Using a key category in his *ordo rei*, Luther asserted that "under Christ, law is in a state of being done, not having been done."[191] Christ's example gave a "double testimony" of what God wills the Christian to do and thus reinforced his perspective that another type of law fulfillment is yet to occur in the Christian.[192] The Spirit is given under Christ for precisely this purpose, Luther argued, "so that the law's righteousness might be fulfilled in us."[193] Though justified passively by Christ's own righteousness, the Christian was yet to fulfill the law in some way through the Spirit's help as sanctification. Contra Agricola, Luther presented a multilayered view of law in which justifying law fulfillment in Christ did not exclude other types of law fulfillment in the human person via the Spirit.

In view of this non-justifying, sanctifying type of law fulfillment, Luther described two additional functions of law vis-à-vis the Spirit: admonishment and exhortation. Admonishment has to do with a particular use of law, which the Spirit speaks to the Christian as a monitor against sin. In the second disputation, Luther admitted that "even the saints need the law as a kind of admonishment (*monitore*) since there is a constant war between spirit and flesh in them."[194] Preaching the law in this way helps the Christian to identify her "vices and sins" in support of what Luther called

190. WA 39/1:456.15–18.
191. WA 39/1:374.11–12.
192. WA 39/1:464.3–5.
193. WA 39/1:367.10–11.
194. WA 39/1:432.14–15.

the "formal" (*formaliter*) and "purging" (*expurgative*) removal of sins.¹⁹⁵ He differentiated this formal, purging removal of sins from the imputed (*imputative*) remission of sin in Christ. Whereas the salutary law accused the Christian of sins to support lifelong repentance, the law as admonishment or monitor helps the Christian to resist sin in the cradle-to-grave life after justification. She reduces her sin in a "formal and purging manner" and "purges and mortifies more and more the sin that remains in [her] flesh."¹⁹⁶ The law's admonishment facilitates this secondary law fulfillment in the Christian after justification by helping the Christian to identify and resist sinful urges in the flesh.

Exhortation is a third way Luther described the law to function in the Christian life under Christ and in the Spirit. In the second disputation, Luther asserted that before justification (*ante iustificationem*) the law terrifies, but for the pious (*pii*), the law ought to be taught to "exhort them to the good (*ut hortetur ad bonum*)."¹⁹⁷ In contrast to the accusing law, Luther asserted that the law is to be softened (*mollire*) for the justified such that it can be taught as an exhortation.¹⁹⁸ The content of the exhortation as Luther imagined it echoes the law/gospel/law pattern we have seen elsewhere with Christ's example. According to Luther, the law exhorted the Christian to the good by acknowledging the Christian's place under Christ, then pointing toward future action: "Now, offer your bodies to righteousness . . . put away desires of the flesh . . . [and] be imitators of the righteousness of good works."¹⁹⁹ Referencing the *exemplum Christi*, Luther understood the law to present the Christian with directives for good actions they were to undertake as they developed their own righteousness after justification.

To demonstrate the Spirit's application of these two functions of law in the Christian life, Luther provided a narrative example of the Christian's inner battle against sin and for righteousness. He framed the narrative around a Christian youth experiencing sexual temptation. As the temptation was presented to the Christian's flesh, Luther attributed an intellectual judgment against the temptation to the Spirit speaking in the Christian's mind. "The Spirit and the heart cried out against the flesh," Luther said.²⁰⁰

195. WA 39/1:432.13–14; 431.10; 432.7.
196. WA 39/1:432.7.
197. WA 39/1:474.20–22.
198. WA 39/1:475.2.
199. WA 39/1:475.3–5.
200. WA 39/1:500.21.

The Spirit and the heart's outcry had two components: "Leave the girl in peace" and "wait on the wife" God planned for him.[201]

The first part of this outcry echoed the prohibition against lust and coveting in the Decalogue, which per Luther the Spirit had written on Moses's tablets of stone. Thus, the appearance of the prohibition in the Christian's mind takes the form of an admonishment against the temptation; this desire violates the law! In his own analysis of the example, Luther claimed that the Spirit was "admonishing" (*admonenti*) the Christian on the will of God.[202] The admonishment has a clear pedagogical function. In the very moment that the desires of the flesh awaken for the pretty girl, the Spirit is there reminding the Christian to resist the sinful urge. This application of law is devoid of an accusing edge. Rather, the Spirit speaks the law in the gentle way of a parent who catches and redirects her child before he does something that could harm himself or others.

The second part of the outcry, to wait on the wife God has promised, functioned as an exhortation. Whereas the prohibition stopped the Christian from doing something, the exhortation provided a directive of what to do instead—to wait, to trust God's promise, to sit tight and be patient. There is, again, a gentle parenting quality to this—devoid of a punitive quality, it functions as a redirect, like a parent speaking gently to a child "go do this instead!" Just like a child could obey a parent in that type of redirect, Luther attributed a positive outcome to the Christian's actions. Despite the temptation, the Christian "obeyed the Spirit [and] averts (*deprecans*) by prayer the evil he feels . . . and did not enter (*non intret*) into temptation."[203] Even if the Christian is unable to obey the law in a justifying way, Luther narrated a manner in which the Spirit uses the law to guide the Christian away from the temptations of the flesh and toward acts congruent with the law under Christ.

Just as Luther parsed the human affective dimensions of law and gospel using the penitential language of sorrow and the good intention, so too he mapped the admonishing and exhortation functions of law in the Spirit back onto this anthropological matrix. The Spirit spoke the law to the Christian as admonishment and exhortation to support the good intention as love of God and hatred of sin.[204]

---

201. WA 39/1:500.24–25.
202. WA 39/1:501.11.
203. WA 39/1:501.3–5.
204. Kärkkäinen connects the gift of the Spirit in Luther's pneumatology to the

Luther never questioned his view that the human person herself cannot assent to the good intention apart from grace. However, in defense of the law contra Agricola, he argued that the benefits of faith elevate the human to the good intention by liberating her from sin and directing her toward love of God. Critiquing what he saw as a Pelagian view amongst the Nominalists like Biel, Luther asserted in his first set of theses from December 1537 that the human person is unable to formulate the good intention unless she is "elevated" by the gospel.[205] Luther connected this elevation to the benefits of faith. The first benefit, the remission of sins through Christ, liberates the human out of servile love of God as attrition. This freedom opens her up to what Luther calls a "filial" (*filialis*) fear of offending God.[206] Filial fear is not rooted in terror, but in love. The Christian is now able to fear offending God for God's sake rather than from her own fear of punishment.

Luther credited the second benefit of faith—the gift of the Spirit—with elevating the human to the good intention. He said, "[God] gives the Spirit (*spiritum*) to those who believe in order that, from the soul (*ex animo*), they might begin to hate sin ... and to love, worship, and to call on God."[207] Luther's location of the hatred of sin and love of God *ex animo* is key. This is not the same kind of justifying good intention that occurs vis-à-vis the promise of the Gospel about Christ—the trust in God's promise. Rather, Luther keyed in on the good intention being produced in the human soul itself. The good intention of faith is a gift from the outside; the good intention from the Spirit is productive from within the human herself.

The Spirit works the good intention in the Christian by elevating her capacity for the good intention vis-à-vis the law. In contrast to his depiction of the Spirit as the terrifying author of the law "before Christ," Luther appropriated the traditional pneumatological office of "vivifier and sanctifier"

---

medieval concept of infused charity. See Kärkkäinen, *Luthers trinitarische Theologie*, 107.

205. WA 39/1:345.28–29.

206. WA 39/1:395.18–19. Thomas Aquinas formulated a similar notion of the good intention vis-à-vis filial and servile love when he expanded Lombard's volitional orientation to contrition by overlaying Lombard's view of contrition with Augustinian notions of servile and filial love. Thomas determined that contrition must result from filial love of God for God's own sake, not fear of punishment or servile love. Filial love for God could only be elicited in the human through the infusion of divine charity; cf. Aquinas, *ST* III, q.90, a.2; *Suppl.*, q.1, a.2, r.1; q.1, a.3.

207. WA 39/1:383.10–11, 13. Anderas notes that "this purgation [of sin] by the gift of the Spirit is no monergistic affair, for the Spirit's operation quickens and sustains a spiritual agency on the part of the redeemed person himself" (Anderas, *Renovatio*, 84).

here under Christ.[208] The Spirit as vivifier allowed Luther to address the anthropological problem in the will, which he understood to cause sin through unresponsiveness and active disobedience to the law.[209] As vivifier, the Spirit supplies the solution to this anthropological problem by actually recreating the human soul with the law in view. In a striking portrayal of the Spirit's work in this regard, Luther explained that "[Christ] brings the Holy Spirit into those who believe in order that they might have delight in the law of the Lord ... and in this manner, their souls are recreated according to [the law] and this Spirit gives to them the will that they might do it."[210] Unlike Biel, who Luther understood to give too much credit to human volitional capacity, Luther located an alternative for generating the good intention. The good intention "under Christ" and "in the Spirit" does not result from the human's natural volition but rather a revivified willpower that is distinct to Christians who have received the Spirit as gift.[211]

The Spirit also orients this new will to the law so that the will produces the good intention. Luther stated, "By faith, we receive the Holy Spirit, who produces new motions and fills the will so that it begins to truly love God and hate sin."[212] As the "sanctifier," the Spirit moves the will to the good intention to love God and hate sin. The Spirit accomplishes this orientation of the will to the law by speaking the law in the soul. Just as he described in the Christian youth narrative, Luther affirmed that the Spirit "causes remarkable and indescribable cries against sin in your heart" and that the Spirit gives a "certain testimony in our hearts" against sin.[213] Where Biel and the Nominalists permitted that the human will could, according to its nature, ascent to love of God with laborious effort, Luther is able to claim that the

---

208. WA 39/1:370.21.

209. WA 39/1:379.6; 372.7–9; cf. 419.19—420.1 for Luther's critique of the Nominalists' elevation of unaided human reason.

210. WA 39/1:373.1–4.

211. Anderas interprets this claim as "Luther's *donum*-rendition of the traditional *gratia cooperans* . . . [because] the Spirit's operation quickens and sustains a spiritual agency on the part of the redeemed person himself" (Anderas, *Renovatio*, 84). The Spirit's recreation of the human will here is an intriguing development in light of Dieter's observation in Luther's marginalia to Lombard's *Sentences* that the indwelling Spirit as caritas works "durch etwas Geschaffenes im Menschen." In this instance, that "something created" appears as a renewed human volitional power vis-à-vis the Spirit. See Dieter, "Du mußt den Geist haben!," 69.

212. WA 39/1:395.22–23.

213. WA 39/1:526.5–6.

Spirit transforms the law's requirement for perfect obedience, fear, and love of God into something "enjoyable and easy."[214]

The reason is the Spirit sustains the movements of the recreated human as it ascents to the good intention. Luther described this new motion, saying: "After receiving the Spirit, I begin to hate from the soul everything that offends [God's] name and I am made a doer of good works."[215] Here, we see Luther assert that the gift of the Spirit realigns the soul's affections. Where previously the soul could only love itself, now the soul is able to produce a negative affective response to that which violates the divine will. The extent to which Luther understood this change to occur in the person herself through the Spirit's support is captured in a remarkable reversal of the so-called bondage of the will. Volitional consent to sin occurs "against my will" because the Spirit has recreated and moves the Christian's will according to the law.[216]

For Luther, the Spirit's offices as both the author of the law and the vivifier and sanctifier are vital for sustaining the production of the good intention in the Christian. The Spirit as vivifier and sanctifier recreates the justified soul, but because the Spirit is also author of the law, the Spirit does so in light of the law. This insight leads Luther to conclude, "It is true, *we* are not able to intend the good, but the Spirit who is given to believers readies it."[217] Again, weaving a path between Biel's Pelagian view and Agricola's antinomianism, Luther asserted that it is not in fact human natural powers that muster a true good intention out of love of God. Instead, the Spirit as gift works in the human soul as part of the benefits of faith in justification.

The connection between the Spirit as gift, the law, and the Christian's good intention leads Luther to a bold claim: the Christian herself begins to fulfill the law "in the Spirit." The law, he said, "is to be fulfilled by the pious also" because it is God's will that we begin to fulfill the law here.[218] Luther's reference to "the pious," or the justified soul, positions us "under Christ" in his *ordo salutis* and signals that he was referencing a sanctifying type of law fulfillment rather than a justifying one.[219] The larger context of

---

214. WA 39/1:388.5–6, 11–12; cf. 387.10 in reference to the law as it is defined by Christ.

215. WA 39/1:434.8–10.

216. WA 39/1:514.6–7.

217. WA 39/1:378.8–9.

218. WA 39/1:381.3–8.

219. Anderas emphasizes the complementary nature of Christ's justifying gift of law

the statement deals with the burden of law fulfillment and sees Luther to distinguish between law fulfillment apart from Christ and law fulfillment under Christ. It is the latter about which he claims is also required for the pious. A sanctifying law fulfillment is in view.

Even this sanctifying law fulfillment does not occur through human natural powers. Rather, the Spirit, as agent of the law ameliorated by faith, sustains it. Luther stated that the Spirit "drives [believers] to begin to fulfill the law in this life."[220] The Spirit's connection to law enables Luther to claim that under Christ and in the Spirit the Christian "firmly obeys the word and law of God, which says 'you shall not covet,' and the Holy Spirit admonishes him concerning this will of God and he does not succumb [to sin]."[221] Importantly, Luther also never suggested that this sanctifying law fulfillment was completed in the temporal life. Rather, we begin (*incipere*) to do it with the Spirit's help. "In the Spirit," the Christian begins to fulfill the admonishing and exhortative law as it is opened up in relation to the Spirit "under Christ." This law fulfillment is sustained by Christ's gift of the Spirit, who recreates and orients the recreated human will to the law by speaking the law in the soul.

Luther used this auxiliary stage "in the Spirit" under the rubric of gospel to connect the Spirit to the gifts of faith in justification. The Spirit is given over to the Christian as part of Christ's gift. But because the Spirit is agent of the law, Christ's gift of the Spirit actually gives over the Spirit and the law in a mollified way. As author of the law, the Spirit's relation to the human is transformed. By developing his pneumatology in this way, Luther carved out new functions of law under Christ that see the Spirit to speak the law to the soul as an admonishment against sin and exhortation toward action rooted in love of God and hatred of sin. The gift of the Spirit is vital to Luther's correction of Agricola because the Spirit elevates the soul to produce the good intention by simultaneously recreating the human will and orienting it to the law. Now, contra Agricola, Luther could maintain the ongoing place of the law in the Christian life because he was able to contend that the Christian begins to fulfill the law herself, with the Spirit's help.

---

fulfillment *ex nobis* with the Spirit's sanctifying gift of law fulfillment *in nobis*, stating: "The gift of law-keeping by the Spirit, so far from being rendered superfluous by Christ's grace, is in fact rendered possible by the transformation—through that great grace—of an intolerable burden into the light and easy *iugum Christi*. Once again, grace in Christ is ordered to the gift of the Spirit" (Anderas, *Renovatio*, 82).

220. WA 39/1:380.4–5.
221. WA 39/1:501.9–11.

In this section we have seen that Luther introduced the stages of "before Christ," "under Christ," and "in the Spirit" to discuss stages of human penitential experience in relation to law and gospel. Before Christ, the law functioned to accuse the human and to elicit the human experience of sorrow, driving the person to Christ. Under Christ, the law is placated by the remission of sins by means of Christ as the divine agent of justification. In the Spirit, the law takes on new functions in relation to the Spirit as gift. It functions to instruct the believer to form the good intention to love God and hate sin by means of the recreated will. Luther used "before Christ" and "under Christ" to discuss the person before and after justification. However, the stage "in the Spirit" allowed him to nuance the Christian life after justification by focusing on the works of particular trinitarian persons—especially, the Spirit as Christ's gift.

Luther reconnected the law to the Spirit in relation to human penitence to address the way Agricola's antinomianism challenged the law/gospel principle. In doing so, he also expanded his pneumatology. This expansion allowed him to analyze the Spirit's role in sustaining new volitional moments in the justified soul vis-à-vis the law. Luther's introduction of the Spirit's office as "author of the law" presents the Spirit as the source of law, as its efficient cause. As such, the Spirit causes human sorrow by means of a mediate cause, the law. Similarly, Luther showed the Spirit in its office as gift to recreate and orient the human will to the law in part through the Spirit's other office as the law's author. He made the Spirit the speaker of the law to the soul. Because the Spirit is mediated through Christ as gift, the Spirit does not speak the law to accuse, but to elicit the good intention from the recreated will. By giving the human a new will and filling that will with the proper content of the law, Luther showed the Spirit to work the good intention in the Christian. This process of developing the good intention one temptation at a time meant the Christian was beginning to fulfill the law in the temporal life through sanctification.

Chapter Conclusions

In the summer of 1537, Luther made a significant pneumatological discovery as he prepared sermons on the Gospel of John. Christ identified the Spirit as the cause and agent of the law in John 16:8. This revelation presented Luther with a troubling pneumatological picture to resolve. The Spirit, whom Scripture calls the paraclete and comforter, also causes the law's accusations leading to despair and death. Around the same time, Agricola publicly espoused the antinomian view that the law ceased in the Christian life after the human person received the promise of the gospel in faith. This position echoed Luther's arguments in his 1531 *Lectures on Galatians*. From the perspective of Luther's John 16:8 connection between the law and the Spirit, Luther now saw Agricola's antinomianism as a challenge to both the ongoing use of the law and the role and efficacy of the Spirit in the Christian life. Luther needed to determine how the Spirit could be both the agent of law and also of consolation in the gospel in order to refute Agricola's antinomianism.

This chapter has shown that Luther reconciled the Spirit and law with the gospel by articulating a more nuanced notion of the human in relation to law from the perspective of the human under gospel. Luther introduced medieval penitential language of sorrow and the good intention to describe human responses to law under both law and gospel. Under his analytical category "law," he showed the human to respond to the accusing law through sorrow for sin. In the move to "gospel," Luther identified a transformed and mollified law that admonishes and exhorts the justified human to produce the good intention. These admonishing and exhortative functions allowed him to maintain the ongoing role of law contra Agricola.

After examining Luther's preservation of law under gospel, we then explored how Luther resolved the Spirit's connection to law in John 16:8 with the Spirit's paracletic activity in eliciting faith in the believer under gospel. This goal saw a further investigation of the human under law and gospel through Luther's introduction of new sequential categories for analyzing stages in the Christian relation to God. These categories bore certain likenesses to the medieval tradition begun by Lombard. The categories "before Christ," "under Christ," and "in the Spirit" revealed the Spirit as efficient cause of law in terms of law's changing relation to the human. Luther determined that "before Christ" the Spirit in its office as author of the law caused the law to accuse of sin, which is consistent with Luther's traditional concept of "law." Consistent with Luther's classic concept of "gospel," the stage "under Christ" saw Christ as the divine agent of justification in fulfilling the law. Thus, we were able to see Luther maintain his classic position that the accusing law and its cause in the Spirit were satisfied through Christ's righteousness, which was given over to the human in faith.

But because Luther understood the gift of the Spirit to be one of the benefits of faith, we also saw that Luther devised an auxiliary stage under the rubric of gospel called "in the Spirit." In the Spirit, Luther made sense of the Spirit's connection to law by showing the Spirit to speak the law in admonishing and exhortative ways to the justified soul in order to elicit the good intention to love God and hate sin. Luther connected the Spirit and law to the human through penitential language and anthropological categories mapped according to law and gospel. This enabled him to successfully preserve a role for law in the Christian life against Agricola while also making sense of the pneumatological picture he found in John 16:8.

The connection between the Spirit, the law, and human penitence examined in this chapter reveal increasing anthropological and trinitarian depth to Luther's law/gospel paradigm. The John 16:8 discovery prompted Luther to articulate the divine dimensions of law and gospel more carefully. While he maintained his classic position that sees Christ as the divine agent of justification, he newly emphasized the Spirit's relation to law as the law's efficient cause and to gospel as Christ's gift. The Spirit's capacity to be given as gift in the gospel hangs on Luther's theology of the cross, and the gift of the Spirit specifies the indwelling in the human person, specifically, of the divine cause of the law.

This pneumatological insight opens up new anthropological dimensions to law/gospel. Justification can no longer be seen simply as a forensic notion of imputation of Christ's righteousness. Rather, Luther understood a certain kind of law fulfillment to occur *in* the human herself on the basis of imputation. The static notion of the passive human in faith vis-à-vis Christ is thereby expanded to permit a more dynamic notion of the human in relation to the Spirit. This dynamic anthropological picture imagines changes to human volition resulting from the gift of the Spirit as agent of the law. These changes are not accounted for in the static picture that scholars typically attribute to Luther.

These anthropological and trinitarian insights deepen the relation between law and gospel in Luther's paradigm. Luther's classic idea about the accusing function of law is maintained and clarified through the identification of the law's efficient cause in the Spirit. However, Luther's notion of law is made more dynamic by Luther's association of law with the *exemplum Christi*, which led him to identify new functions of law under gospel. The law's connection to the Spirit supports Luther's development of a third use of the law, a view powerful voices in Luther scholarship have opposed despite numerous studies showing internal consistency with Luther's larger theology. While Agricola restricted law to the civil use, Luther carved out a third use in which the Spirit causes the law to guide the Christian's conscience to produce the good intention.

Thus, to counter Agricola, Luther introduced language of medieval penance to demonstrate the role of law after gospel for formulating the good intention. Luther tied the law to the Spirit as author and gift in order to grant divine causality to law in its functions before and after gospel. But by doing so, Luther also made it necessary to clarify Christian obedience to the law. This would require that he also revise his classic anthropological concept of "simultaneously just and sinner" (*simul iustus et peccator*) to clarify, once again, human agency before the law. We turn to these topics in the chapters ahead.

Chapter 4

Purgation and Prayer "in the Spirit"

HUMAN FULFILLMENT OF THE law was a problematic thesis for Luther. Remember, Luther thought justification occurred by divine agency without any human merit acquired through law obedience. Yet we have shown in the previous chapter that the Spirit has a specific function in Luther's late theology to present the law to the justified soul. The Spirit's activity elicits a desire to fulfill the law in the justified soul. Thus, as we have seen, Luther does subscribe to a specific notion of law fulfillment, namely a law fulfillment for sanctification after justification. This is not the accusing law but rather the sanctifying law that admonishes sinful inclinations and exhorts good works after justification and in relation to the Spirit.

For Luther, the law is connected to sin. The more a person tries to obey the law herself, the more the law exposes her sin. This epitomizes the law's accusing function. The only solution is Christ's righteousness applied from outside the sinner. Luther appeared to change his tune, however, on the topic of the sanctifying law. He distinguished between justifying law fulfillment and an incipient sanctifying law fulfillment. This distinction is evident in his remarks that "it is necessary that both justification and law fulfillment take place in us"[1] and that "the Spirit is given to us in order that the law's righteousness might be fulfilled *in us*."[2] While Luther thought

---

1. WA 39/1:443.14; cf. 374.11–12: "Under Christ, law is in a state of being done, not of having been done. Here believers need to be admonished by the law."

2. WA 39/1:367.11 (emphasis added).

justifying law fulfillment must occur through Christ *extra nobis* on account of sin, he advocated for sanctifying law fulfillment *in nobis* on account of the Spirit.³ So the question we have now is how does the sanctifying law relate to sin? We know that the accusing function of the law accuses of sin, but how does the sanctifying law function such that it can be fulfilled *in* the Christian herself as a process distinct from justification?

I will show that for Luther the sanctifying law functions as a guide to sin and righteousness in the Christian life. Through admonition, the sanctifying law helps the Christian to recognize her ongoing sinful inclinations after justification. Through exhortation, it guides her to resist those inclinations in favor of good works. In sections two and three, I will look at the way Luther used the accusing and sanctifying functions of law to address two distinct aspects of sin, original sin in human nature and actual sin acted out by individuals. Luther was interested in how each type of sin was resolved in relation to divine Persons. Therefore, we will examine the way he introduced a medical metaphor known as "Christ the Physician" into his discussion of sin and law. He used the metaphor to show how Christ *healed* sin in human nature diagnosed by the accusing law and *is healing* the sin in individuals through the Spirit and the sanctifying law. This means we will look at the role of the sanctifying law in the healing process.

Finally, sections four and five will look more carefully at the justified person's experience of the healing process in relation to the sanctifying law. We will look at how Luther constructed the sanctifying law as a way of treating the actual sin in the Christian using the language of disease and healing. Because Luther was interested in the human person's experiential aspect, we will look at the way he narrated the temporal process of treating actual sin through the sanctifying law in very practical terms through an anecdote about a Christian youth struggling with lust. Then, we will turn to look at prayer as the key practice the Christian must engage to overcome sin and to produce good works as righteousness.

---

3. Anderas introduces this distinction in relation to sanctification, stating that "both in Christ *extra nos* and by the Spirit *in nobis*, the law is confirmed because it is kept. On the basis of Christ's fulfillment of the law in the sinner's place, God justifies the ungodly with full respect to the infinite perfection of his own justice as it is expressed in the law; and this forensic, atonement focused justification in Christ is intrinsically ordered to the *Gerechtmachung*, the *iustificatio legis in nobis*, that begins to take shape in the redeemed by the power of the Spirit's *primitiae*" (Anderas, *Renovatio*, 81).

The Soteriological Solution to Sin and Law

The aim of this chapter is to clarify how Luther opens the Christian life "in the Spirit" to good behavior in relation to the sanctifying law. This requires that we determine the anthropological object of the sanctifying law and the means and mechanisms of the human response. To position ourselves to begin clarifying this anthropological dimension of law fulfillment, we must first investigate Luther's understanding of the soteriological resolution for law vis-à-vis human sin. With a clearer conception of the relation between law and sin, we will be able to see how Luther used the law to encode good behavior in the Christian life "in the Spirit."

When Luther discussed law, he posited law as a divine word in relation to certain anthropological conditions. These conditions see change and alteration as the Christian progresses through the stages of the *ordo rei*, what we have identified as "before Christ," "under Christ," and "in the Spirit." To define these anthropological conditions, Luther looked to concepts from medieval doctrines of sin, namely the distinction between original and actual sin (*peccatum originale et actuale*). Luther introduced original and actual sin in the *Antinomian Disputations* to distinguish himself from medieval Nominalists like Gabriel Biel. While Biel and others dealt only with actual sin, or so Luther claimed, he was interested in how the human relation to God resolves "sin in its entirety, original and actual."[4] Luther correlated these hamartiological categories to the accus-

---

4. WA 39/1:398.18–19. The distinction between original and actual sin originated in Anselm of Canterbury's *On the Virgin Conception and Original Sin* when Anselm inquired into how God assumed human nature without becoming sinful and, then, how God's action in restoring human nature restores individual persons. To do this, Anselm distinguished between nature and person. Anselm, *On the Virgin Conception* c.1. Ebeling interpreted Luther's concept of sin as radical discontinuity with medieval theology; it was "entirely in opposition to the theology and piety of the Middle Ages!" (Ebeling, *Lutherstudien*, 3:115, translation mine). Through this interpretive lens, he concluded that Luther's doctrine of sin included both a sharp escalation in the essence of sin and a collapse between the universal sin in human nature and the particular sins of an individual: "*peccatum originale*, understood as *peccatum radicale*, constitutes the essence of sin [for Luther], while individual sins are only its consequences." This view of collapse and radicalization is repeated in Kleffmann, *Die Erbsündenlehre in sprachtheologischem Horizont*, 107–9; Lohse, *Martin Luther's Theology*, 250; Leppin and Schneider-Ludorff, *Das Luther-Lexikon*, s.v. "Sünde." Oswald Bayer also interpreted Luther's notion of sin as a collapse but framed the collapse through his Word theology. Original and actual sin in Luther, per Bayer, did not have to do with individual actions, but rather a fundamental attitude of "refused communication" with God. Individual sins were refused communication made concrete. Bayer, "Being in the Image of God," 85–86.

ing and sanctifying law in order to make room for good behavior as law fulfillment "in the Spirit."

Original and actual sin, as Luther understood these terms, have to do with human nature as a universal category and with particular persons and their temporal actions as instantiations of this universal.[5] Luther defined original sin as "corruption of the entire [human] nature." The original sin was concupiscence, or a sinful affection in the human will for an object other than God, namely the self.[6] Original sin generates a corresponding "inclination" (*pronitas*) to sin in human nature. This sinful inclination is a predisposition to love God and other objects only based on the pleasure these objects offer to the self. Because Luther thought that human reason is also blinded by original sin, reason offers no check on the will's sinful affections.[7] The result is what Luther called "actual sin." Luther's definition of actual sin appeared within one of his frequent aspersions against Jews, Muslims, and papists, who he criticized for repenting only of actual sins of a temporal nature, like murder, theft, and adultery, rather than the entire life.[8] While original sin affects human nature universally, actual sin pertains to particular individual persons as they consent to and act upon the inclination generated by original sin.

This way of defining original and actual sin has important antecedents in medieval Scholasticism, which Luther inherited through his study of Lombard's *Sentences* and Gabriel Biel's *Commentary on the Sentences*. The distinction between original and actual sin began with Anselm of Canterbury, who in the eleventh century differentiated between sin in universal human nature and sins of particular persons.[9] Lombard picked up this distinction and supplied the terminology of original and actual sin

---

5. Jared Wicks interprets Luther's understanding of original and actual sin in relation to Romans 4:7, claiming that Luther understood actual sins via Paul as sins in thought, word, and deed. These actual sins are forgiven by God, but nevertheless rooted in sinful passions and concupiscence inherent in nature because of original sin. It is these ongoing concupiscent inclinations after justification that produce sins in particular human choices and actions. Wicks, "Living and Praying," 527.

6. WA 39/1:397.23-24. Lohse suggests that Luther redefined concupiscence away from its Augustinian legacy as "selfish love" to mean sin against the Holy Spirit or disbelief in Lohse, *Martin Luther's Theology*, 55. This is in contrast to Anderas's claims that Luther actively deployed this Augustinian ordered love framework in Anderas, *Renovatio*, 88-100.

7. WA 18:675.22-34.

8. WA 39/1:395.13-14; 396.1-4.

9. Anselm, *On the Virgin Conception* c.1-2.

(*peccatum originale et actuale*) used by Luther and medieval Scholastics before him.[10] Lombard defined original sin as a "weakness" in human nature.[11] This weakness is transmitted, like a disease, to all individual persons through propagation. Each person is born with damage to their human nature, passed on by his/her parents. This damage is called the *fomes peccati*, the "tinder of sin" or sinful inclinations in the human will. Through the *fomes*, Lombard saw original sin to incentivize the "actual sin" of individuals, which he defined as a "[disobedient] act or movement of soul or body." Luther picked up this distinction between original and actual sin, distinguished as both a universal and particular and as a quality of nature and act. He used these hamartiological categories to nuance the soteriological and anthropological dimensions of law fulfillment.[12] The main challenge he faced was that the sinful inclination, what the Medievals called the flames of sin, is not extinguished, but continues to burn after justification as an "ember" (*carbo*) of sin that is inflamed by desires.[13]

Healing Original and Actual Sin from the Accusing Law "Under Christ"

First, Luther described the soteriological dimension of law fulfillment "under Christ." Under Christ, law no longer accuses because Christ hides original and actual sin. To arrive at the conclusion that original and actual sin are covered under Christ, Luther looked to cultural history combined with a theological trope called "Christ the Physician" (*Christus medicus*). The *Christus medicus* trope dates to the era of the Apostolic Fathers, when Ignatius of Antioch coined the phrase based on Jesus's healings and raising of the dead in the Gospels. Throughout much of the early church, the trope was used theologically to describe miraculous physical healings, medicine, and, especially, Christ's work in justification. In the fourth century, Latin Fathers such as Tertullian and Augustine applied

---

10. Cf. Biel, *Collectorium* II, d.30, q.2, art.2, conclusion 1; II, d.42, introduction; II, d.43, introduction; Biel, *Canonis* III, lectio 72, M–N.

11. Lombard, *Sentences* II, d.30, c.8.

12. Lohse adds to this the helpful insight that Luther gleaned his understanding of the nature of sin from early exegetical work on the Psalms and Romans with an obvious sharpening between his 1509 marginalia notes on Lombard's *Sentences* and his 1513 *Lectures on the Psalms*. See Lohse, *Martin Luther's Theology*, 53–55, 249.

13. WA 39/1:501.8.

the trope to theological anthropology to discuss the effects of justification in the soul.[14] In 1537, Luther picked up the trope and used it in this final sense.[15] As the Good Physician, Christ heals original sin and the actual sins spurred by the sinful inclination.

The *Christus medicus* trope had real significance in the late-fifteenth and early-sixteenth centuries as the black plague finished another death march through western Europe. By all accounts the suffering—and the fear—were great.[16] Symptoms of plague began with the appearance of buboes, blister-like abscesses the size of eggs or larger. Filled with puss and blood, buboes appeared in the groin, neck, and armpits. Then came fever, vomiting of blood, and, finally, death.

Monasteries served as late-medieval hospitals—monks as nurses, physicians, and pharmacists. Cloister walls separated the dead and dying from the living. Outside the walls, life was fear, which sundered friendships and fostered suspicions. Inside, cheerful flowers and herbs meant for tinctures and medicines grew eerily beside the sights, sounds, and smells of suffering and death. Medical treatments were paltry. Some tried bloodletting. Others looked to theriac or electuary, "medicinal" pastes made of snakeskin, stag bones, precious metals and gems, or rare plant extracts thought to neutralize poison in the body.[17] The medieval hospital was a place of tremendous

---

14. An intellectual history of the term can be found in Porterfield, *Healing in the History of Christianity*. Modern interest in the topic began with Adolf von Harnack's *Medicinisches aus der Ältesten Kirchengeschichte*. Harnack covers not just the soteriological application of the Christ the physician trope, but the application of Christ's healing to psychology, illness, and even exorcism.

15. On Luther's use of the *Christus medicus* trope, see Steiger, *Medizinische Theologie*, 3–50. Luther used the trope across the duration of his career. In both his 1518 *Sermon on Indulgences and Grace* (WA 1:239–46) and argument 20 of his 1536 *Disputation Concerning Justification* (WA 39/1:112–14), Luther deployed the *Christus medicus* concept to discuss moral improvement and healing from sin in the temporal life after justification. This span suggests a consistency in Luther's understanding of sin and sanctification that warrants greater exploration, opening insight into Luther's early theology.

16. David Nirenberg has shown that religious persecutions rose after plague outbreaks as communities, lacking the knowledge of modern epidemiology, blamed outbreaks on marginalized groups. Reasoning that only divine wrath could cause such horrendous suffering, Christians looked to sources of communal sin, curses from witches, or poisoning by Jews. Nirenberg, *Communities of Violence*, 231–49. Geraldine Heng set these persecutions in the framework of premodern racial construction in *Invention of Race*, 380. Modern analogs of anti-Asian racist violence occurred during and since the onset of the COVID-19 pandemic spurred suspicion and fear of Asian communities worldwide. Lim et al., "COVID-19 Pandemic."

17. Aberth, *From the Brink of the Apocalypse*, 116–17.

suffering—not for help and healing, but a place to die.[18] With monks at hand, last rites were readily available, ensuring the greatest possible chance of one's final resting place near God in heaven.

The prevalence of illness and death, quarantine, and the closure of cities perpetuated an atmosphere of fear to which no one was immune, clerical or lay. With ineffective and even harmful medical treatments, the death toll of the plague between the fourteenth and sixteenth centuries was as high as 60 percent of the population, killing more than 100 million people over the course of 150 years.[19] Records show the death rate in Germany was somewhat lower—20 percent instead of 60. In this unsettling environment, snakeskin and stag bones could not save you. The only hope for physical or spiritual healing was Christ the Good Physician.

Luther inscribed his analysis of original and actual sin into this cultural history when he equated original sin with the plague, or what Luther called "black cholera."[20] Moving between theology and real life, Luther related the technical language of theology to the everyday, using biblical metaphors his audience understood—both theologically *and* experientially. Original sin is "cholera," "a grave illness," the "original disease," and the "disease and sin of nature."[21] This plague of sin corrupts and perverts "human nature itself."[22] While just over half of the population would get the black plague, *all* suffered from the disease of sin and needed the very best hospital, the Church.[23] Like the plague's buboes, original sin presented with particular symptoms. The main symptom was "an inclination to sinning" that spurred sin in each individual's actions.[24] The black plague and its buboes were terrifying, but it had nothing on the disease of original sin.

Reflecting both the fears and the hopes of his day, Luther linked the disease of original sin to the *Christus medicus* trope. Christ is the Good Doctor who treats and heals the disease of original sin. But he must first

---

18. Risse, *Mending Bodies, Saving Souls*, 208.

19. Aberth, *Plagues in World History*, 37.

20. WA 39/1:427.2. Luther used the term "cholera" for the black plague. However, cholera as defined by modern epidemiological criteria was not present in Europe until the nineteenth century, when it was transmitted from India through trade routes. See Aberth, *Plagues in World History*, 101–2.

21. WA 39/1:426.4–19; 350.18.

22. WA 39/1:397.23–24.

23. WA 39/1:350.14–15.

24. WA 39/1:397.24.

diagnose it and convince the sick patient of her disease.[25] In this sense, Luther linked Christ to the accusing law. "First, [the doctor] diligently enquires about the disease and the cause of the disease. Later, he reveals these causes to the ferocious sick person and persuades him that he is infested with a very grave disease."[26] To do this, Christ the Good Doctor "preaches and expounds the law or wrath."[27] Christ uses the law because "the disease is shown in order to heal it."[28] The law is useful here because the law diagnoses "the damage into which we have fallen since the beginning."[29] Therefore, Christ uses the law to show the human person the "black cholera that torments" her with the aim that she will accept his treatment.[30] The accusing law supplies the diagnostic criteria necessary to diagnose and convince the person of her diseased nature.

Once the patient is thoroughly convinced that she needs medicine to heal her diseased nature, Christ the Physician prescribes his healing medicine. Luther depicted Christ the Physician to announce the gospel promise. The clinical language of the diagnosis and prescribed remedy show Christ's comforting bedside manner. He says,

> Behold, you are saddened, you are afflicted, you have been led into hell by the law and the black cholera that torments you. Do not despair; a good rhubarb is at hand and it is the best by far—that you might know Christ, receive him, and live.[31]

Here Christ functions as both physician and medicine. As physician, he prescribes himself as the best medicine to heal the disease of original sin. But Luther did not see Christ as just the medicine but also as the cure for the disease: "Christ is given so that this disease might be healed . . . so that he might restore corrupt nature to its integrity."[32] Christ the Physician

---

25. WA 39/1:425.13—430.11.
26. WA 39/1:424.10-12.
27. WA 39/1:425.1-2.
28. WA 39/1:424.18-19.
29. WA 39/1:424.4-9.
30. WA 39/1:427.1-4.
31. WA 39/1:427.1-4; cf. 424.16-18. On common late-medieval medical approaches to plague, see Garza, *Understanding Plague*; Byrne, *Encyclopedia of Pestilence*; Gilman, *Plague Writing*.
32. WA 39/1:386.9-11. Steiger describes the distinction between physician and remedy as an important feature of Luther's medical theology. The christological office (*Amt*) is to protect and to heal. Steiger, *Medizinische Theologie*, 28-29.

prescribes himself as the theriac to cure original sin, to heal human nature, and return it to good health.

The sick patient ascertains Christ as the medicinal rhubarb by means of faith. She is then deemed to be healed. For the Christian, Luther said the diseased nature and its sin is "hidden in Christ."[33] This means that, under Christ, "sin is dead . . . in an imputative manner, when I by means of faith in Christ accept the remission of sins and am utterly liberated from sin."[34] Because the sick patient has received the medicine that will restore her, she is deemed healthy on account of Christ. Her remaining symptoms no longer confirm the law's diagnostic criteria.[35]

Christ's medicine ought to bring signs of new health. Luther reflected this expectation when he said, "You are sprinkled and washed by the blood of Christ. Therefore, offer your bodies to obey justice. . . . Be imitators of the justice of good works . . . you have Christ."[36] When the Christian receives Christ as the best medicinal rhubarb to heal human nature, the law deems her to be healthy and she should have new signs of health in just actions. The problem is the effects of the medicine are not instantaneous but require time to fully heal the disease. To this point, Luther noted that "in faith, we are not yet perfectly healthy, but healing . . . the disease is not yet totally healed."[37] He acknowledged that the symptoms of the disease persist for the

---

33. WA 39/1:551.15.

34. WA 39/1:431.9, 10–12. The specific way that Christ heals human nature concerns the role of the incarnation in Luther's Christology. Like Anselm and Aquinas, Luther understood the permeation of original sin in terms of universals and particulars. Sin entered particular human persons through the sin of the one man in whom all of humanity in that moment was contained. Imputation of Christ's righteousness functions similarly through a propagation model; Christ contains all human nature within himself. Thus, when Christ perfectly fulfills the law, that righteous attribute of Christ's human nature can extend by propagation to all of Christ's heirs through faith. On this point, Luther further echoed medieval discussions about liability for original sin. Anselm, Lombard, Aquinas, and Biel all agreed that original sin was absolved in Christ's remission of sins given in the sacrament of baptism. Cf. Anselm, *On the Virgin Conception* c.22, 29; Lombard, *Sentences* II, d.32, c.3; Aquinas, *ST* I-II, q. 81; Biel, *Canonis* III, lectio 72, M-N. To this, Thomas added that, just as original sin was spread through propagation, so also remission of sins was spread through propagation of Christ's heirs (Aquinas, *ST* I-II q. 81). Luther adopted this perspective in his 1519 "Sermon on Two Kinds of Righteousness," noting that just as we inherit culpability of Adam's sin, so also Christ grants an alien righteousness that removes culpability through an alien process. See WA 2:145.9–25.

35. WA 39/1:436.1–2, 6.

36. WA 39/1:475.1–6.

37. WA 39/1:376.6–8.

duration of the healing process. While Christ's medicine takes effect, the sinful inclination remains in the human will and intellect to spur actual sin. To get rid of the sinful inclination and actual sin, something else is needed to help guide and support the human will and intellect.

To summarize, under the soteriological dimension of law fulfillment, Luther used the *Christus medicus* trope to separate original and actual sin from the accusing law. Under Christ, original and actual sin are as though they are nothing. Christ the Physician heals human nature from original sin. Particular individuals participate in Christ's just human nature by faith. Thus, both original and actual sin are covered by Christ in justification.

The problem is Luther's account of law fulfillment under the soteriological dimension does not ensure the good works in the Christian life that are supposed to result from faith. The "ember" of sin, the sinful inclination, persists in individuals. Here, Luther's distinction between "healed" as a completed act and "healing" provides an opening. When the work of divine grace is understood as an ongoing process in the Christian life, the healing process in the human person contextualizes the lingering "symptoms" of sin within a temporal dimension in which improved health can occur. The actual sins that result from the ongoing sinful inclination can be "healed" in favor of good works. But something is required to guide the human will and reason to choose God and the good behaviors over the sinful inclination during the healing process. By further probing the temporal dimension of the sinful inclination and actual sin, we can begin to see how Luther carved out an anthropological dimension of law fulfillment in the temporal realm that attends to the good behaviors that should exhibit from faith.

Actual Sin and the Sanctifying Law

In the previous section, we clarified Luther's view that original and actual sin are hidden from the accusing law under Christ. The anthropological problem with which Luther must now contend is that the Christian maintains the inclination to sin under Christ because she is "healing," and not yet fully healed. Objects of desire continue to activate the *fomes peccati* inborn in her, driving her to further sinful acts known as actual sin. Now we see Luther make sense of good behaviors in the Christian as a practical, anthropological dimension of law fulfillment by focusing on affections generated by this ember of sin. This section investigates how Luther understood the Christian to control her affective responses to the sinful inclination to diminish actual sin and to produce good works after justification. To answer this question, we must examine the way Luther increased the anthropological language of the emotions in relation to the Holy Spirit and the sanctifying law's admonishments and exhortations.

First, I want to introduce a fantastic story Luther told at the end of the antinomian controversy about a "Christian youth" dealing with the ongoing experience of the ember of sin. I introduce this narrative here at the beginning of this section because it will be structurally important for the remainder of the chapter. Luther narrated the story in this way:

> If I, a Christian, still strong in my youth, were to fall in love with a beautiful girl or woman, unless I were a total tree trunk, I could not [help] but feel affection for her and desire to attain her, even if I were baptized and justified, were it only permitted by disgrace or another punishment that I fear. Yet, nevertheless, if I am a Christian, the heart and the Spirit in the heart right away exclaim: "Get behind me, Satan! Do not speak! No, do not rule, flesh! Be completely silent! You should not persuade me or incite me to fornication, adultery, passion, or to do any other shameful acts against my God in this way. Instead, I will wait until God will give a woman to me whom I love! I will make an end with her! I will leave her [i.e., the desired girl/woman] to her bridegroom and family." These and such words are not man's, but Christ's and the Holy Spirit's, who says in the heart: "Let the girl in peace. I will give you another in due time, whom you will easily love." This Christian, even if he is affected by sexual desire, nevertheless obeys the Spirit, averts by prayer the evil he feels, and prays that he might not enter into temptation.
>
> Therefore, this already is what it means to overcome sin, even if it cannot be done without trouble and much difficulty. . . . The Christian stands firm and obeys God's word and law which says: "You shall not covet," and with the Holy Spirit admonishing him concerning this will of God, he will not give in.[38]

Here we see Luther rehearsing the temporal experience of the sinful inclination in the Christian life after justification vis-à-vis the law, Christ, and the Holy Spirit. Much of what Luther said about the changing human relation to law contra Agricola throughout the *Antinomian Disputations* coalesces in this narrative. Throughout the remainder of the chapter, we

---

38. WA 39/1:500.16—501.6, 9–11.

will examine this narrative from multiple angles as we discuss the anthropological dimension of law fulfillment.

The "Christian youth" narrative begins with a young man experiencing sexual desire for a pretty girl. In medieval moral theologies and theological anthropologies, these feelings of desire had to do with affections in the human will. Affections were understood as an inclination or leaning toward a particular object that moved the lover toward or away from a virtuous end. Just affections inclined the will toward love of God as virtue, but sinful affections inclined the will toward vice based on disordered love. When desirable objects were presented to the human will, these affections for love of God or the self were activated, prompting the human will to choose for or against attainment of the object. Human reason, or the intellect, was charged with judging the lovability of a desired object determined by an object's proximity to God, and thus to guide the will in choosing, or not choosing, to act on an affection.

In Luther's early *Disputation against Scholastic Theology* and his controversy with Erasmus over the freedom of the will, Luther infamously rejected this structure for moral reasoning in relation to the doctrine of justification. He saw original sin to completely ruin both human reason and volition. Humans were incapable of knowing or willing the good of love of God. But now we see Luther reposition this language of medieval moral reasoning to discuss the anthropological dimension of law fulfillment after justification in view of divine grace. The context of the discussion in the *Antinomian Disputations* was not the human's natural powers, as it was with Erasmus, but in view of the Christian's relation to the sanctifying Spirit as Christ's gift in justification.

Luther introduced the sanctifying law as the Spirit's tool in helping the Christian overcome the ongoing sinful inclination. The sanctifying law is the law that redirects the Christian's sinful inclinations; it admonishes against sinful inclinations and exhorts to good instead. We know we are dealing with the sanctifying law, not the accusing law, because we are discussing the Christian as she is positioned after justification. Luther used the terminology "under Christ" to designate the Christian position after justification. In this location, the accusing function of law is removed because the Christian's original and actual sin are hidden under Christ. Luther also positioned the Christian in proximity to Christ's gift, the Holy Spirit, who newly speaks the law to the Christian as it is transformed by gospel to admonish to good.[39] For this reason, this transformed law is "highly commended"[40] to the Christian to help her contend with her ongoing inclination to sin after justification.

Luther framed the sanctifying law's effect on the Christian in terms of ordered love. The sanctifying law helps the Christian by identifying and redirecting the sinful affections created by her ongoing inclination to sin. Luther thought that the Christian needs the law to "reveal sins" after faith to direct her away from the remaining inclinations to sin generated by the ember.[41]

At the same time, the law also "admonishes to good."[42] Thus, he presented the law as a bidirectional guide to the Christian's affections. This function is evident in the "Christian youth" narrative introduced at the beginning of this section. When the Christian experiences sexual desire for the pretty girl, the commandment against adultery appears in his thoughts. "You shall not covet" functions to judge against the desire as a wrong affection. As a result, the Christian recognizes the desire as part of the remaining sinful flesh. Interestingly, the law does not rebuke the desire itself, but the direction of the desire. It is directed toward the wrong object: the Christian desires a pretty girl, not the wife God has for him as his "good end."[43] The command against adultery then redirects the Christian's sexual desire toward his future wife. The sanctifying law does not have the natural sexual desire itself in view but rather the wrong object for those affections. The sanctifying law's admonishment and exhortation direct those natural inclinations, not to extinguish them but to order them toward the correct object. This helps the Christian to recognize and judge against sinful affections created by the remaining inclination to sin, redirecting these affections toward a good end.

At the anthropological level, the sanctifying law's admonishment against sinful affections helps the Christian to respond with a new set of negative and positive emotions in the will. Luther brings back the penitential responses of sorrow and the good intention in relation to the sinful affections. Luther brought these two emotional responses together as a corollary to the sanctifying law's admonishment and exhortation: "I hate everything

---

39. WA 39/1:474.21–22.
40. WA 39/1:444.9–10; cf. 455.8–13.
41. WA 39/1:474.17–18.
42. WA 39/1:474.21–22.
43. WA 39/1:500.24.

that offends God's name and I become a pursuer of good works."[44] When the sanctifying law admonishes against the sinful affection, the Christian responds with "a hatred of sin remaining in the flesh."[45] Similarly, the law's exhortation toward a good end redirects the affection to coincide with a good intention against sin out of love of God.[46] When the law identifies and redirects the Christian's sinful affections, she generates new sorrow for sin and good intentions against sinful inclination in the will.

The issue of volitional consent is critical at this anthropological level. Consent has to do, not with *feeling* an affection or desire, but with volition—the will's choice to follow or act on that affection. Luther's medieval predecessors William of Ockham and Duns Scotus recognized two alternatives here: one could consent *to* the affection and, thus, will to sin; or one could consent *not* to sin and, thus, will against (nill) the wrong affection. The medieval opinion was that sin resided in one's response to a desire, not necessarily in the desire itself, which could be natural.[47] Here, Luther seemed to agree: though the Christian may feel a sinful affection because of the sinful inclination, she has an option—she can "not consent to sin, but drive it back."[48] The Christian may feel the affection, but she may also will against, or nill, the affection with the help of the sanctifying law.

This notion of consent plays out in the "Christian youth" narrative. The Christian youth feels sexual desire for the pretty girl, and this desire is identified by the commandment against adultery. At this point in the narrative, consent becomes a main theme. The Christian cries out against the affection, declaring that he *will not* be incited to fornication; he will not sin against God. Here, we see that the Christian youth hates what is offensive to God. He does *not consent* to sin. Instead, the Christian consents to law obedience. We see Luther say that the Christian youth *will* wait on the wife God will give him as an end and leave the pretty girl for her future husband. This positive consent is the good intention, which gets formulated as consent *to* a good exhorted by the sanctifying law. The Christian youth will act on the affection as it is redirected by the sanctifying law's exhortation to love God and the wife God has for him.

---

44. WA 39/1:434.9–12.
45. WA 39/1:394.14–15.
46. WA 39/1:350.24–27.
47. Cf. Adams, "Structure of Ockham's Moral Theory," 614.
48. WA 39/1:436.10–11.

At this point, Luther had brought together the sanctifying law with the Christian's sinful affections. The sanctifying law admonishes against the Christian's sinful affections that are generated by the lingering sinful inclination and activated by objects of desire. It also redirects these affections toward God through exhortation. Luther also had the Christian controlling these affections as they are revealed by the sanctifying law through new emotional responses having to do with volitional consent, but the human will is corrupted by sin. Therefore, the will requires assistance to not consent to sin in accord with the sanctifying law. To address this, Luther incorporated the Holy Spirit into the consent process.[49] The Spirit appears not only as the divine agent of the law, as we saw in chapter 3, but also to support human volitional capacity to resist—to *not* consent—to the sinful affection.

The Holy Spirit supports the Christian's volitional activity to resist the sinful inclination by recreating the will and filling it with new affections aligned to the law. Referring to the Antinomian controversy in his 1539 treatise, *On Councils and the Church*, Luther asserted, "Christ did not earn only *gratia* for us, but also *donum*, 'the gift of the Holy Spirit,' so that we might not only have forgiveness, but also cessation of sin."[50] Christ gives the gift of the Holy Spirit specifically to help the Christian deal with the sinful inclination. To aide the cessation of sin, Luther suggested in the *Antinomian Disputations* that the Spirit recreates the will in line with the law.[51] Within this new will, "the Spirit elicits new motions and fills the will so that it truly loves God and hates remaining sin in the flesh."[52] Luther adopted the medieval view that the affections move the human will. When he showed the Spirit to fill the will with new motions, these motions should be understood as new affections that move the Christian away from sin and toward God in the act of consent. The Spirit supports the Christian's volitional activity to resist, to not consent to, her sinful affections by recreating the will and filling it with new movers, new affections.

---

49. In his reading of this passage, Anderas interprets this phrase "*hic spiritus*" in terms of Luther's appropriation of the Augustinian *spiritus/caro* distinction. "Hic spiritus" is not the Holy Spirit but rather the Christian's recreated spirit which helps her to reign in the flesh. He then understands the nonconsent in this passage in even stronger terms of human agency than I am suggesting given I interpret this as an example of medieval *cooperatio* motifs. See Anderas, *Renovatio*, 98.

50. WA 50:599.32–34.

51. WA 39/1:373.2–3. See chapter 3.

52. WA 39/1:395.22–24.

PURGATION AND PRAYER "IN THE SPIRIT"

The way Luther depicted the Spirit's work to recreate and sustain the will's new movements results in a new subjective experience for the Christian. It is not the Spirit but the Christian herself who can now say, "After receiving [the Spirit], I begin to hate wholeheartedly everything that offends God's name."[53] The Spirit is not the subject of the "I" in this statement.[54] Rather, the "I" is the Christian herself, even as the Spirit is the source of the new will and the affections.

This blurring of volitional subjects is another element that appears in the "Christian youth" narrative. When the Christian does not consent to sin and cries out against his sinful desire for the pretty girl, Luther states that it is "the heart and the Spirit in the heart" crying out against the affection.[55] In this telling of the narrative, cooperation seems to be in play. However, Luther also attributed the action to the Christian youth himself. In the third analysis of the narrative, Luther claimed that "the Christian stands firm and obeys" and the Christian "averts the sin he feels."[56] The Christian himself, but also together with the Spirit, consents against the sin and for obedience to the law. The Spirit is at work in the Christian's volitional activity, guiding the Christian regarding the will of God and judging against the sinful affection.

In summary, Luther introduced the sanctifying law and the Spirit in relation to the anthropological language of the emotions to clarify how the Christian manages her sinful affective inclinations in the stage "in the Spirit." Luther maintained his pessimistic view of human intellectual and volitional capacities. Bound by original sin, the intellect and will are no longer able to judge and will rightly. However, Luther showed that when the will's affections are activated by objects of desire, the Spirit speaks the sanctifying law to admonish against the sinful affections, elevating blind

---

53. WA 39/1:436.9–10. Anderas refers to this as a "*donum*-rendition of the traditional *gratia cooperans*" (Anderas, *Renovatio*, 84).

54. Saarinen claims that Christ is the subject of good works in the human person via the *fides Christo formata*, the faith in Christ in the form of the Christian's soul. Saarinen, "Einige Themen," 295. Theodor Dieter points out, however, that in Luther's discussions of the will and affect, the will and affect are not the Spirit's will and affect, but the person's. He raises the question, "Wie also kann das Wirken des Hl. Geistes im Menschen so gedacht werden, daß es zugleich das Wirken des Menschen ist, der darin 'Ich' sagen kann? Und wie kann umgekehrt das Wirken des Menschen in der Gemeinschaft mit Christus und dem Hl. Geist so verstanden werden, daß es nicht als verdienstliches aufgefaßt werden muß?" (Dieter, "Du mußt den Geist haben!," 71–72).

55. WA 39/1:500.21.

56. WA 39/1:4–5.

human reason. In speaking the sanctifying law, the Spirit both instills a negative judgment against the sinful affection and redirects this affection toward a good, namely God, as an exhortation.

Luther also introduced the Spirit in conjunction with increased emotional language vis-à-vis human volitional capacity. He showed how the Spirit props up human volitional capacities to consent against a sinful affection and, instead, to consent for the good affection as it is redirected toward God. Unlike the intellectual function of the sanctifying law, Luther blurred the volitional subjectivity between the Christian and the Spirit. We will return to this blurring of volitional subjects in the section on prayer below. At this point, we see how Luther put the sanctifying law and the Spirit in place as mechanisms to support human reason and will. Now, we must clarify how Luther understood these moral reasoning processes in the anthropological dimension as they worked with the Spirit to control sinful affections and to produce good behavior in fulfillment of the sanctifying law.

Purgation of Sin and Formal Righteousness "in the Spirit"

To review, we have been tracking the way Luther opened the anthropological dimension of law/gospel to good behavior as fulfillment of the sanctifying law in the stage "in the Spirit." We have seen that Luther utilized robust medieval hamartiological categories. Rather than a nebulous concept of sin that encompasses all spiritual and physical incursions against God, Luther separated sin into two distinct categories. *Original sin* mars human nature universally. *Actual sin* is particular to individuals. Christ hides both kinds of sin from the accusing law in justification and heals human nature in the soteriological dimension of law fulfillment. However, the sinful inclination continues to undermine the Christian's good behavior in the temporal life, spurring her to further actual sins despite her justification under Christ.

In the previous section we began to clarify the anthropological dimension of law fulfillment by examining the inner moral processes to resist the ongoing inclination to sin. Of special interest was the way the Holy Spirit and the sanctifying law prop up human reason and will. Together, the Spirit and the sanctifying law help the human person produce intellectual judgments against and volitional nonconsent to the sinful affections that are stirred up by the *fomes peccati*. The current section examines how these inner moral processes lead to good behavior as fulfillment of the sanctifying law in the Christian. Because Luther distinguished two kinds of sin, only one of which is healed in justification, we will now attend to a second process for removing sin from the Christian after justification in the stage "in the Spirit" and a second kind of righteous result. The second process is purgation. Purgation results in "formal righteousness."

Purgation as a Second Process for Removing Sin

Luther introduced purgation (*purgatio*) as the process for "routing out" and "driving out" remaining sin after justification.[57] Purgation is a medieval concept that Luther would have frequently encountered in two of his medieval sources: Gabriel Biel and Johannes Tauler. The fifteenth-century Augustinian Scholastic Gabriel Biel was one of Luther's favorite foes.[58] In his *Canonis Misse Expositio*, Gabriel Biel posited purgation as the process of overcoming one's actual sin in ascent to love of God.[59] Biel positioned purgation *prior to* the infusion of justifying divine grace into the soul as a means of preparing the soul for God. Luther critiqued Biel in the *Antinomian Disputations* because Biel's system did not account for the ongoing experience of the sinful inclination.[60]

Instead, Luther looked to the fourteenth-century Dominican mystic Johannes Tauler. Tauler understood purgation as an effect or consequence of the divine-human relationship. In his *Predigten* (Sermons), Tauler taught that the gift of the Holy Spirit leads to transformation of vice and the inclination for vice into virtue through purgation.[61] By slowly extinguishing the inclination, the *fomes peccati*, in the soul, purgation elevates the soul to God such that God further enlightens and works in the soul.

57. WA 39/1:350.26-27.

58. See, for example, Luther's *Disputation against Scholastic Theology* (WA 1:221-28, esp. 224.18, 29; 225.20, 23).

59. Biel, *Canonis* III, lectio 72, M-N.

60. In the prefaces to the second and third disputations, Luther identifies the Nominalist theologians, Ockham and Biel, as Pelagians, suggesting that like the Nominalists, Johann Agricola posited Christians are able to formally remove sin themselves without the aid of divine grace. Luther's reference to the Christian "traveler" (*peregrinus*) in the preface is a thinly veiled reference to Biel's Christian "pilgrim" (*viator*), who Biel posited as striving against actual sin in the ascent to love of God (cf. WA 39/1:419-22, 489-96, esp. 490.9).

61. Tauler, *Die Predigten Taulers*, 238. Volker Leppin describes Luther's developing reliance on Tauler throughout the 1510s, explaining that by the beginning of the sixteenth century, Wittenberg had emerged as the center for the study of Tauler. Leppin, "Luther's Roots," 55; cf. Kieckhefer, "Notion of Passivity," 203.

Per Tauler, purgation is a process after the infusion of justifying grace that escalates the real effects of that grace in the soul. Contra Biel, Luther took over Tauler's understanding of purgation, replacing the language of virtue and vice with righteousness and sin.

Echoing Tauler, Luther brought in purgation as a secondary process for removing ongoing sin after justification. Just as he coupled original and actual sin, Luther now brought together imputation and purgation. The first way that sin is removed is "by reputation or imputation, which means the mercy and grace of God has removed sin."[62] Imputation means that "God does not impute sin"; God does not attribute sin to the Christian. Rather, Luther introduced purgation as a process after the justifying imputation of Christ's righteousness. He remarked that "all good works done after justification are . . . the good intention against sin. For nothing else happens than that the sin, which is shown by the law and forgiven in Christ, is purged."[63] Purgation is a process that involves driving out the sin remaining in the Christian after justification even though this sin is hidden from the accusing law by imputation of Christ's righteousness.

The Spirit speaks the sanctifying law to spur purgation. In imputation, the accusing law functioned to reveal sin and drive the sinner to Christ. Now, in purgation Luther claimed that "the remaining sin in the flesh . . . is being purged by the law."[64] The law supports purgation because the law "exposes" the remaining sin to be driven out of the Christian herself.[65] Luther was careful to say, however, that this is not the law exposing ongoing sin in an accusing way. He insisted that "we are not under the law that accuses us. For we have received the Holy Spirit in whom we begin to detest and hate sin, and we purge it."[66] As we saw in chapter 3, this Spirit is the divine agent of the law. Therefore, both the Spirit and the sanctifying law are operating in

62. WA 39/1:491.24–25.

63. WA 39/1:350.24–27.

64. WA 39/1:474.17–19.

65. WA 39/1:350.26. Jared Wicks has shown that in Luther's 1517 *Tractatus de indulgentiis*, the reformer claimed that post-justification penitence must accompany God's inner healing and renewing influences through *gratia sanans*. As we saw in chapter 3, the changing functions of law support and duplicate penitence after justification. Wicks, "Catholic Encounters," 3. Where Anderas connects Luther's *donum*-motif to *cooperatio*, Wicks connects the *donum* in Luther's thought to *gratia sanans*, healing grace, which then permits and sustains the cooperation. See Wicks, "Catholic Encounters," 5; Anderas, *Renovatio*, 84.

66. WA 39/1:436.9–10.

purgation to reveal the Christian's ongoing sin—the sinful inclination and resulting actual sin—so that it may be driven out.

Purgation has to do with removing human sin before the law. Luther used several names for this: the "remaining sin that adheres in the flesh"; the "old leaven"; the "Old Adam."[67] Luther used all these terms for the ongoing remnant of sin that is left after justification, the *fomes peccati*. Purgation sees the slow, steady diminishment of this remaining inclination to sin. To make this clear, Luther links purgation to the Pauline notion of "dying to sin." He says, "To be dead and to die to sin is [sic] a Pauline phrase for battling against sin and not allowing it to rule in us."[68] Dying to sin is purgation. "The pious die in this life to sin, that is, to the world with all of its concupiscent desires."[69] Purgation is dying to the remnant of sin, driving out that remnant and its sinful affections. While imputation removes the guilt for original and actual sin from the accusing law, the second process of purgation sees the Christian, by means of the Spirit and the law, to work against the inclination to sin in the particular person herself.

Finally, just as imputation was correlated to Christ, purgation occurs in relation to the Spirit. Luther remarks that the law is fulfilled "imputatively" in Christ. Then, the law is also fulfilled "in a purging manner because the Holy Spirit is given me . . . what is left in me of sin, this I purge until I become totally pure, and this in the same Spirit who is given on Christ's account."[70] The Christian does not purge sin on her own, by her own powers apart from divine aid, but rather the Holy Spirit is the divine person operative in sustaining this activity in her. One way the Spirit supports purgation

67. WA 39/1:492.3-4; 474.17-19; 396.10-13; 493.14.

68. WA 39/1:551.2-4. It is important to note that it is the sinful inclination, not the self, that is dying and being mortified here.

69. WA 39/1:551.11-12.

70. WA 39/1:434.4-12. Oswald Bayer claims that there is no metaphysical progress in the moral improvement of sanctification, only ethical progress. Bayer, *Living by Faith*, 64-65. However, Bayer's anti-metaphysical claim is inconsistent with the theological reasoning Luther used, which sees the gift of the Spirit to support the purgation of the sinful inclination in the soul's moral powers. The ethical progress Bayer advocates requires nothing more than an increasingly voluntary adherence to the civil law, not the Spirit. Wicks points to a more metaphysical explanation here when he shows that around 1518 Luther replaced the medieval language of *gratia sanans* (healing grace) with the language of *gratia* and *dona*. The *dona*, gifts, come to fill the position of *gratia sanans* in the moral change the Christian ought to experience after justification. Luther includes the Spirit in the *dona* in the Antinomian Disputations. Wicks, "Catholic Encounters," 5. This is in agreement with the argument here as well as Anderas, *Renovatio*, 83; Lund, "Luther's 'Third Use of the Law,'" 180-81.

is through the law. As we saw in the "Christian youth" narrative, the Spirit "admonishes" the Christian youth about the commandment against adultery, which enables the Christian to resist and redirect the sinful inclination. The Spirit also supports purgation by guiding and sustaining the Christian's volitional responses. Luther reports that "after receiving the Spirit, I begin to hate from my whole heart everything that offends [God's] name."[71] Thus, purgation is a secondary process to imputation for removing remaining sin. The Spirit works alongside human action in purgation.

Formal Righteousness as a Secondary Result of Removing Sin

The result of purgation "in the Spirit" is "formal righteousness" (*iustita formaliter*).[72] As we saw above, Luther took over Tauler's understanding of purgation, but he abandoned the language of virtue and vice. In Luther's alternative terminology, "formal righteousness" replaced "virtue." Therefore, "virtue" lies in the background of Luther's notion of formal righteousness. Luther's understanding of virtue came from Aristotle by way of William of Ockham and other medieval Scholastics. In the *Nicomachean Ethics*, Aristotle defined virtue as "moral excellence" that is formed as a state in the soul by exercising virtuous habits across the span of an entire life.[73] Aristotle understood the virtuous disposition in the soul to be formed by virtuous actions.[74] As virtue in the soul increased, virtuous actions became an outgrowth of the virtuous disposition. Virtuous disposition and virtuous actions were mutually reinforcing. Luther scholarship has emphasized Luther's rhetorical critique of philosophy in theology and, with it, Aristotle's philosophical contributions in understanding the human person.[75] Yet,

---

71. WA 39/1:434.4-12.

72. In the 1519 "Sermon on Two Kinds of Righteousness," Luther developed the notion of two kinds of righteousness, alien and proper (formal), corresponding to two kinds of sin, original and actual. He explained that the alien righteousness given to the believer through imputation leads to proper righteousness in a life spent profitably in good works and "slaying the flesh" (cf. WA 2:145-52).

73. Aristotle, *Nicomachean Ethics* II.1 (1103a-b).

74. Aristotle, *Nicomachean Ethics* II.2 (1104b).

75. Cf. Ebeling, *Luther*, 77. Although Ebeling's opinions still loom large in Luther scholarship, significant work is underway to more carefully parse Luther's use of philosophy over and against Luther's rhetorical critique of it. For example, Helmer, *Trinity and Martin Luther*; White, *Luther as Nominalist*; Dragseth, *Devil's Whore*. At the time of writing, the Luther and Logic group, headed by Christine Helmer, meets on a monthly basis

while Luther distanced himself from the language of virtue and vice, here in the context of the *Antinomian Disputations*, he leaned into other philosophical categories of causality from Aristotle to explain the effects of the Spirit's relation to the soul in sanctification.

Luther preferred the biblical language of "sin" and "righteousness" over the philosophical categories of virtue and vice. However, he utilized this biblical language of righteousness alongside a philosophical distinction between relative and formal relations. In the context of a prolonged discussion differentiating imputation and purgation, Luther stated,

> We are pure and holy, but first by way of imputation, because sin is not imputed to us. Second, we are also *formally righteous* as soon as I, by virtue of these first fruits and the Holy Spirit given to me from heaven, begin in faith to struggle and battle sin.[76]

The reference to holiness from imputation in this quote has to do with what Luther called the "relative" removal of sin, the removal of sin by means of "reputation," "because of Christ," and "in the reckoning and forgiveness of the pitying God."[77] Relative has to do with a particular relation; in this case, the justifying relation between Christ and the soul in faith that hides, but does not remove, an individual's sin.

By contrast, "formal" has to do with an Aristotelian notion, namely, the formal cause of a thing. Using the example of a bronze sphere, Aristotle explained that form is "whatever we ought to call the shape of the sensible thing," for example, the spherical shape of the bronze.[78] The formal

---

to discuss Luther's use of philosophy and to deepen our own scholarly understandings of philosophical terms and constructs.

76. WA 39/1:493.25—494.3.

77. WA 39/1:491.24; 356.33; 356.29-30. This final quote reflects the distinction between Luther's theses, reflected here, and his development and debate of those theses in the disputations themselves, reflected in the long quote comparing formal and imputed righteousness. While Luther maintained that sin is "only" removed relatively by reputation in the theses, when he expanded his discussion of this thesis in the argument, he used the thesis to contrast relative and formal righteousness for justification. Relative righteousness, by reputation, alone suffices to justify. However, Luther made clear in his development that relative righteousness does not preclude but leads to formal righteousness. This opens up Ebeling's elevation of the Theses to the *Disputatio de homine* as authoritative on Luther's anthropology to considerable critique. White framed this in terms of "disputation without debate." See White, *Luther as Nominalist*, 60-80.

78. Aristotle, *Metaphysics* VII.8 (1033b). According to Mannermaa, *forma* in Luther's medieval parlance refers to "actual reality," such that *forma iustitia* must mean real righteousness. Mannermaa only associates formal justice with Christ himself, which remains

cause of the human person is the soul. Aristotle sees this as a generative process; the formal cause of the human does not receive its final shape until reaching its final end.[79] Therefore, when Luther says the Christian becomes formally righteous by battling or purging sin and through "first fruits" of good works, he is appropriating Aristotelian language to stake a claim about the shape of the Christian subject, specifically her soul. In this case, the Christian's form is being transformed from a sinful shape into a righteous shape. Through purgation, the justified soul is being reshaped to be less sinful and more righteous.

Imputation confers an immediate transformation of sin into relative righteousness. However, purgation is not instantaneous. Rather, formal righteousness overtakes sin in the flesh across the duration of a lifetime. Luther set this process into the small moments of the everyday life:

> Sin is removed in a formal and purging manner because here day by day and more and more, I purge and mortify sin that yet adheres in my flesh, until finally everything that is the old person is elevated and consumed and a pure and clarified person emerges without any pollution or stain.[80]

As the Christian daily engages the activity of purgation, remaining sin is slowly and progressively transformed into formal righteousness. Luther concedes that this process is never fully completed in the temporal life and is only done with difficulty.[81] Yet, moving against the moral laxity threatened by Agricola's antinomianism, Luther advocated an increase in formal righteousness and a parallel decrease in actual sin in the Christian life after justification.

Formal righteousness displays itself as good behaviors, or good fruits, and resisting sin. In Matthew 7:17, Jesus states, "Every good tree

---

distinct with reference to essence when it is present in the Christian. The *iustitia Christi* must ever remain *extra nos*. He adds to this the view that alien righteousness is alien, but "in faith this alien reality *really* determines the believer's being." See Mannermaa, *Christ Present in Faith*, 24–26.

79. Falcon, "Aristotle on Causality."

80. WA 39/1:432.7–11.

81. WA 39/1:501.6. Mannermaa distinguishes between human and divine perceptions of the Christian's moral progress on the basis of Christ. While progress seems like a crawl to the human, God views it as "successful running" on account of Christ present as the *forma fidei*. Mannermaa, *Christ Present in Faith*, 65. Saarinen suggests that Luther understood the difficulty as an involuntary act of *peccatum regnans*, ruling sin. Saarinen, *Weakness of Will*, 123.

yields good fruit." This theme gets picked up by Paul in Galatians 5 as the fruits of the Spirit. Luther used this biblical imagery to talk about formal righteousness as good behavior. He says that battling sin and "the first fruits of the Spirit" constitute formal righteousness.[82] Luther grabbed Jesus's language to name the good fruits as "good works and virtues."[83] Active resistance of sinful urges works alongside these active good works. Inverting the Pauline construct of the bound will in Romans 8, Luther put voice to the Christian experience in sanctification: "Even though I have the occasion, place, and time to fornicate, commit adultery, steal, etc. without any disgrace or punishment, still I do not do it. Here I experience truly and in myself that the Spirit dwells in my heart and is efficacious."[84] Luther was describing the freedom to sin without divine punishment because the Christian's sins are hidden under Christ. Yet, Luther turned Paul's construct on its head. The bound will is freed; the Christian *chooses not to sin* despite the guilt-free opportunity. To resist sin through formal righteousness both reaffirms the indwelling presence of the Spirit and shows the Spirit to have a real effect on the Christian's behavior.

Finally, Luther framed formal righteousness as law fulfillment "in the Spirit." Distinguishing between imputed and formal righteousness, Luther suggested that "Christ came and killed that sin by sin . . . so that the justice of the law may be fulfilled in us first by way of imputation, then also formally."[85] A few arguments earlier, Luther stated something similar. He claimed that "under Christ, the law is in a state of being done, not in that of having been done . . . among those who are under Christ, [the law] begins to be done as something enjoyable, possible in the first fruits."[86] The formal fulfillment of the law's justice sequentially follows the imputed justice and, as such, requires the Spirit's help. Because Christ gives the Spirit as a gift to the Christian—moving her from the stage "under Christ" to the stage "in the Spirit"—Luther says, the Christian "being driven by [the Spirit] . . . also in this life begins to fulfill the law."[87] Luther's "Christian youth" narrative

82. WA 39/1:494.1–2.

83. WA 39/1:464.21–22. On the legal function of Christ as example, see chapter 3. Luther oriented good works and virtues here to the doctrine of the three estates, three categories Luther understood to structure social life. On the ethical dimensions of the three estates, see Saarinen, "Ethics in Luther's Theology."

84. WA 39/1:436.16–17.

85. WA 39/1:383.7–13.

86. WA 39/1:374.11–12, 15–16.

87. WA 39/1:365.3–4.

exemplifies this process in narrative form. There, Luther boldly asserts that the Christian begins to fulfill the law when he obeys the Spirit, who speaks the law, to resist sin and act well.[88] As the result of purgation, formal righteousness begins to fulfill the sanctifying law "in the Spirit."

In conclusion, this section has shown how Luther connected the inner moral processes for intellectual and volitional resistance of the sinful affections to good behavior through the concepts of purgation and formal righteousness. Luther identified two types of sin: original and actual. He addressed each hamartiological category through a corresponding process for removing sin: imputation and purgation. Although Christ hides guilt for both original and actual sin from the law, Christ only restores human nature as a universal from original sin. Therefore, the sinful inclination and actual sin in particular individuals remained after justification. He looked to purgation as the process for decreasing actual sin by resisting the sinful inclinations after justification "in the Spirit."

Similarly, we found that Luther identified two distinct outcomes of these sin-removal processes: relative righteousness and formal righteousness. Relative righteousness results from imputation of Christ's righteousness. As such, relative righteousness is a righteousness by reputation alone. Formal righteousness emerges through purgation as the Christian's form is transformed from sin to righteousness. Thus, we see a decrease in sin and an increase in formal righteousness as good behavior in sanctification in the Christian life. Although Luther repudiated the adoption of Aristotelian virtue ethics in Scholastic discussions of justification, Luther's understanding of purgation reflects certain similarities to these medieval conversations. This is particularly evident in his descriptions of the decrease in actual sin and increase in actual righteousness. These residual intonations of virtue likely resulted from Luther's reliance on Tauler's descriptions of purgation, which we saw to have a significant role in Luther's thinking.

Purgation and formal righteousness in the Spirit are critical concepts for Luther's claim that both justification and law fulfillment must take place *in* the Christian herself. By introducing processes and outcomes to the anthropological dimension that parallel the soteriological aspect, Luther was able to retain both Christ's agency in justification and to make room for law fulfillment in the Christian life as sanctification. To do this, he positioned law fulfillment in relation to the Spirit and the soul's volitional activities to resist sin and do good works. Christ confers fulfillment of the accusing law

88. WA 39/1:501.9–11.

in the soteriological dimension to preserve divine agency in justification. We also see law fulfillment at the anthropological dimension sustained through shared activity between the Spirit and the human soul. Up to this point, Luther's discussion of law fulfillment in the anthropological dimension has remained highly theoretical. Now, we will turn to look at Luther's more pastoral explanations for how the Spirit supports purgation and formal righteousness in the Christian through the sanctifying law.

Prayer as the Penitential Tool for Purgation and Formal Righteousness

To review, this chapter investigates Luther's claim that law fulfillment must occur *in* the Christian herself as a secondary process to justification. Luther was interested to clarify not just how a person is justified but also how good works result from justification in her temporal life as sanctification.[89] This chapter has explored Luther's claim by identifying his use of a medieval distinction between original and actual sin correlated to the accusing and sanctifying law. Luther saw Christ to fulfill the accusing law's demands on the Christian's behalf by hiding both original and actual sin from the accusing law. Simultaneously, however, the Spirit speaks the sanctifying law to the justified soul, identifying and judging against the remaining inclination to sin with which the Christian must contend "under Christ" and "in the Spirit." Thus, law fulfillment *in* the Christian herself emerges as a work to purge actual sin in obedience to the sanctifying law in the stage "in the Spirit." Purgation names a process of divine and human activity in which the Christian's inclination to sin is transformed into formal righteousness—a slowly, perhaps imperceptibly, incipient righteousness that occurs in the Christian herself.

Now we turn to examine the more practical realities of how purgation and law fulfillment occur in the Christian's daily experience. It is important to remember that Luther was first and foremost a pastor concerned with the spiritual wellbeing of his flock. That means Luther often explored topics from several vantage points, through systematic as well as pastoral and practical theology applied within the daily experiences of ordinary people. The topic of law fulfillment in the Christian life is

---

89. This idea emerged in Luther's third set of theses (WA 39/1:352–54), harkening back to Anselm's inquiry into how human nature can be restored in *On the Virgin Conception*.

no exception. Therefore, this section examines the practical and pastoral aspects of Luther's approach to the topic of sanctifying law fulfillment in the human person under Christ.

We will use two interrelated questions to structure this query. First, exactly how does Luther understand the Spirit to speak the sanctifying law into the soul? Does the Spirit have a voice? Or is the law infused into the mind by some other means? Second, how does the Christian hear and respond to the sanctifying law to purge ongoing sin and to develop formal righteousness? When and how does this activity occur? What spiritual or ritualized tools are at the Christian's disposal to support this sanctifying action? By attending to Luther's practical theology, we will begin to see how he understood law fulfillment to be realized in the daily life of the Christian.

Prayer (*oratio*) supplies Luther's practical, pastoral response to these questions. Luther depicted prayer as cultivating a discursive, relational space between the Spirit and the soul. In experiential moments of temptation (*Anfechtung, tentatio*), this discursive relation takes on a particular function that helps the Christian to resist and overcome the inclination to sin. By investigating how Luther described this to occur, it becomes possible to clarify how he understood the Christian to overcome sin and obey the law in cooperation with the Spirit.

Prayer Pronounces the Sanctifying Law under Gospel

Luther claimed that prayer is the fundamental work of the Christian life.[90] Therefore, it is striking that he linked prayer to law in the Christian life under gospel. In theses proposed for the third *Antinomian Disputation*, Luther asserted, "The Lord's Prayer ... is full of the teaching of the law."[91] Prayer makes the law known. In other writings, Luther suggested that the act of prayer originates from a divine command. "The first thing to know," Luther wrote, "is this: It is our duty to pray because of God's command."[92] He taught that prayer extends from a positive restatement of the second commandment. This is reinforced through the dominical injunction. "Do not take the Lord's name in vain" implies via the negative a command to call on God in times of need.[93] Christ doubles down on this command

---

90. WA 51:455.9–10.
91. WA 39/1:351.2.
92. WA 46:81.30.
93. WA 30/1:139.26–27.

when he "urgently demands" prayer as the true worship and proper work of Christians. In the *Antinomian Disputations*, Luther did not present prayer as obedience to God's command. Rather, prayer functions as a particular type of proclamation and application of the divine command for the Christian life. The Lord's Prayer, and in some cases prayer of the Ten Commandments, *communicates* the sanctifying law.

In the most practical sense, Luther understood the act of prayer to involve repetitive recitations of the Lord's Prayer, the Ten Commandments, the Psalms, the Creed, and even the example of Christ.[94] Of these sources, Luther isolated the Lord's Prayer as the best because "the real master [Christ] composed and taught it."[95] While Luther did not exclude spontaneous prayer, he certainly valued preformulated prayers more highly because God himself arranged the words of the prayer.[96] No prayer could be better than the one taught by Christ himself! Thus, Luther was interested to show in his arguments against Agricola how the Lord's Prayer, as the very words of Christ himself, communicates law to the Christian after gospel.

The practice of prayer is also shaped by a fourfold meditative structure that expands the meaning of preformulated prayers. In 1535, Luther wrote an instructional booklet on prayer for his barber, Peter. In this booklet, Luther drew on the medieval monastic practice of *lectio divina* to structure and deepen Peter's prayer practice. *Lectio divina* has its origins in the monastic traditions of the patristic period. Origen (third century CE) believed Christ, the divine Word, was incarnate in Scripture and devoted reading could reveal Christ to the reader of Scripture in new, efficacious ways. This tradition passed from Origin through Ambrose to Augustine. By the sixth century CE, *lectio divina* had a concrete fourfold structure for reading Scripture to access Christ: reading (*lectio*), meditation (*meditatio*),

---

94. Luther named these sources for prayer in a number of important texts from the late 1520s and 1530s, including the *Large* and *Small Catechisms* (*kleine/große Katechismus* [1529] in WA 30/1:57–122); "A Simple Way to Pray" (*Wie man beten soll, für Meister Peter den Barbier* [1535] in WA 38:358–75); and *On Councils and Churches* (*Von Konziliis und Kirchen* [1539] in WA 50:488–653).

95. WA 38:364.20. In the third set of theses, prayer refers exclusively to the Lord's Prayer. In the arguments for the third disputation, however, Luther typically mentioned prayer in relation to temptation (*tentatio*) and sanctification without specifying the content. Luther's elevation of the Lord's Prayer should be understood in light of John Tauler's claim that the *Pater noster* is the most devout and valuable of oral prayers; cf. Tauler, *Predigten*, 101. I will discuss the influence of mysticism on Luther's understanding of prayer more fully in the next section.

96. WA 30/1:196.9–10.

prayer (*oratio*), and contemplation (*contemplatio*). The role of *lectio divina* in medieval monastic life was solidified in the twelfth century by Bernard of Clairvaux, who understood the Holy Spirit to be operative in this practice to shape the Christian life.[97]

Luther is not commonly associated with the *lectio divina* tradition. Yet, as Kang Chi-Wan has pointed out, Luther was after all an Augustinian monk whose daily life was devoted to prayer shaped by this monastic practice.[98] Luther's indebtedness to Bernhard is also well established[99] and, as we have seen elsewhere in this study, Bernhard was vital in shaping Luther's arguments about the Christian life during the Antinomian controversy. Resonances of the *lectio divina* are evident in many other aspects of Luther's thinking as well. These include his foundational framework for theology as *tentatio-meditatio-oratio* and his hermeneutical presupposition that Scripture conveys Christ the Word.

When Luther described a fourfold way of reciting the Ten Commandments in prayer for Peter Barber, he expanded this monastic practice of *lectio divina* to shape the everyday religious life of the laity. Luther taught Peter that the Christian can pray each of the Commandments in four ways: (1) as instruction about God's demand; (2) as thanksgiving and praise; (3) as confession of the failure to obey the command and of ingratitude for the divine goodness articulated in the command; and (4) as prayer and supplication for help in fulfilling the command.[100] The Lord's Prayer, the Creed, the Psalms, and Christ's example in the Sermon on the Mount supplied other preformulated prayers that Peter and other members of the laity could pray using this fourfold structure. Each of the preformulated prayers supplies the Christian with robust theological content when the Christian

---

97. Smits, "Practice, Process, and Performance."

98. Kang, "Die Lectio Divina," 112.

99. Cf. Leppin, "Luther's Roots," 49–61; Posset, *Pater Bernhardus*.

100. WA 38:365.1–4. Luther used the example of the first commandment to have no other Gods. He placed this command within the fourfold structure to show: (1) the instructive component: God expects complete trust in his purpose as God; (2) the thanksgiving component: How great and fatherly, how unmerited that God offers to be my God; (3) the prayerful confession: I have violated and been ungrateful for this; (4) the supplication: God please help me fulfill this command." Jared Wicks related prayer to the Christian as *simul iustus et peccator*, suggesting that both dimensions of the *simul* require a particular intention in prayer. The just dimension requires gratitude and humility. The sinful dimension uses prayer to take up the struggle against sin. On this basis, Wick asserted that for Luther prayer is an instrument of purgation along with reading the word and the sacraments. Wicks, "Living and Praying as *Simul*," 537, 543.

reflects on the preformulated words through the various lenses of instruction, praise, confession, and supplication.

In the *Antinomian Disputations*, Luther applied this structure to the Lord's Prayer to show that the preformulated words of each petition communicates a divine command. Each petition of the Prayer communicates law when the Christian meditates on its instructive dimension. For example, the petition "thy will be done" includes within it, Luther said, a command that the Christian speaks to herself *that* God demands that God's will be done.[101] The same is true for every petition of the Prayer.[102]

In this way, prayer constitutes an iteration of law after gospel in both content and form. Prayer is one way that "the law is to be taught to the pious."[103] The preformulated words of the Lord's Prayer along with the Ten Commandments, Creed, the Psalms, and Christ's example communicate what the Christian is to do. She is to hallow God's name, to bring about God's kingdom, to do God's will, etc. The Christian repeats these commands to herself in prayer. Embedded within the repetition, however, is also praise for God's goodness revealed in these commands, confession of her failure to obey and her sorrow, and supplication for divine help in her future efforts to obey.[104] Thus, prayer communicates a sanctifying law after gospel. This pronouncement of law does not condemn but guides and supports the Christian's efforts to purge sin and develop righteous. Luther framed this notion of sanctifying law in prayer through the framework of the medieval practice of *lectio divina*.

In Prayer, the Spirit Speaks the Sanctifying Law in the Soul

Luther elevated prayer as a key aspect of Christian piety in which law gets communicated to the Christian after Gospel. The Spirit is a keystone of Luther's teaching here because the Spirit speaks the law through the preformulated words of prayer. As we will see, Luther constructed prayer

101. WA 39/1:351.9-10.
102. WA 39/1:351.3-24.
103. WA 39/1:513.5-6.
104. In contrast to the perspective offered by Wicks, Matthias Mikoteit advances a nonontological interpretation of Luther's understanding of prayer as *confessio peccatorum*; the "man of faith" affirms God's pronouncements of sin as true in Mikoteit, *Theologie und Gebet bei Luther*, 246. Oswald Bayer distinguished five marks of prayer. However, similar to Mikoteit, each mark is reducible to divine promise and the trust of faith; Bayer, *Martin Luthers Theologie*, 315-16.

as a relational, discursive space in which the Spirit admonishes the Christian by speaking the law to her.[105] Moreover, the way the Spirit speaks the law in prayer is specified to the Christian's particular sinful affections. The Christian receives the Spirit's admonitions through prayerful listening. This discursive exchange did not occur in just any kind of prayer, however. Luther thought that meditative prayer was required to open the mind to the Spirit's exhortations.

The medieval mystics, especially Johannes Tauler and Jean Gerson, shaped Luther's understanding of meditative prayer in stimulating the Spirit-human relationship. The fourteenth-century German mystic Johannes Tauler employed language reminiscent of Luther's when he claimed that prayer initiates "*das heiße Liebesfeuer*," the hot fire of love, in the soul.[106] Tauler's fire imagery represented the mystical union or the inward connection with God established in prayer.[107] Tauler thought that "true prayer" began with meditation on the Lord's Prayer. True prayer facilitates the mystical union because it consists of elevating the mind to God in inner yearning and humble submission.[108] Luther borrowed Tauler's fire imagery to explain how prayer, especially the Lord's Prayer, opens the mind to the Spirit's admonitions.

When it came to the anthropological attribute involved in the Spirit-soul relation in prayer, Luther seemed to combine Tauler's insights with those of Jean Gerson, the fifteenth-century French mystic and Chancellor of the University of Paris. Tauler thought that the mystical union occurred in the ground (*der Grund*) of the soul. The Spirit of God used the light of reason to reform and renew the ground of the soul in prayer.[109] Gerson, on the other hand, emphasized the affective powers. Because he thought

---

105. In his introduction to Luther's letter on prayer to Peter Barber, Peter Zimmerling noted the incredible "dialogical character" of prayer in Luther. He observed that at first prayer is speech to God, but "alongside the expressive side of prayer is also a receptive moment," which he notes is a "verbal experience of the Holy Spirit" (Zimmerling, "Einleitung," 15–16). A contemporary analog is the prayer practices amongst American Evangelicals, who have theological genealogies running back to Luther. Tanya Luhrmann sought to understand in cognitive psychological terms how Evangelicals come to "hear God's voice," which she concluded was a type of participatory theory of mind in which one learned to attend to certain types of emotionally powerful, spontaneous thoughts in the mind. See Luhrmann, *When God Talks Back*.

106. Tauler, *Predigten*, 166.

107. Tauler, *Predigten*, 101.

108. Tauler, *Predigten*, 101.

109. Tauler, *Predigten*, 101.

the affective powers to be less affected by sin than the cognitive powers, he elevated the affect as the seat of the mystical union. Volition became the vehicle for reforming the entire soul as intellectual content was interjected into the soul through the affect.[110] In the union, Gerson understood the Christian to be "made as if one" with God. This implied a spiritual union modeled after Aristotle's notion of friendship: there was a conformity of wills among friends.[111] This union, however, was in the alignment of the will and affect, not in the substance itself. Luther's language suggests he combined Tauler and Gerson to emphasize equally the role of the intellectual and volitional powers in constructing and sustaining a type of human-Spirit union, established in prayer, to guide the soul's penitential responses.

Luther did not hypothesize a mystical union in prayer per se, as Tauler had done. However, Tauler's mystical influences appear in Luther when the Reformer portrayed prayer to create a special kind of relation between the Spirit and the human soul characterized by a unique discursive quality. The Spirit speaks to the Christian. In his *Small Catechism*, Luther claimed that the second petition of the Lord's Prayer, "may your kingdom come," means "that we ask in prayer that [God's kingdom] come to us." This occurs, he claimed, "whenever our heavenly Father gives us his Holy Spirit."[112] Expanding his use of Tauler's mystical imagery, Luther

---

110. Ozment, *Homo Spiritualis*, 70–73. More recently, Jeffrey Fisher has questioned Gerson's confidence in the affect as the ground of knowledge of God in the mind, noting Gerson's late "recognition of the relative inefficacy of both affect . . . and intellect in the journey of the mind toward God." Luther's reliance upon the Spirit's creative activity to reconstitute the will as a locus of the divine-human relation may be seen as, in part, an awareness of and a correction for Gerson's late rethinking of the affective capacities. See Fisher, "Gerson's Mystical Theology," 214–15. An important transmitter between Gerson and Luther was Gabriel Biel. Biel used Gerson's concept of prayerful union in his *Canonis misse expositio*, which Luther is known to have studied at great lengths. Biel critiqued Gerson's location of the mystical union in the affect or will, countering a more intellectual position. See Stanciu, "Accomplishing One's Essence," 143–44. Supplementing my arguments about Luther's medieval theological influences, Anderas tracks Luther's affective language back to Augustine's *motus* concept interpreted through Luther's reading of Valla and Cicero, pointing to the additional influences of Renaissance thought on Luther's understanding. See Anderas, *Renovatio*, 94–100.

111. Ozment, *Homo Spiritualis*, 74.

112. WA 30/1:302.21. Luther's point that the Spirit is given in order that we live godly lives temporally confirms the larger argument in this chapter that the Holy Spirit makes possible law fulfillment in the Christian by rehabilitating and supporting her volitional capacity. Martin Brecht indicates that part of Luther's critique of monastic prayer was the motivation to pray in angst. Luther corrected this by linking prayer to the Holy Spirit. Brecht, "Und willst das Beten von uns han," 272.

also explained to Peter Barber that prayer "kindles a fire in the heart" and, in this fire, "the Spirit continually instructs us."[113] Prayer creates a discursive space for the Spirit-human relation through which the Spirit speaks instructive content on the law to the soul.

Meditative prayer using the petitions of the Lord's Prayer sustains this relational, discursive space. Advising Peter Barber, Luther reported "getting lost" in prayer as he meditated on the petitions of the Lord's Prayer. He wrote:

> I stay, however, as nearly as I can with the same general thoughts and sense [of the petition]. Often it occurs that I get lost among so many ideas in one petition that I leave the other six. When so many rich, good thoughts come, one should let the other petitions go and give room to such thoughts and with quiet listening and with love, not hinder them. Because the Holy Spirit himself preaches here and one word of his sermon is far better than a thousand of our prayers.[114]

Revealing again his indebtedness to Tauler and *lectio divina*, Luther placed the petitions of the Lord's prayer into the fourfold structure of instruction, praise, confession, and supplication. Prayer using the Lord's Prayer begins as preformulated speech to God. Yet, as the Christian repeats the petitions over and over again, the repetitive fourfold contemplation opens the Christian up to the Spirit's instruction. The Spirit begins to speak in what appears to be the Christian's own "good thoughts." Luther was clear in his instruction to Peter that the Christian ought to attend carefully—with love—to these thoughts. The Spirit speaks here.

Through the Christian's thoughts in prayer, the Spirit speaks the law for the purpose of sanctification. In the 1535 letter to Peter Barber, Luther advised that "when the Spirit speaks in prayer, heed it and write it down [because you] receive a miraculous experience with the law of God."[115] The tone of Luther's advice construes the prayerful experience with law more positively than we typically expect when Luther talks about law. Here, the Spirit brings the law to the Christian in prayer as something to be noted and obeyed, not as something that terrorizes the mind. Luther expressed a similar sentiment in *On Councils and Churches* (1539) where he discussed

---

113. WA 38:372.31—373.1.

114. WA 38:362.37—363.15.

115. WA 38:366.11-15. Zimmerling suggests that the heart and reason are stimulated by prayer, which seizes the affect in spiritual experience. Zimmerling, "Einleitung," 17.

prayer vis-à-vis sanctification in the Spirit. In this text, the Ten Commandments and the Creed are operative forums where the Spirit uses prayer to help us mend our ways.[116] In the 1530s, we are seeing prayer emerge in Luther's thought as a key site in which the Spirit speaks the sanctifying law to the Christian mind for sanctification.

In the *Antinomian Disputations*, Luther repeated this idea that the Spirit speaks in the Christian's own thoughts through prayer. In the "Christian youth" narrative, he presented a Christian tempted by sexual lust at the sight of a pretty girl. Luther depicted the youth to combat the lust through prayer. At the presentation of the temptation, Luther reported that "right away, the heart and the Spirit in the heart" cry out against the temptation.[117] Simultaneously, the Spirit and the heart reject the temptation through a thought in the Christian's mind. Within the thought, a moral decision emerges: "I will wait on the wife God will give me." Here, Luther presented the Christian and the Spirit to share responsibility. In a cascade of attribution, the Spirit and the Christian both produce the thought to reject the temptation and decide on a more obedient action. This cooperative framing allowed Luther to conclude that the Christian obeys the Spirit and "averts by prayer" the temptation to sin. Prayer facilitates the shared divine and human authorship of the Christian's moral judgments.

The "Christian youth" narrative also reveals that the Spirit gives meaning and specificity to the legal content embedded within the preformulated words of prayer. Luther analyzed the Christian's thoughts twice more in his discussion of the narrative. As he did, he related the content of the Christian's thoughts back to the divine command and the Ten Commandments. In the first instance, Luther shifted the source of the content of the thoughts away from human authorship. "These and similar words are not the person's, but Christ's and the Holy Spirit's, who say: 'Leave the girl in peace, I will give to you another, whom you will easily love, at the appropriate time.'"[118] Here, Luther linked the words to their divine authors. The second and third Persons of the Trinity supply the content of the Christian's thoughts. These words take the form of an admonition and a promise linked to the offices of these divine Persons.

---

116. WA 50:641.20–34.

117. WA 39/1:500.21–24.

118. WA 39/1:501.1–3. Luther's interpretation of the content of the Christian's thought in this second instance follows the format of a command and promise in line with Bayer, *Martin Luthers Theologie*, 315–19; Haemig, "Praying Amid Life's Perils," 187.

In the second instance of Luther's analysis, he linked these words to the Ten Commandments. After the Christian resists the temptation through prayer, Luther stated that the Christian stands firm in his resistance to the temptation. The Christian "obeys God's word and law which says, 'You shall not covet.' With the Spirit admonishing him about this will of God, [the Christian] will not give in."[119] At this deepest stage of analysis, the command in the prayer, reformulated as the Christian's own thought, extends from the divine will expressed in the Decalogue. But it is the Spirit in its punitive and sanctifying offices who translates the command in the Decalogue into an admonishment tailored to the particular temptation and sinful affection facing the Christian. Christ stands as the mediating figure in the shift of the command into an admonishment, reflecting Luther's strong commitment to the proper order of "under Christ" and "in the Spirit." In prayer, the Spirit specifies and clarifies the abstract legal content of the divine command in the Decalogue to a particular moment of human experience. In this moment, the Christian can either follow the sinful inclination or resist it with the help of the Spirit's admonition.

Prayer constitutes a bilateral discursive space through which the Christian also responds to the Spirit's commands. The Spirit speaks the law through the words of the Prayer and the Christian's thoughts. So, too, Luther described the petitions of the Lord's Prayer to communicate the Christian's penitential response to the law back to the Spirit in confession and supplication. As a venue for the law, the Lord's Prayer elicits sorrow and confession of sin. Luther staked the claim that Christians are "often sad and grieving because of sins," but this sadness (*tristor*) exists because "the law of God drives them in this way."[120] The Lord's Prayer, which is "full of the teaching of the law," elicits this response.[121] Drawing on the fourfold structure of prayer, Luther linked the first petition of the Lord's Prayer to the law: "God's law teaches that God's name is to be hallowed."[122] When the Christian prays this petition, Luther claimed that the Christian "confesses that the name of God has not yet been perfectly sanctified"[123] and "praying, [she] bears witness that [she] has not fulfilled this law." Thus, she "truly confesses with [her] own

---

119. WA 39/1:501.9–11.
120. WA 39/1:350.34–35.
121. WA 39/1:351.1–2.
122. WA 39/1:351.11–12.
123. WA 39/1:351.5–6.

PURGATION AND PRAYER "IN THE SPIRIT"

voice that [she] sins against the law and repents."[124] Prayer supplies the means by which the Christian articulates her sorrow for disobeying the law; she confesses her sin and repents.

Prayer also supports the good intention in response to law. Luther identified the fourth moment of prayer as supplication. He claimed that in supplication the Christian asks and expects in faith that God give her what is needed to obey. "Who asks for something, first confesses herself not to have that which she asks and expects to be given [to her]."[125] The confessional moment of prayer encompasses supplication within it. In confessing her lack, the Christian asks God to give her what she needs to obey. Luther understands this request to be intertwined with the good intention. Prayer does not only teach the law but also creates a forum in which the Christian responds to the legal content of the prayer through sorrow and the good intention.

These penitential responses to the Spirit's command in prayer are evident in the "Christian youth" narrative. When the Spirit cries out in and with the Christian's heart, Luther depicted the Christian's response as hatred of sin: "Do not persuade me to fornicate ... or other shameful sins against my God."[126] It is this same hatred of sin that Luther correlated to the penitential experience of sorrow. The good intention appears in the Christian's determination to wait on a wife. Both responses emerge within the Christian's prayerful relation to the Spirit. Confirming this, Luther asserted that "by prayer" the Christian youth obeyed the Spirit and did not give into the sinful affection.[127] Prayer constitutes the Christian's discursive response to the law articulated as sorrow and a good intention.

To summarize, Luther's writings on prayer during the 1530s reveal the strong influence of medieval mysticism in Luther's approach to prayer. In his mystical view, Luther saw prayer as a relational, discursive space in which the Spirit speaks to the Christian in and through the Christian's own thoughts. Luther guided the Christian to use prayerful attention to identify the Spirit's instruction in those thoughts and in a penitential response. In the *Antinomian Disputations*, Luther added several clarifications to this more general approach to prayer. Of relevance to this discussion, he maintained that the content of what the Spirit speaks in prayer is

124. WA 39/1:351.1–4.
125. WA 39/1:351.23–24.
126. WA 39/1:500.21–24.
127. WA 39/1:501.4–5.

a type of admonishment and exhortation of the law. These are the attributes he correlated with the sanctifying law. Additionally, he showed that the Spirit's admonishments within prayer are specified to the Christian's affections in a particular moment. The following section will more closely examine Luther's distinction between meditative prayer in the petitions of the Lord's Prayer, Creed, and other sources and the prayerful appeal specifically in the moment of temptation.

Prayer as a Defense Against Temptation

The previous section examined Luther's teachings on prayer in various texts from 1529 to 1539. These texts contextualize Luther's approach to prayer in the *Antinomian Disputations*, unveiling continuities and expansions. Both sets of texts underscore Luther's mystical presupposition that prayer establishes a relational, discursive space between the Spirit and the human soul. By means of the preformulated words of the Lord's Prayer and other texts from the Catechism, the Spirit speaks the sanctifying law as an admonition and exhortation to the soul in the form of the Christian's own thoughts. The way the Spirit expounds on the law within the Christian's thoughts is particularized to the Christian's own situation. The content of the thoughts judge and reorient the Christian's sinful affections.

Luther made an important addition to his appeal to prayer in the *Antinomian Disputations*, however. He used prayer in the *Disputations* as a recourse and defense against temptation (*tentatio*, *Anfechtung*) and ongoing sin. He said, Christians pray fervently "that they might be able to live as holily and piously as they desire."[128] Later, he added that "we ought to pray, lest we fall into temptation."[129] Luther's earlier writings present prayer as a meditative practice set apart from the activities of daily life. For example, Luther designates the quiet hours of the morning and evening for prayer in his instruction to Peter Barber.[130] While meditative prayer in the morning or evening orients the Christian's daily life to God through the law, prayer in the moment of temptation delivers the Christian from the flesh, world, and devil by establishing the discursive space of prayer in a critical

---

128. WA 39/1:512.16–17.

129. WA 39/1:527.12.

130. WA 38:359.4–5. Luther also distinguishes a second categorical time for prayer, namely, in *Not* or emergency, see WA 38:359.11; cf. Zimmerling, "Einleitung," 28–30.

experiential moment.[131] In this way, prayer becomes the Christian's tool for purging actual sin and cultivating formal righteousness.[132]

Luther adopted the link between prayer and temptation from Johannes Tauler. In his *Sermons*, Tauler taught that prayer is the best reaction to temptations (*Anfechtung*) because prayer places "fiery bonds" on the devil.[133] Tauler defined prayer in mystical terms as an "inward connection" to God.[134] As such, he reasoned that prayer is well-suited as a tool in temptation because prayer constitutes a glance toward the divine. It redirects the soul to God, heightening the inward connection. This glance aids in temptation because it produces divine things in the Christian. What are these divine things? Tauler seemed to think that these noble things have to do with virtue. He suggested that temptation itself becomes a noble deed with God[135] and that virtue is obtained and perfected in temptation as one sinks further into God.[136] Luther's position reflects Tauler in yet another way. Tauler specified that the prayerful glance toward the divine brings the Christian to the *exemplum Christi*, showing her what she is to do to resist the devil.[137] Thus, the utility of prayer amid temptation for Tauler extended from the bidirectional effect of prayer. It both binds the devil and connects the soul to God to produce virtue and virtuous deeds. Luther adopted Tauler's elevation of prayer in the moment of temptation with a similar bidirectional effect, replacing the language of virtue with the language of formal righteousness. Prayer helps to restrain, or purge, sin and to develop formal righteousness instead.

In the *Antinomian Disputations*, Luther approached temptation as an opportunity to sin that provokes the sinful inclinations in the human soul. Temptation itself is no sin, but it makes righteous action difficult. Luther had a broad view of temptation. It comes from both within the human subject and from objects external to the self. "The devil, the world, and the flesh" present many obstacles and annoyances that snare and overthrow

---

131. See Luhrmann, *When God Talks Back*, 60–68.

132. Wicks suggests that the believer's prayer is for the Spirit to purge out *ruled* sin (*peccatum regnatum*) so it cannot rise back up and destroy her. Wicks, "Living and Praying as *Simul*," 543.

133. Tauler, *Predigten*, 425.

134. Tauler, *Predigten*, 101.

135. Tauler, *Predigten*, 189.

136. Tauler, *Predigten*, 404.

137. Tauler, *Predigten*, 208.

the Christian's aspirations for righteousness.[138] In the "Christian youth" narrative, Luther contextualized temptation within the human subject as concupiscence. The pretty girl pricks the Christian youth's innate sexual desire. It's not the desire itself that Luther sees as sinful. Instead, the desire is misguided. It is directed toward the wrong object—toward the pretty girl rather than the wife God has planned for this youth. This misdirectedness is caused by the residue of sin—the *fomes peccati* that remains for the duration of the Christian's temporal life.[139] The Christian's justification is not at risk in this scenario. Rather, the temptation sets the Christian youth into a moment of opportunity. He can act on the concupiscent desire and commit an actual sin. Or he can resist the sinful desire in the Spirit and build formal righteousness.[140]

Luther's concern about temptation was rooted in the insidious effects of temptation on the Christian's spiritual life. Temptation itself was not sin per se. Rather, temptation results from the sinful inclination spurred by the *fomes peccati*. The real danger of temptation was that it leads to further sin.[141] Luther understood temptation in terms of his own experience of *Anfechtung*. Doubt and its kind—unbelief, despair, and hatred of God—are the "gravest temptations for true saints."[142] Doubt undermines faith by questioning the efficacy of justification under Christ.

Inversely, Luther feared an over emphasis on the inner, spiritual relation to Christ would diminish the importance of outer righteousness, leading to complacency.[143] As the error Luther most associated with the Antinomians,[144] complacency conflates imputed and formal righteousness. The Christian's own formal righteousness developed with the Spirit in sanctification is collapsed into the righteousness credited to the Christian on Christ's behalf in justification.[145] False security was a chief concern. Luther

---

138. WA 39/1:520.1–6.

139. Birgit Stolt depicts temptation in terms of the human moral powers. She suggests that the "heart," which stands for the intellect, will, and affect, is like a ship that is tossed to and fro by its moral faculties. These "Stürmwinde" are emptied with the honest confession and open heart created in fervent prayer. Stolt, "Herzlich lieb habe ich dich," 408.

140. Cf. WA 39/1:525.13—526.8.

141. Cf. WA 1:436.9—437.1; 506.11—507.4.

142. WA 39/1:501.20-22.

143. WA 39/1:489.20—490.5.

144. Cf. WA 39/1:491.13; 527.14—528.2.

145. WA 39/1:356.31-32; 491.23—492.4.

worried the complacent Christian would assume a false security about her own moral condition and abandon the sorrow and good intention of penitence.[146] In turn, false security threatened to diminish the Christian's felt need for Christ and the Spirit's sanctifying work.[147] The real danger of temptation therefore lay not in the ongoing experience of feeling desire and the sinful inclination but in complacency about acting upon it.[148]

Temptation also presents an opportunity to purge sin and to enact formal righteousness. Temptation, Luther said, must "heal from within, from the heart"[149] with the help of the sanctifying work of the Spirit. The gift of the Spirit is effectual in initiating the purgation process. Luther claimed that the Christian "begins to detest sin, to hate it, and to purge it with the help of the Holy Spirit [by] not consenting to it, but driving it back."[150] Temptation presents the Christian with the opportunity to purge sin by not consenting to the sinful inclination expressed in response to temptation. Through cooperative activity with the Spirit, Luther claimed that "even though I have the occasion, place, and time to fornicate, commit adultery, steal, etc. without disgrace or punishment, I do not do it." Together with the Spirit, the Christian resists temptation.[151] This insight leads Luther to the conclusion that "here I experience truly and in myself that the Holy Spirit is in my heart and is efficacious." The experience of temptation is upended when the Christian has an opportunity to purge actual sin and to develop formal righteous. In doing so, the Christian's fortitude to resist temptation confirms the Spirit's indwelling presence in the soul.

Echoing Tauler, Luther posited prayer as the effective means for resisting temptation and overcoming sin. "Even if [the Christian] is affected

146. WA 39/1:352.20–21, 28–29.

147. As a corrective, Luther separated these two types of righteousness across the stages of his *ordo rei*. Imputed righteousness occurs in the stage "under Christ" while formal righteousness is worked temporally and progressively in response to the sanctifying law "in the Spirit."

148. Here, we see Luther link spiritual and corporeal human existence through the effects of temptation. By combining the spiritual and corporeal, the inner and outer, in Luther's parlance, he opened his discussion of prayer and temptation up to the topic of purgation and formal righteousness. The temporal activity of purging sin and enacting formal righteousness has spiritual effect for driving out doubt and complacency. See WA 39/1:436.13—437.3.

149. WA 39/1:526.13–14.

150. WA 39/1:436:9–11.

151. This is contra Bayer, who claims that prayerful opposition to *Angst, Not,* and *Anfechtung* is the work of God, not the human. See Bayer, *Martin Luthers Theologie*, 322.

by sexual desire," Luther claims, "nevertheless . . . he averts by prayer the evil he feels and prays that he might not enter temptation. This, therefore, is what it means to overcome sin."[152] Prayer helps the Christian to resist sensual desire in temptation by redirecting the sinful inclination away from the object of desire. By resisting the opportunity to follow a sinful affection, the Christian does not succumb to sin but actually overcomes it.

One way prayer enables the Christian to resist sin is by elevating the mind to Christ. Speaking of the constant bombardment of temptation in the temporal life, Luther noted:

> Neither the devil, the world, nor our flesh will cease [sending labors, difficulties, and annoyances]. Unless we watch extremely carefully in prayer, they will build for us as many snares as possible until they finally overthrow us . . . but this is the remedy: that we have our eyes and mind focused on Christ himself.[153]

Prayer is watchful preparation for the temptations thrown at the Christian from the devil, the world, and the flesh. In prayer, the Christian "considers the sin in his flesh against which he battles day and night."[154] In this struggle, Luther set prayer back in the terms of the *exemplum Christi*, as seen with law in the previous chapter. Prayer both facilitates a meditative introspection on the reality of the person's ongoing sin and it directs the mind to Christ's example. In the face of temptation, the Christian "immediately runs to the word, according to Christ's example."[155] The *exemplum Christi* functions to reassure the Christian against doubt because Christ's example communicates forgiveness of sins, saying, "Do not fear little flock, because the Father is pleased to give you the kingdom."[156] The *exemplum Christi* also demonstrates what the Christian is to do. As Luther notes, Christ tells his followers to "go, and do likewise!"[157] Prayer functions at two levels here. It facilitates the Christian's reflection on her ongoing, actual sin. Prayer also elevates the mind to Christ, connecting the mind to the promise of the gospel and Christ's example of righteous action.

Prayer also connects the Christian to the sanctifying work of the Holy Spirit. Luther asserted that in the face of temptation, the Christian

152. WA 39/1:501.3–6.
153. WA 39/1:520.1–7.
154. WA 39/1:501.17–18.
155. WA 39/1:501.20–21.
156. WA 39/1:501.24–25.
157. WA 39/1:464.13—465.1.

PURGATION AND PRAYER "IN THE SPIRIT"

must "learn to pray for sanctification and not to be secure as the Antinomians are."[158] The reason for this prayerful appeal for sanctification (*sanctificatio*) is that "impious things," the inclinations to sin susceptible to temptation, "do not heal from the outside, but it is necessary that [they heal] from inside, from the heart."[159] With this statement, Luther moved against both the Antinomians and the Nominalists, like Biel. Impiety and temptation cannot be resisted by human efforts alone. Divine grace must be added. As we have seen, Luther framed this in terms of the *ordo rei*. Healing in the heart extends from both justification under Christ and the gift of the Spirit. The gift of the Spirit in justification permits the "healing from the inside" as the Spirit recreates and redirects the soul's inclinations. Prayer connects the Christian to sanctification in the Spirit because the Christian invites the Spirit to elevate her volitional capacity to resist the temptation. This coincides with Luther's more sweeping statement linking prayer and temptation a few moments prior:

> Christ fulfilled the law, but it must be added: "Later see to it that you lead a holy, pious, and irreproachable life, as is fitting for a Christian.... I will give you my Holy Spirit, who makes you a soldier; he will even produce mighty and unspeakable cries against sin in your heart, so that you finally do what you wish." But am I not unable? "Pray that I may hear you, and I will make you able."[160]

Here, Luther reiterated the necessary result of justification in Christ, namely that the Christian live a holy life. He credited the Spirit with creating the Christian's capacity to perform this activity, but not without human participation. In prayer, the Christian appeals for the Spirit's help in elevating her volitional capacities to resist temptation.

By means of prayer, the Spirit creates the human capacity for a holy life by orienting human noetic powers to the sanctifying law. Part of the Spirit's office that Luther identified is to vivify the will, recreating it according to the law.[161] Temptation functions as an incursion of the old, misdirected will into the new one. Echoing Paul's lament in Romans 8, Luther noted, "Often I am seized by bad things which are against my will. Even saints bewail this.

---

158. WA 39/1:527.7-8. This is one of the rare instances where Luther used the terminology of sanctification in this disputation, clarifying the doctrinal region he has in mind when he discussed the Spirit's use of the law after justification.

159. WA 39/1:526.13-14.

160. WA 39/1:526.2-8.

161. Cf. WA 39/1:373.3-4.

But, this is your remedy: that you pray."[162] Temptation lures the Christian to go against her own will as it is recreated and redirected by the Spirit. But Luther posited prayer as a solution.

Luther's "Christian youth" narrative clarifies how prayer aids the Christian to overcome temptation as the Spirit bolsters the will in prayer. When the Christian youth experiences a "natural" desire for the pretty girl, his desire is rooted in human sensory experience. Luther framed it in Aristotelian moral decision-making processes as the sensory affection moves across the intellect and will into action. The Christian first feels the concupiscent desire for the pretty girl. As the Christian works to resist the temptation, Luther described the Spirit as redirecting the Christian's affections toward the law in the mind. In response to the desire, the Spirit and the Christian's heart together cry out against, make a negative judgment against, the temptation coming from Satan and the flesh. Finally, Luther described the Christian, together with the Spirit, to decide that "I will wait until God gives me a woman whom I will easily love! With her, I will make an end."[163] Luther then concluded, "This Christian, even though he is affected by sexual desire, nevertheless obeys the Spirit, averting by prayer this evil he feels and praying not to enter into temptation."[164] By speaking within the Christian's own thoughts in prayer, Luther showed the Spirit to redirect the Christian's affections away from the concupiscent desire for the pretty girl and toward the wife that God has in store for him.

Notably, when Luther explained the content of the Spirit's instruction within the Christian's thoughts, he reexamined the Spirit's words as a reiteration of law. The Spirit's words specified the Tenth Commandment, "You shall not covet."[165] In doing so, Luther depicted the Spirit as redirecting the Christian's affections in line with the law. The Spirit moves the Christian toward an object that accords with the divine will in the form of a "wife God has for you." This renders Luther's claim that the Christian "obeys the Spirit" quite remarkable. The Spirit is speaking the law, so Luther has depicted the Christian in this way to be obeying the law in a moment of temptation. Thus, we can see that Luther understood the Spirit to redirect disordered human affections in line with the divine will in the law via prayer. This solution echoes the "conformity of wills" we saw in Gerson.

162. WA 39/1:514.6–8.
163. WA 39/1:500.20–25.
164. WA 39/1:501.3–5.
165. WA 39/1:501.10.

PURGATION AND PRAYER "IN THE SPIRIT"

The Spirit's movement of the will coincides with an infusion of intellectual content about the law in prayer. As discussed above, Luther asserted that "the Lord's Prayer . . . is full of the teaching of the law."[166] This parallels Luther's position that the law must be taught to admonish and exhort in the moment of temptation such that *in* that moment, the Christian knows the law and is able to combat the temptation in her flesh.[167] Thus, prayer teaches the law so that in temptation the Christian is able to resist. In the "Christian youth" narrative, this legal content emerges in the Christian's own thoughts as negative judgments against a desire. Luther attributes these thoughts to both "the heart" and "the Spirit in the heart."[168] As we saw in Luther's advice to Peter Barber, this indicates that during prayer the Spirit speaks law in thoughts that arise within the Christian's own mind. When Luther reexamined the Christian's and the Spirit's shared judgments against the desire for the pretty girl, he reframed these judgments as a declaration and specification of the Tenth Commandment. These specifications come to the Christian in the moment of temptation precisely because he prays.[169] Prayer sustains the discursive space within the experiential moment of temptation in which the Spirit both speaks the law to the Christian in and through the Christian's own intellectual content and conforms the Christian's affections and volitional movements to that legal content.

To purge sin and obey the law through prayer, the Christian formulates and acts on a good intention. In Luther's third set of theses against the Antinomians, he posited that "all works done after justification [are] nothing else than repentance or the good intention against sin. For nothing else happens than the sin, which is shown by the law and forgiven in Christ, is purged."[170] After justification, in the stage identified here as "in the Spirit," the Christian's good works constitute good intentions against the sins exposed by the law. By means of the good intention, these sins are purged from the Christian life.

The "Christian youth" narrative reflects this movement between the good intention and purgation in prayer. In conjunction with the Spirit, the

---

166. WA 39/1:351.1-2.
167. WA 39/1:513.5-7.
168. WA 39/1:500.21. In the letter to Peter Barber, Luther exhorted Peter to "heed and write down" these thoughts in prayer because "the Spirit speaks here" and "here, you receive a miraculous experience with the law of God" (cf. WA 38:366.11-15).
169. WA 39/1:501.5, 10.
170. WA 39/1:350.24-27.

Christian formulates a good intention against the temptation of the pretty girl. The Christian youth declares, "I will wait until God gives a woman to me whom I will love! With her I will make an end!"[171] By waiting for the wife God has in store for him, the Christian youth intends *not* to succumb to the sinful desire he feels in violation of God, but *to follow* God's will. These intentions align to the formation of a good intention not to sin in moral decision-making. Luther showed the Christian youth to act on this intention when he claimed even though the Christian is affected by sexual desire, he obeys the Spirit and averts the evil he feels by prayer.[172] The Christian acts on his good intention by resisting the temptation of the pretty girl and waiting on his wife.

Luther used this insight to link prayer to purgation and sanctifying law fulfillment after justification. He concluded that "this is what it means to take sin captive," that this Christian "obeys the Spirit . . . and God's word and law . . . with the Holy Spirit admonishing him about this will of God."[173] The Christian in Luther's narrative overcomes an actual sin when he purges the concupiscent desire for the pretty girl. Because this sin was first revealed by the Spirit speaking the law to the Christian's own thoughts in prayer, Luther showed the Christian to also obey the sanctifying law when the Christian follows his good intention to wait on the wife. Prayer in temptation connects the Christian to the Spirit and the law in a way that opens possibilities for law fulfillment *in* the Christian herself when she resists the temptation with the Spirit's help.

This section has shown that the Christian fulfills the sanctifying law in the Spirit through prayer. Prayer creates a discursive space in which the Spirit speaks the sanctifying law to the soul. By exploring Luther's broader discussion of meditative prayer in the 1530s alongside of the *Antinomian Disputations*, we saw that Luther isolated the pre-formulated words of the Lord's Prayer, the Ten Commandments, the Creed, and the Psalms as sources of law for the Christian after justification in Christ. Through meditative prayer in the morning and evening, Luther understood the Spirit to elucidate the law through the Christian's own thoughts. This rabbinic practice of elucidating the law meant the Spirit interpreted the law in ways relevant to the Christian's particular circumstances and temptations. The "little thoughts" that arise in the mind during meditative prayer

---

171. WA 39/1:500.24–25.
172. WA 39/1:501.3–5.
173. WA 39/1:501.4–5, 10.

were key for Luther. These little thoughts are the Spirit's voice, where the Spirit relates the law to one's life. Luther called this a "miraculous experience with the law" because it infuses intellectual content of the divine command into the Christian's mind through prayer. Thus, we see Luther apply his mystical notions of an immediate God-human relationship in the soul broadly to locate the sanctifying law in the Christian life through prayer. The Spirit communicates the sanctifying law immediately within the Christian's mind through an intensified spiritual connection built as a discursive space in prayer.

We have also isolated temptation (*tentatio, Anfechtung*) as a key experiential moment in sanctification. Luther recognized two experiential moments for prayer: meditative prayer and prayer in temptation. In temptation, prayer becomes an effective practice for overcoming sin in obedience to the Spirit and the sanctifying law after justification. Prayer during temptation builds a discursive space in which the Spirit speaks the sanctifying law as a specific admonition against a particular sinful affection the Christian feels because of the *fomes peccati*. These remaining sinful affections in the flesh are the site of ongoing, or actual, sin.

Temptation opens the Christian up to a moment in which a sinful affection can be resisted and redirected toward God as formal righteousness. The redirection of the affection comes via the relation to the Spirit which is grounded and made effective in prayer. Here, the Spirit elevates the intellect and will to oppose the affection through the good intention. Luther depicts the Christian as overcoming actual sin and obeying the law through good behavior when the Christian resists particular desires in the good intention and resulting action in prayer. Thus, prayer in temptation becomes the tool and experiential moment in which the Christian—together with the Spirit—purges actual sin and fulfills the sanctifying law *in* herself.

Chapter Conclusions

Luther's expanded connection between the Spirit and the law in the summer of 1537 led him to bold new claims contra Agricola. In Luther's view, Agricola's castigation of law denigrated the role and efficacy of the Holy Spirit in the Christian life. In response, Luther asserted that not only is law fulfillment incomplete as a distinct process from justification, but also that incipient law fulfillment is required. The Christian must fulfill the law in herself in sanctification. This is a bold claim considering Luther's typical emphasis on human moral passivity in justification. Law fulfillment "in the Spirit" witnessed the Spirit's indwelling presence and effect in the soul after justification. But given Luther's previous emphasis on human passivity, he needed to clarify Christ's and the Spirit's effect on human sin for righteousness in the Christian life.

This chapter has examined the way Luther opened the anthropological dimension of law/gospel to good behavior in sanctification. He formulated an anthropological framework for sin and law fulfillment parallel to his soteriological framework. Both frames employ the categories of sin, identify a process for removing sin, and a new moral condition that results. At the soteriological dimension, we saw Luther formulate this framework as *original sin*; original sin is removed by *imputation* of Christ's righteousness; imputation results in *relative righteousness*. The problem was this soteriological framework failed to address the ongoing presence of the sinful inclination after justification because the result of imputation was righteousness by reputation alone. Imputation conferred no ontological change in the human person herself. Something else was needed.

To resolve this problem, Luther introduced the medieval hamartiological category of *actual sin* and *purgation* into his discussion about law fulfillment in the temporal life as sanctification. Actual sin is purged in the Spirit by admonishing the sinful inclination. Purgation results in the transformation of the Christian's form of sin into the form of righteousness. *Formal righteousness* becomes the sanctifying corollary of actual sin, rooting righteousness in both eternal and temporal realms. This hamartiological logic included an escalation of anthropological language having to do with the emotions, moral reasoning, and moral action. As the Christian works to resist her inclination to sinful affections in the will, the Spirit and the sanctifying law come in to support moral decision-making in the human intellect and will as resistance to the sinful affections. The result of these renewed inner moral reasoning capacities is "good fruits" or good behaviors. These behaviors occur in three distinct loci of human social relations, namely, in family relations, political relations, and spiritual (ecclesiastical) relations. Unlike imputation, which sees only divine agency in Christ, purgation in the temporal realm opens law fulfillment to shared moral agency between the human person and the third person of the Trinity, the Holy Spirit.

When Luther discussed this new framework for purging sin and fulfilling the law in pastoral or practical terms, prayer and temptation

PURGATION AND PRAYER "IN THE SPIRIT"

emerged as key human experiences in which the Spirit-human relation is strengthened and made efficacious.

Noteworthy developments in Luther's pastoral discussion had to do with the Spirit's connections to both the law and the soul. For law fulfillment to occur at the anthropological level, Luther showed the Spirit to speak the law as admonishments specified to the Christian's particular affections experienced in the moment of temptation. In contrast to the accusing law, these admonitions did not appear as abstract moral injunctions. Thus, the injunction against adultery in the "Christian youth" narrative was particularized as "leave this girl in peace, wait on your wife." This more specific pronouncement of the divine command supported the human person's intellectual capacity for judging the moral value of an affection. To overcome the blindness of reason, Luther understood the Spirit to apply the sanctifying law as an admonishment against an affection for the Christian and to speak these judgments within the Christian's own thoughts. Echoing an Aristotelian notion of "likeness of wills between friends," Luther showed the Spirit-soul connection established in prayer to align the soul's affections to the divine will in the person of the Spirit. This results in a shared, cooperative, and volitional subjectivity between the Spirit and the Christian in resisting the sinful affections and pursuing good works as law fulfillment in sanctification.

In this chapter, we have more carefully examined the anthropological dimension of law fulfillment "in the Spirit." In the next chapter, we will discuss modifications to Luther's key formula for articulating the human condition after justification, the *simul iustus et peccator* (simultaneously just and sinner). Luther now needed a way to talk about the human being after justification that permits temporal effects of divine grace. This will be the topic of the next chapter.

Chapter 5

The Human Subject After Justification

THE PREVIOUS CHAPTERS HAVE shown that Luther connected the Holy Spirit to the divine word of law before and after justification in the *Antinomian Disputations*. To describe the human person's changing relation to the law and the Spirit, Luther articulated an *ordo rei* for the Christian life that runs parallel to law/gospel. This *ordo* uses four sequential categories: "before Christ," "under Christ," "in the Spirit," and "after Christ." This study has focused on the first three. These categories see the Spirit to speak the law to the Christian in distinct ways—either to accuse and elicit sorrow or to admonish and guide her to the good through the good intention. The stage "in the Spirit" is particularly important to the current discussion. It opens new possibilities for human righteousness after justification vis-à-vis the Spirit. Luther called this "formal righteousness." In chapter 4, we saw that formal righteousness has to do with the transformation of the Christian's "form," which is the formal cause or shape of her soul. Through the Spirit's vivifying activities, the soul is recreated from the form of sin into the form of righteousness. Luther was describing temporal anthropological effects of divine grace through the Spirit.

The problem is that scholarly interpretations of Luther's anthropology exclude temporal effects of divine grace on the human person *qua* human. Gerhard Ebeling's analysis of Luther's theological anthropology orients this conversation around an anthropological dialectic in Luther's theology, *simul iustus et peccator*—simultaneously just and sinner.[1] Ebeling rooted the *simul* formula in a forensic understanding of Luther's doctrine of justification. In justification, the human person is deemed to be righteous through a divine pronouncement of justice. This pronouncement does not actually change anything having to do with the Christian herself—her human nature, substance, or essence that constitutes her as her. Instead, the divine pronouncement establishes a relation to God through faith in Christ, which Ebeling called a "relational ontology."[2] The Christian in herself remains sinner, *peccator*. The new relation to Christ infers justice to her, but this justice is restricted to God's declaration and does not substantially adhere at all in the Christian herself.[3] Per Ebeling, the anthropological *simul* construct results from this relational ontology and affirms his view that the real effects of divine grace occur only eschatologically. Yet, this relational ontology and the resulting *simul* cannot account for the anthropological effects of Luther's robust pneumatology in the *Antinomian Disputations*.

Therefore, this chapter analyzes how Luther formulated a more complex anthropological picture vis-à-vis the sanctifying work of the Holy

---

1. The *simul* formula was first elevated by Kjell Ove Nilsson in his 1966 book, *Simul*. Nilsson outlined a series of *simul* constructs in Luther's thinking, spanning his concept of God, Christology, ecclesiology, and anthropology.

2. Ebeling, "Luthers Wirklichkeitsverständnis," 423. Theodor Dieter has critiqued scholarly interpretations of the relational ontology as merely descriptive and not efforts to work out the philosophical implications of Luther's theology as a true ontology of relation. Thus, descriptive approaches get stuck in negating substance as a category. To understand the true philosophical implications of Luther's thinking here, per Dieter, scholars must engage the medieval scholastic discussions about relation familiar to Luther. Dieter, *Der junge Luther und Aristotles*, 635.

3. As the relational ontology seeks to clarify, the Christian in the temporal life *coram mundo* is and remains a sinner. Her declared status as righteous speaks about her only eschatologically *coram deo*. When Ebeling diagrammed this relational ontology according to Aristotelian causes taken from Luther's 1536 *Disputation on Man*, the Christian "herself" as temporal sinner is placed onto a horizontal axis. The Christian's substance and accidents represent the formal and material causes through her soul and body. The Christian's eschatological determination as "just" is placed onto a vertical axis, which then sees God as the Christian's efficient cause in creation and her final cause in eternal life. God is the mover, the agent, of the Christian's ontological being, while the Christian only supplies form and matter, which temporally construed, remain substantially unaffected by the vertical axis in justification and ultimately pass away. This relational ontological picture of the Christian person does not allow for the kind of formal righteousness in the Spirit that Luther describes in the *Antinomian Disputations* because the Christian's temporal being is seen as static and unaffected by the God-relation. See Ebeling, *Lutherstudien*, 2:334–38, 354.

Spirit. By sharpening our view of this picture, Luther's understanding of the temporal effects of justification on the Christian's temporal moral agency will also become clearer. The first step is to clarify how in the *Antinomian Disputations* Luther reconciled the *simul* construct with the two kinds of righteousness, relative and formal, discussed in chapter 4. Then, we will zoom in on the temporal dimension of the *peccator* to try to ascertain how the sinner can become righteous in her form, the soul. Here, we will see that Luther's *simul* formula is more dynamic than the relational ontology concept suggests. Then, we will turn to another anthropological construct that Luther used to describe the Christian person in the temporal life after justification: "the militant Christian." Alongside the *simul* formulation, this construct offers more robust possibilities for articulating human agency and moral progress in the Christian life than currently understood.

The *Peccator* Dimension of the *Simul* Formula

In order to account for human agency and moral progress as sanctification in Luther's theological anthropology, we must first reconcile an apparent contradiction between the *simul* construct and the two kinds of righteousness. The *simul* construct holds a paradox in tension: "We are certainly righteous, pure, and holy and that we are unrighteous, sinners, and condemned."[4] The Christian is righteous via her relation to Christ but in herself remains a sinner. This seems to contradict Luther's ideas about two kinds of righteousness. Luther thought that relative righteousness comes from Christ, but the Christian's formal righteousness has to do with the human soul itself. Luther also claimed that Christians begin to become formally righteous in themselves when they begin to fight against sin "in the Spirit."[5] Luther's descriptions of the just part of the *simul* accord

---

4. WA 39/1:492.19–20. Ebeling determined that these two paradoxical dimensions are established solely by divine pronouncements of righteousness or unrighteousness. The pronouncement of righteousness is eschatological and exists in total opposition to the unrighteous determination of the earthly existence, laying weight on the eschatological. See Ebeling, "Luthers Wirklichkeitsverständnis," 417. Wilhelm Christe reinvigorates this eschatological focus, applying Ebeling's "coram relations" (relation before God or before the world) to the *simul*. Christe claims that the *simul* has to do primarily with confession and prayer—that the Christian is just through the confession of faith and prays as *peccator* for the coming of righteousness. See Christe, "Gerecht und Sünder zugleich," 66–67, 83–85.

5. WA 39/1:494.1–3.

with his descriptions of relative righteousness. Both come from Christ and refer to Christ. The contradiction is at the temporal, anthropological level where the *peccator* meets formal righteousness. The static view of the justified human person as sinner is too blunt to account for the development of formal righteousness in the temporal life. We need a sharper tool. The question is, what? This section examines the way Luther brings the *simul* together with the two kinds of righteousness in the *Antinomian Disputations* so that we can begin to answer this question.

Neither the *simul* construct nor the two kinds of righteousness are new developments in the *Antinomian Disputations*. Luther first introduced his *simul* formula to define the anthropological condition of the Christian person in his *Lectures on Romans* chapter 7 in 1515/1516. The concept saw further development in the *Freedom of a Christian* (1520), the *Lectures on Galatians* (1531/1535), and the *Disputation on Man* (1536), among other places. Luther's *simul* concept percolated in the context of a late-medieval trend in increased scrupulosity, or sin-burdened conscience.[6] He used it to rail against later Scholastic theological anthropologies, which he understood to grant too much credit to human action in justification.

One of Luther's main adversaries on this topic was the fifteenth-century Nominalist Gabriel Biel, whose commentaries on Lombard's *Sentences* Luther read while studying theology in Erfurt. Biel's doctrine of justification relied on a notion of "doing one's best" (*facere quod in se est*).[7] Biel thought that the penitent sinner could ascend to a justifying love of God for God's own sake "by doing what was in her," by trying her best. God would then accept the sinner's best as though it were just. Biel did not discount human intellectual and volitional capacities. He thought human intellection was able to determine that God ought to be loved above all else and that human volition could then actually love God for God's own sake in contrition. Distinct to Biel's theology was the idea that the Christian could ascend through attrition (sorrow for sin out of fear of condemnation) to true contrition (sorrow for sin out of love of God). Luther deemed Biel's notion of doing one's best as Pelagianism.[8] This led Luther to escalate human passivity and moral incapacity in the *peccator* and to emphasize divine

---

6. McCue, "Simul iustus et peccator," 90.

7. The most comprehensive exposition of Luther's reaction to Biel remains Oberman, *Harvest of Medieval Theology*.

8. WA 39/1:419.18.

action in justifying the sinner. The human would become righteous in relation to God but in herself she remained as she was, a sinner.

Luther problematized the notion of doing one's best on an anthropological basis. Biel, like other later Scholastic theologians, agreed that postlapsarian condition was characterized by the effects of original sin. The residue of original sin, what medievals called the "tinder of sin" (*fomes peccati*), hampered human intellectual and volitional powers for morally good action. Original sin "darkened" rational powers[9] and the flames of sin expressed themselves in the volition as wrong affections or desires, known as "concupiscence" (*concupiscentia*).[10] Luther quibbled with Biel's doctrine of justification precisely because of the ongoing residue of original sin, what Luther called the ember (*carbo*) of sin. Intensifying the rational and volitional effects of the ember, Luther decided that under no circumstances was the human person capable of ascending to love of God apart from divine grace. "Doing one's best" could only ever result in loving oneself.

Luther saw Augustine's controversy with Pelagius to mirror his own struggles with Scholastic theology. When Luther read Augustine's anti-Pelagian writing *On the Spirit and the Letter*, Luther saw Augustine describe a similar experience to Paul's struggle between spirit and flesh in Romans 7 and Galatians 5.[11] Augustine's distinction between spirit and flesh thus gave shape to Luther's *simul* formula, which the Reformer reworked to fit his critique of Biel and the Nominalists. Just as we have seen Luther do, Augustine depicted the Christian life through the language of disease and healing[12] to describe the reconciliation between two contrary dimensions of the Christian after justification, the "spirit" and the "flesh." Augustine said, "While the flesh so lusts against the spirit, and the spirit against the flesh, that we do not the things we would; whilst also another law in our members wars against the law in our mind."[13] Augustine saw the Christian's "diseased old nature," the flesh, to be at war with the Christian's new righteous nature, the spirit. Thus, he conceptualized the Christian life as the experience of these warring inner factions. When Luther invoked his *simul* formula, he typically did so using this Augustinian language. Just and sinner correlated to

9. Cf. Oberman, *Harvest of Medieval Theology*, 131.
10. Oberman, *Harvest of Medieval Theology*, 122–28.
11. Cf. Anderas, *Renovatio*, 88.
12. Disability theologians have critiqued the tradition of sickness and disease in the Christian tradition. See Brock, *Wondrously Wounded*.
13. Augustine, *On the Spirit and the Letter*, 59.

a (righteous) spirit and (sinful) flesh as two dialectical anthropological and moral determinations that characterized the Christian person.

Notably, however, Luther made this Augustinian trope more complex. *Simul iustus et peccator* actually had two aspects: total and partial.[14] The total aspect (*totus-totus*) ascribed the moral determination of sinner or righteous to the person in her entirety *coram deo* or *coram mundo*. In this total aspect, the relation to Christ bestowed the righteous determination *coram deo* while she remained in her entirety sinner *coram mundo*.[15] The partial aspect (*partim-partim*), however, had to do with the person herself in her temporal life *coram mundo*. Here in this partial aspect, Luther could specify greater nuance into the function or disfunction of human intellectual and volitional powers as they conferred changing degrees of justice and sin in the human soul.[16]

Luther had also developed a notion of two distinct kinds of righteousness in his early theology independent of the *simul* construct. His 1519 sermon "On Two Kinds of Righteousness" (*De duplicii iustitia*) is the paradigmatic text for this idea. In the sermon, Luther posited two kinds of righteousness as moral corollaries to the two kinds of sin, original and actual. "Alien righteousness" is given over to the Christian from Christ through no merit of her own to rectify original sin, which was also given over to her through no fault of her own.[17] Proper righteousness, what Luther also called formal righteousness, is a righteousness worked "with that first and alien righteousness" in a life spent overcoming sin through good works.[18]

---

14. Cf. Nilsson, *Simul*, 312–29.

15. Luther articulated the total aspect in at the end of the third disputation. He stated, "By way of reputation we are truly and totally righteous even though sin is still there ... when someone was wounded and is already healed, then the entire man is called healed. We likewise say that the man is wounded, even though barely one limb is wounded" (WA 39/1:563.13—564.3).

16. Cf. WA 39/1:504.24–25; 542.6, 18–19. The *partim, partim* distinction is taken up in Mannermaa, *Christ Present in Faith*, 58; Christe, "Gerecht und Sünder zugleich," 78–79; Dieter, *Der junge Luther und Aristotles*, 330–31; Anderas, *Renovatio*, 87–88. Christe echoes Ebeling in negating the *partim-partim* aspect, concluding that the *partim-partim* stands "behind" the "real righteousness" that is found only in Christ. See Christe, *Gerechte Sünder*, 283.

17. WA 2:146.16–19.

18. WA 2:146.34–37; 147.7–11. Christe argues that the *simul* construct represents two structural "moments" of justification. The first is positive imputation of Christ's righteousness and nonimputation of sin to the human. He describes the second moment as the fruit of the renewed life of the "*homo christianus*." See Christe, "Gerecht und Sünder zugleich," 72–73. In a similar way, Mannermaa describes faith as the beginning of "real

Formal righteousness is the product, the fruit and consequence, of alien righteousness, completing alien righteousness, according to Luther, by purging actual sin. These are themes we already saw in chapter 4. Now, in the *Antinomian Disputations*, Luther will bring the *simul* construct from Paul and Augustine together with the two kinds of righteousness to develop an anthropology constitutive of moral action and progress.

The *Simul* Formula in Luther's Lectures on Galatians (1531/1535)

In order to clarify how the relative and formal moral determinations align to the anthropological dialectic between *iustus* and *peccator*, we must first dive further into what Luther actually meant when he described the Christian as *simul iustus et peccator*. One of the mainstays for scholarly understanding of Luther's *simul* construct is Luther's 1531 *Lectures on Galatians*, the same text where Luther elaborated his law/gospel paradigm discussed in chapter 3. The *Lectures on Galatians* are important for Luther's anthropology of the justified Christian because in Galatians 5 the Apostle Paul writes about the Christian's struggle between "spirit" and "flesh."

In the *Lectures on Galatians*, Luther defined the Christian person as "righteous and sinner at the same time."[19] The *simul* refers to an anthropological condition based on the Christian's position under law/gospel. Gospel comes as a justifying divine word that deems the Christian as righteous on account of Christ but without affecting her herself as sinner. The resulting anthropological condition is that the Christian is both "holy" and "profane." She is just and sinful. This condition rests on the Christian's relation to God. She is both a "child of God" and "God's enemy." The *simul* is the paradox between the Christian's condition in herself and what she is in relation to God.

The *simul* formula in the *Lectures on Galatians* grew out of Luther's understanding of sin and righteousness in his doctrine of justification. For justification, the Christian must overcome sin with "perfect Christian righteousness."[20] Luther broadly defined the sin of human nature in an Augustinian way, according to a notion of concupiscence. The sin inborn in the Christian by human nature, the flesh, is wrong desire.[21] This over-

---

righteousness" (Mannermaa, *Christ Present in Faith*, 56).

19. WA 40/1:368.9.
20. WA 40/1:366.10.
21. WA 40/2:87.11—88.2.

arching category of wrong desire, or concupiscence, incurs a host of other sins: sexual sins, pride, anger, despair, impatience, and unbelief. Here, Luther plainly commented on human incapacity to overcome this condition. Paul's words in Galatians 5:17 mean incapacity: "To prevent you from doing what you want . . . you are unable to do what you want."[22] Sin puts righteousness out of reach.

In order to get to "perfect Christian righteousness" from human incapacity, Luther looked to Christ. "Perfect Christian righteousness" consists of faith and imputation.[23] To align these two components of righteousness with the Christian involved three steps. The Christian first requires faith in the heart as "trust in the Son of God or trust of the heart in God through Christ."[24] This faith, Luther decided, is a divinely granted gift. Next, faith is imputed to the Christian as righteousness for Christ's sake. God "reckons" the Christian's imperfect faith as perfect righteousness because the Christian's faith believes in Christ, who suffered and died for the sins of the world.[25] Finally, on account of faith, the Christian's own sin is not imputed to her. Instead, the Christian's sins remain proper to her and are covered by Christ as a hen protects her chicks with her wings.[26] Because God can no longer see the Christian's sin, her sin becomes "as if" it is not sin. God reckons her imperfect righteousness as perfect righteousness, her sin as not sin. Thus, Luther concluded, to create perfect Christian righteousness out of human incapacity requires God to work faith in the person. God must see something that is not there, namely Christ's righteousness, and *not* see something that is there, i.e., the Christian's sin.

The result of this understanding of justification is further specification of the Christian's *simul* condition. "*Simul iustus et peccator*" means the Christian is now simultaneously "flesh," which is the concupiscent, sinful human nature, and "spirit," the dimension of the Christian *deemed* righteous by God through faith.[27] As scholars typically interpret this construct, the human in the temporal life remains perpetually sinner, "flesh," in her nature because the "just" dimension is merely attributed to her from the

22. WA 40/2:88.3-4.
23. WA 40/1:367.6.
24. WA 40/1:366.6.
25. WA 40/1:366.9-10.
26. On Luther's broad use of this imagery, see Holm, *Gabe und Geben*, 159-60.
27. WA 40/2:88.9. This represents the *totus-totus* aspect of the *simul* that is premised on imputation. See Mannermaa, *Christ Present in Faith*, 60.

outside—from God on account of Christ. The Christian is never actually made just in any ontological or substantial way in herself during the temporal life.[28] The Christian life is then marked by battle and struggle between the spirit and the flesh. The flesh rises up against the spirit because of its ongoing concupiscent desires. The Christian's task is to struggle against the flesh, which Luther presented as futile. Human incapacity emerges to assure the Christian's failure and to drive her back to Christ where she again finds Christ's "perfect righteousness," comfort, and consolation.[29] The way Luther presented the *simul* formula in the *Lectures on Galatians* suggests that the *peccator* dimension of the Christian person speaks only to the moral incapacity of the sinful flesh.

The Form of the *Peccator* in the *Antinomian Disputations*

Much like he did in his 1515 *Lectures on Romans*, Luther brought in the *simul* concept in the *Antinomian Disputations* to position his anthropology between the Nominalists and the Antinomians. Luther viewed both as extreme positions on moral agency before the law. The Nominalists, who Luther deemed to be semi-Pelagians, granted too much moral agency to the human person and, in doing so, escalated the law to the detriment of consolation.[30] By contrast, Agricola gave too little credit to the person for moral agency and rejected the law, thereby risking moral laxity and spiritual pride.

Despite their seemingly contrary positions, Luther identified a common problem between Nominalism and Antinomianism. Both positions erred in their treatment of formal righteousness. They both understood sin to be formally removed from the Christian life.[31] In Luther's view, the

---

28. This has to do with a distinction between divine and human substances. The divine substance cannot be intermingled with the human substance without compromising the divine substance; God would cease to be God were God to share substances with humans. Mannermaa explains that Luther's critique of Scholastic doctrines of justification was the determination of divine grace as an accidental property applied to the human substance. In Mannermaa's words, "Grace is not—as one could say in this context—an 'accident,' but its nature is precisely that of a 'substance.' To rephrase, grace is God in Christ. This reality has its being in itself—not in or from something else . . . the *formalis iustitia* is Christ himself, and even when this righteousness is present in a human being, it remains what it is with respect to essence—namely, it remains God's own righteousness, of which the human being cannot boast" (Mannermaa, *Christ Present in Faith*, 25).

29. WA 40/2:89.7.

30. WA 39/1:420.1–13.

31. WA 39/1:490.6–13.

THE HUMAN SUBJECT AFTER JUSTIFICATION

Nominalists erroneously understood sin to be formally removed in the ascent *up to* the infusion of justifying grace. In this Nominalist picture, the human reckoned with sin before justification could occur through merit. The Antinomians, on the other hand, mistakenly thought sin was formally removed through justification in Christ. Thus, they took too far the notion that Christ reckons with sin once and for all in justification, positing that after justification the Christian no longer needed to concern herself with sin. Instead, Luther wanted a middle way. Christ's sole agency in justification had to be maintained without negating human capacity to reprove sin and strive for righteousness on account of justification. In the *Antinomian Disputations*, Luther carved out a new anthropological space between the Nominalists and Antinomians to correct the false conclusion that sin is formally removed all at once and once for all. To do this, Luther returned to the *simul* formula and more carefully parsed the *peccator* dimension of this formula in relation to the law and the Spirit to clarify how and when sin is formally removed and righteousness developed.

Consistent with his earlier positions, Luther used the *simul* formula in the *Antinomian Disputations* to diagnose the anthropological paradox in the Christian. "Two contraries are in one and the same subject."[32] He had defined the contraries earlier: "We are certainly righteous, pure, and holy and that we are unrighteous, sinners, and condemned."[33] The subject in this paradox is "the pious" (*pii*), Luther's designation for the human person after justification. The pious have a unique moral status. They are "righteous ones who live in the flesh."[34] As he did in the *Lectures on Galatians*, Luther labeled these contraries using Augustinian terms: "spirit"[35] and "flesh."[36] The "spirit" is the inner person, the aspect made just in Christ. Thus, "spirit" aligns with the anthropological condition of *iustus*. The "flesh" refers to human nature, namely, the temporal aspects of the person still marred by the ember of original sin.[37] While the flesh is not the body, for Luther flesh is still somehow bound to and by the body, subject to its desires and passions. Luther positioned the flesh temporally. The pious "live in the flesh ... insofar as they

---

32. WA 39/1:515.6–7.
33. WA 39/1:492.19–20.
34. WA 39/1:356.1–2.
35. Please note that "spirit" with a lowercase "s" will refer to an anthropological label. "Spirit" with a capital "S" will refer to the divine person, the Holy Spirit.
36. WA 39/1:350.22; cf. Anderas, *Renovatio*, 98.
37. WA 39/1:492.4.

are not yet dead."[38] The anthropological paradox of the temporal human person after justification is that one Christian subject has two "natures"; she is righteous as spirit and sinner as flesh simultaneously. We seem to have an anthropological picture akin to the *Lectures on Galatians*.

Despite initial similarities, in 1537 Luther mapped the just/sinner paradox according to the two moral determinations discussed in chapter 4: relative and formal righteousness. In the *Lectures on Galatians*, any movement toward human righteousness failed and led back to Christ. In the *Antinomian Disputations*, only the *iustus* anthropological dimension is linked to relative righteousness: "We are righteous [*iustus*] ... by the reputation or mercy of God promised in Christ, that is, according to Christ in whom we believe."[39] This reputation grounds what Luther called "relative righteousness."[40] Relative righteousness is handed over, attributed, to the Christian through faith in Christ. When the Christian is deemed to be just, her justice is derived from and measured according to Christ alone.[41] The just dimension of the spirit in the *simul* formula extends from the relation to Christ in faith.

Luther linked the *peccator*, the sinful anthropological dimension, to the Christian's formal righteousness, which has to do with the Christian's formal cause, the soul. According to the "form and substance, according to us ourselves, we are sinners."[42] Luther did not view the human person "by nature" very favorably because human nature remains tainted by the ember of sin, an inherent inclination to sin. As you may recall from the

---

38. WA 39/1:356.5–6. Vind rejects the possibility that the *simul* construct refers the Christian's condition before and after justification. She maintains that *peccator* is a theological determination of the human person and must, therefore, be separated from the philosophical person, which has to do with human nature in the temporal realm. This position derives from Ebeling's assertion that theology takes the future, eschatological form of the human person as its object and, therefore, is only able to speak of the human in this life as sinner. Because theology derives its pronouncements from God, the theological determination of the person is always separate from what philosophy has to say about the person. See Vind, "Human Being According to Luther," 76; Ebeling, *Lutherstudien*, 1:37.

39. WA 39/1:492.19–23.

40. WA 39/1:356.31–34.

41. Mannermaa emphasizes the *forma fides*, which he claims begins in the human and is then perfected through imputation of Christ's righteousness when Christ is given to the believer as a gift. In this way, Mannermaa excludes the Holy Spirit in his treatment, linking sanctification, perfection of the *forma*, instead to Christ as gift. Mannermaa, *Christ Present in Faith*, 56–57.

42. WA 39/1:492.24.

discussion in chapter 4, the ember of sin is understood to be concupiscence or selfish affections. Concupiscence is created by original sin and passed onto each individual person from her parents through propagation. Individual persons confirm their culpability for concupiscence because it manifests in actual sin. Even after justification when the *iustus* dimension is added to the Christian, the ember continues to burn in the soul as an inclination toward sin. This inclination gets inflamed by desirable objects. What is important is that we see a paradoxical picture of the Christian with two centers of moral determination. One is found in the relation to Christ and the other is in herself.

In light of his earlier writings, Luther did something surprising with the *peccator* anthropological dimension to police antinomian interpretations of his theology. He admitted a degree of moral change into the Christian's form as *peccator*. This change appears to occur in the temporal life. "Here sin is removed in a formal and purging manner because *day by day, more and more* I purge and mortify the sin that remains in my flesh."[43] Luther later positioned this change in terms of the effects of gifts bestowed in justification. "We are formally righteous when by these first fruits and the Holy Spirit given to me from heaven by faith, I begin to fight and wrestle with sin."[44] The Spirit's presence is critical here. In the Spirit, Luther seems to have seen the justified soul in dynamic terms. He permitted progressive, daily change as a decrease in sin and an increase in righteousness.[45] The Christian as *peccator* seems capable of moving between the form of sin and the form of righteousness in the soul.

In the *Lectures on Galatians* Luther depicted the *peccator's* sin as *leading infinitely back* to Christ. However, contra the Antinomians, he showed the moral change in the *peccator's* form *to extend from* the just anthropological dimension established in relation to Christ. "Grace and forgiveness of sin do not make us such who are secure in relation to sin ... but rather such who are diligent and scrupulous that we might overcome [sin]."[46] Justification *sola fide* actually incites the scrupulosity against sin that so tormented Luther as

43. WA 39/1:432.7-9.

44. WA 39/1:494.1-3.

45. Mannermaa tries to make room for Christ's sanctification of the human person by linking sanctification to Luther's description of Christ as leavening in the Eucharist, which slowly suffuses the entire believer until she becomes pure at death. Mannermaa, *Christ Present in Faith*, 60. Though Luther uses imagery of slowly rising in the *Antinomian Disputations*, he does so in relation to the Spirit, not Christ.

46. WA 39/1:353.33-36.

a young monk. Unlike Luther's anxiety-inducing view in his youth, Luther now saw that the Christian does not engage in this battle on her own. The Spirit is given for this very purpose.[47] The formula for moral change in the *peccator* is not human effort, but rather the human person + relative righteousness in justification + the gift of the Holy Spirit.

The problem is the Christian cannot escape the sinful impulses created by the ember of sin in her form. Luther described this inevitability in the "Christian youth" narrative discussed in chapter 4. Luther used the double negative to describe it: the Christian "cannot not" feel desire for the pretty girl even though he is justified.[48] Luther was realistic. Concupiscent affections remain after relative righteousness is conferred in justification. However, the *iustus* dimension created by Christ's righteousness also comes with new affective impulses to love God and hate sin, which are given and sustained by the Spirit.[49] Luther articulated the result in Pauline language. "Our flesh ... strives against the spirit, its adversary."[50] The Christian's paradoxical condition as *simul* actually sets her at war with herself. Something is needed to restrain the sinful inclination and direct her toward good works.

In summary, this section has shown how Luther reintroduced the *simul* construct to position his theological anthropology between the Nominalists and Antinomians. Luther rejected any notion of human moral agency in creating her "just" condition. This is established only through the relative righteousness received from Christ in faith. However, Luther was more optimistic about the Christian's ability to use her just aspect. While the Christian is unable to defeat the sinful inclinations in the form of the soul unaided, Luther introduced a more dynamic notion of moral change in her *peccator* dimension on account of the Holy Spirit. In its movement toward its final end, the soul can move from the form of sin to the form of righteousness. Now, we must determine how Luther increased the "formal"

---

47. WA 39/1:472.13–14. Jared Wicks notes that Luther's early emphasis on *gratia sanans*, healing grace, suggests the *simul* condition was never intended as a static condition to be endured. Instead, the Christian is to struggle against sinful inclinations using the *gratia sanans* to support denial of the sinful self. Luther's use of the *Christus medicus* trope to discuss healing the soul in the *Antinomian Disputations* fits broadly within Wicks's argument. Wicks, "Catholic Encounters," 5; cf. WA 39/1:423–30.

48. WA 39/1:500.16–19.

49. WA 39/1:450.2–4. Wicks shows that Luther's early treatises reflect a view that Christian preaching was to promote penitential purgation of the Christian's concupiscent affections. Through penitence, the sinful drives were to be slowly replaced by longing for God influenced by infused grace. Wicks, "Catholic Encounters," 4.

50. WA 39/1:350.22–23.

language of the *peccator* as a strategy to diminish the sinful impulses and move the Christian toward formal righteousness.

The Noetic Form of the *Peccator*

The previous section examined how Luther correlated the *simul* construct to the Christian's relative and formal righteousness. We discovered that Luther introduced a more dynamic notion of moral change into the *peccator* dimension of the *simul* on the basis of the *iustus* dimension through his *partim partim* distinction. Viewed through this more nuanced vantage point of *partim partim*, Luther admitted movement in the *peccator* between forms of sin and righteousness. However, the ongoing inclination to sin challenged moral progress. Therefore, we must now sharpen our focus on the *partim* aspect and examine this *peccator* dimension in relation to the formal cause to determine how Luther understood the just dimension to affect the form of the soul in such a way that the *peccator*'s moral determination could shift.

When Luther connected the Christian as *peccator* to the form of the soul, he drew on the Nominalist theological anthropologies he learned as a student in Erfurt. A common feature of these later Scholastic anthropologies was a specification of the human's "formal cause" with reference to what is known as the noetic triad. The noetic triad refers to the Platonic tradition of dividing the human soul into memory, intellect, and will (*memoria-intelligentia-voluntas*).[51] Augustine introduced the noetic triad into Christianity in his treatise *De trinitate* when he syncretized Plotinus's idea (the One, the Intellect, the Soul) with the doctrine of the Trinity (Mind, Word, Love). Augustine applied this triad to human persons to describe the ways in which human persons bear the *imago trinitatis*.[52] In the twelfth and thirteenth centuries, Aristotle was reintroduced in the Latin West through human migration between East and West.[53] This philosophical framework brought

---

51. Stolt shows that Luther uses the term "heart" to refer to the intellectual, volitional, and affective dimensions of the Aristotelian rational soul. See Stolt, "Herzlich lieb habe ich dich," 407–8.

52. Augustine, *On the Holy Trinity* 9.3–6; 10.11–12.

53. Western Europeans ventured into the East as part of the series of Crusades meant to save Christian religious sites from Muslims. They brought back manuscripts and writings of classical Greek authors who had been generally lost to the Latin-speaking West. Concurrently, the gradual collapse of the Byzantine empire spurred movement of scholarly classes into the West.

new theological possibilities for Christian theologians in the Latin West. Aristotle's notions of the intellectual appetites of the rational soul in intellection and volition along with the soul's acts in cognition and desire were brought into these medieval discussion of the *imago trinitatis*.

The most influential figure for Luther's understanding of the form of the soul was the early fourteenth-century Nominalist theologian and philosopher William of Ockham. Ockham used Aristotelian metaphysical language to define the human as a rational animal consisting of a body/soul composite as matter and form.[54] The intellectual form as will defines the human as a rational being by means of free voluntary acts.[55] Ockham thought that these free voluntary acts required both cognition and affection (desire).[56] When Ockham linked the will as cognition (right reason) and affection (love, desire) to the human person's moral life, he determined that no one is able to will what she is not able to think. Cognition appeared to determine the scope of the will. Thus, Ockham decided that right reason must be morally normative.[57] Cognition works alongside affection in Ockham's anthropological picture to judge a desirable object as worthy or unworthy of love, then to love it in the will. When it came to movement, Ockham focused on the will as the constitutive power of the form of the soul. The will moved the body (the material cause) by either willing or nilling (consenting or not consenting to) its cognitive and appetitive acts.[58] If reason provided moral norms, then the will was the power to act.

As Pekka Kärkkäinen has shown, Ockham's interpreters Pierre d'Ailly and Gregory of Rimini reapplied Augustine's noetic terminology to

---

54. Ockham understood the body to result from the corporeal form working on and perfecting prime matter. The human soul consists of the sensory and intellectual forms that inhere in the body through the corporeal form and prime matter. The sensory form is important in Ockham's picture as the life principle of the body and the naturally acting subject of the human's animality in cognitive, appetitive, and vegetative acts and habits. The sensory form becomes the conduit by which the intellectual form moves the corporeal form in action. See Hirvonen, "William Ockham on Human Being," 40–43; Adams, "Ockham on Will," 247.

55. Hirvonen, "Ockham on Human Being," 44.

56. Adams, "Ockham on Will," 255.

57. Adams, "Ockham on Will," 255, 259. Adams shows that Ockham understood the task of cognition to be to rightly infer from the divine command, giving right reason its moral normativity. This point distinguished Ockham from Aquinas, who was less optimistic about reason's capacity to judge rightly.

58. Adams, "Ockham on Will" 253–55.

Ockham's anthropological picture.⁵⁹ Luther's Erfurt teacher Jodocus Truttfetter introduced Luther to Ockham's theological anthropology through d'Ailly and Rimini. Ockham thought the intellectual form of the will consisted of two corresponding *acts*, cognition and affection. D'Ailly and Rimini recast Ockham's picture as one soul with two *powers*, intellection and volition. They debated whether the intellect and will are particular *faculties* distinguishable within the soul in which distinct acts of cognition and volition occur or whether "intellecting" and "willing" are two distinct powers that occur within the one soul. Luther took up this specification of the formal cause, the soul, with the noetic triad as powers of intellection, volition, and affection.⁶⁰ This means that in the *Antinomian Disputations*, he combined nouns and verbs to discuss the moral functions of the soul, what he often called simply "the heart."⁶¹ Though Luther almost never used the noun "the intellect," he did speak about "the will" (*voluntas*), reflecting his Ockhamist inheritances. He spoke of intellectual and volitional actions using verbs such as "to perceive" (*intellego*) or "to consent" (*consentio*). When I use the terminology of "noetic forms," the "intellectual form," "volitional form," or the like, I am not referring to distinct faculties per se, but to the powers and actions that constitute the soul as formal cause for Luther.

In two of Luther's most commonly referenced writings, the *Disputation against Scholastic Theology* (1517) and *The Bondage of the Will* (1525), Luther used the language of these noetic forms in the soul while casting doubt on their utility for good works. In thesis 34 of the *Disputation against Scholastic Theology*, Luther rejected outright Ockham's conclusions about the moral normativity of right reason and the power of the will: "In brief, a person by nature has neither correct precept nor good will."⁶² Reflecting his Ockhamist assumption in which the will and

59. Kärkkäinen, "Interpretations of the Psychological," 256–79. Risto Saarinen has shown that the large role played by the affections in Luther's notion of the soul is the influence of the *via Moderna*, transmitted by Luther's Erfurt teachers von Usingen and Truttfetter, on Luther's ethical thought. See Saarinen, "Einige Themen der spätmittelalterlichen Ethik bei Luther," 293.

60. Saarinen, *Weakness of Will*, 117. This is why Luther can talk seemingly imprecisely about the "inner person." He inherited this conceptual shift from "faculties" into "powers" adhering in one soul.

61. Stolt, "Herlich lieb habe ich dich."

62. WA 1:225.37. Mannermaa clarifies that Luther inverted the way medieval theologies mapped the formal and material causes. Medieval theologians made human love in the will to be the formal cause while understanding faith as an intellectual act in the material cause. The problem with this understanding for Luther per Mannermaa was that

intellectual form were connected, Luther focused theses 1–19 specifically to contest the will's capacity to choose the good. After thesis 20, Luther shifted to discuss human merit in relation to divine grace,[63] transitioning from the will to human action without a single proposition related to the intellectual power to determine a right precept. The closest Luther came to clarifying the soul's intellectual capacities is thesis 14, where he posited, "The will can conform to erroneous and not to correct precept."[64] The human person may have intellectual and volitional powers, but their moral orientation as correct and good were in doubt.

In the *Bondage of the Will*, "blind reason" played a larger role. Luther suggested that in even the best persons, free will cannot do anything and does not even know what is just in the eyes of God. The law comes in to reveal one's impotence, which "blinded reason" is not able to recognize without God's admonitions.[65] In these relatively early texts, Luther used the noetic forms of the soul to move against the Nominalists by undermining the moral normativity of right reason and the power of the will to act in accordance with it. Instead, human noetic powers got locked into moral *in*capacity.

Measuring the Moral Function of the Human Intellect and Will in the *Peccator*

In the *Antinomian Disputations*, Luther used this *partim-partim* distinction to work out how righteousness could be developed in the *peccator*. The aim was to support his claim about moral progress after justification. To do this, he needed to show how the noetic form is elevated to the moral task

---

human love was made to form and shape faith, not faith forming human love. As a result, the infusion of grace became an accidental property, while human love remained the substance of faith. Luther sought to correct this by inverting the causal position of love and faith—faith becomes the formal cause. Mannermaa, *Christ Present in Faith*, 24–25.

63. Jared Wicks shows that healing and elevating grace (*gratia sanans, elevans*) were key concepts on Luther's early *Treatise on Indulgences* and *Disputation against Scholastic Theology*. When Luther leaves open the possibility for good works in thesis 40 of the *Disputation against Scholastic Theology*, he is making room for the effects of healing grace on human action. Anderas shows similar developments in Luther's thought in the *Antinomian Disputations* but links it to Augustinian notions of healing and renovation rather than the medieval theology familiar to Luther. See Wicks, "Catholic Encounters," 7; Anderas, *Renovatio*, 88–100.

64. WA 1:224.30–31.

65. Cf. WA 18:675.22–34; WA 18:758.24–27.

of resisting sin and choosing justly after justification, not once and for all but on a case-by-case basis. In view is the Christian "according to herself," which Luther specified as "human nature" and "form and substance," not the Christian's "relative" condition in relation to Christ.[66] This means that Luther examined the Christian's intellectual and volitional form after justification vis-à-vis the Spirit, who recreates and elevates these forms.

The *peccator's* intellectual form after justification remains darkened by sin and susceptible to forgetting God. Luther repeated his earlier critique of Ockham and the Nominalists, who argued that human reason without the Holy Spirit was able to love God as the highest good.[67] Instead, Luther reiterated his traditional claim that the human intellect alone has no unaided knowledge of God's will or even herself.[68] However, Luther also escalated his original position. Although he permitted that the Christian has the "spiritual law" written on the heart, he maintained that the justified Christian's intellectual form is so weak that it is not even able to infer correctly from this spiritual law. He argued, "We are so corrupted by original sin that we are not able to perceive the magnitude of sin. For our flesh, the devil, and the world are at hand who persuade [us] to other things and darken the law of God written in our minds."[69] The intellectual form of the *peccator* suffers under the effects of original sin such that "the flesh breaks in"[70] and draws the mind away from the right precepts of the spiritual law. Thus, the Christian according to herself as *peccator* is prone to error in inferring good precepts even though the spiritual law is written on the mind as a moral guide.

The volitional form of the *peccator's* soul, the will according to the Christian herself, is also weak and susceptible to concupiscent affections.[71] Here, Luther again critiqued the Nominalists. "Even when the law was being taught, nevertheless it was presented to us as if it demanded nothing

---

66. WA 39/1:492.23—493.1. The relative righteousness through relation designates the *totus-totus* distinction.

67. WA 39/1:419.19-20.

68. WA 39/1:507.7-8; cf. WA 39/1:175.22-25.

69. WA 39/1:549.13-16. Kärkkäinen interprets the Holy Spirit itself as the spiritual law, so that with the gift of the Spirit as love, "the true inner essence of the outer written law is fulfilled." See Kärkkäinen, *Luthers trinitarische Theologie*, 146-47.

70. WA 39/1:512.11-12.

71. Saarinen links this to a distinction between "ruled sin" (*peccatum regnatum*) vs. "ruling sin" (*peccatum regnans*). The latter, ruling sin, is the experience of the sinful inclination. Saarinen, *Weakness of Will*, 124.

beyond our powers and was of such a kind that it could be done by human powers and a free will, which they affirmed to remain intact."[72] Luther disagreed at the level of the will's freedom. The problem is that the sinful inclination continues to molest the Christian through sinful affections, robbing the will of freedom to consent to the good precept, were it to exist. Referring to the ember of sin, Luther claimed that "the flesh that is in nature infected by the venom of Satan in Paradise shows itself and agitates the poor Christian to lust, to avarice, to despair, or to hatred of God."[73] The inclination to sin that inheres in human nature spurs the Christian to sins of concupiscence against the neighbor. These sins then feed spiritual sins against God: doubt, despair, and hatred of God. The *peccator's* volitional form lacks freedom, Luther thinks, because the Christian cannot help that these sinful affections rise up in her.

In the "Christian youth" narrative, Luther suggested this inevitability of the sinful affections. He stated that when the Christian youth sees the pretty girl "he *cannot not* feel affection for her."[74] Even though the Christian is baptized and justified, he "cannot not"—he is not able not to—feel the sinful affection of lust for the girl. Luther admitted one exception, however. Playing on Aristotle's concept of the vegetative soul, Luther noted that if the Christian were "a total tree trunk," he might not feel affection for the girl. Luther was making a philosophical joke. In Aristotle's system, the vegetative soul lacked the rational appetites that move it toward or away from the desires of its sensitive appetites.[75] Luther's point was it is natural to feel affections. Those affections are part of human nature. It is the response that matters.

Unfortunately for the ensuing struggle against temptation, the Christian has the substance of human nature, not the substance of a plant. Despite her justice in relation to Christ, sometimes the flesh is going to break in on her volitional form and she will be "reluctantly carried off to sin."[76] This occurs *reluctantly* because the Christian has new affections for God from the Spirit; she does not want to consent to the sin even though she does consent

---

72. WA 39/1:419.11–14.

73. WA 39/1:505.3–6. Luther was interested in moral progress as evidence of the Spirit's presence in the soul. Moral progress creates certainty; cf. WA 39/1:436.9–16.

74. WA 39/1:500.17–18.

75. See Aristotle, *De anima* II.1–2 (413a20–35).

76. WA 39/1:514.6–7. This is an example of the quasi-akratic will discussed in Saarinen, *Weakness of Will*, 122–25.

to it. The Christian's volitional form as *peccator* is bound by the inevitability of experiencing concupiscent affections presented by the ember of sin. Interestingly, Luther softened his earlier insistence on the bondage of the will. The Christian is bound to feel the affections, but she is now able, albeit weakly, to not consent to the sins.[77]

Luther revisited the intellectual and volitional capacities of the form of the Christian's soul and found slight modifications to the Christian "according to herself," or formally, after justification. The intellectual form apart from the Spirit remains severely impaired, though not fully blind, as he had argued in the *Bondage of the Will*. The spiritual law is written on the heart to supply a moral directive, but the intellect's capacity to deduce correct precepts from it are sometimes obscured by inclination to sin. Similarly, the Christian's volitional form, though renewed by the Spirit, remains weak in resisting concupiscent desires. It is sometimes overcome by the desires of the flesh, though not always. Though the moral picture remains bleak, Luther seemed somewhat more optimistic about the Christian's moral capacities after justification viewed from the *partim* perspective. He admitted some new, though slight, improvements in the moral capacities of the noetic forms, but the sinful inclination still sometimes hinders it.

Elevating the Intellect and Will in the *Peccator*

Once Luther had reevaluated the moral functioning of the Christian's noetic forms as *peccator*, he took advantage of an opening for human moral action that he created back in 1517. In thesis 40 of the *Disputation against Scholastic Theology*, Luther posited, "We do not become righteous by doing righteous deeds but, having been made righteous, we do righteous deeds."[78] Even in the midst of his controversies with Rome, Luther was committed to the necessity of good works. What was unique was where he positioned works in the Christian life: *after* justification, not before. In his controversy with Agricola in 1537, Luther connected these noetic forms in the *peccator* to the Spirit and the salutary law after justification. He used this connection to spell out how being made righteous leads to good works as formal righteousness. He is clarifying the dynamic nature of sin and righteousness in the *partim-partim* aspect of the Christian.

---

77. Christe calls this a *"willenstärker Mensch"*; the evil will is still present, but the Christian is able, with difficulty, to resist it (Christe, "Gerecht und Sünder zugleich," 76).

78. WA 1:226.8.

As we have seen at various points throughout this study, Luther escalated his pneumatological language in relation to the human person after justification for the purpose of parsing the human relation to the law. Luther brought in the Spirit again here to buttress the moral powers of the soul, the "form" of the Christian. Christ does not just want to rule the "inner, spiritual man," Luther explained, but the entire person. Christ gives the Holy Spirit as a gift in justification for this purpose. The Holy Spirit admonishes the flesh in the Christian, working in and with the Christian to bring the flesh under Christ's reign.[79] Luther added to this that, because "there is a certain innate inclination in us; in order to elevate and repress it, we need the work of the law."[80] Luther reintroduced the Spirit and the sanctifying law after justification to amend the *peccator* dimension of the Christian and elevate it away from the sinful inclination of the flesh.

Luther first revealed the Spirit to elevate the intellectual form to the correct precept by speaking the salutary law against the inclinations of the flesh. Quoting John 16:8, "The Spirit convicts the world of sin and righteousness," Luther claims that "for this purpose, the Holy Spirit is sent . . . and thereby, sin is made known more and more."[81] The Spirit shows the Christian her sin. As we have seen, Luther understood the Spirit to do this in both accusing and sanctifying ways. After justification, the Spirit accomplishes this by announcing and expounding on the law in the Christian's mind, in her thoughts. For example, in the "Christian youth" narrative, Luther described the Spirit as it declares the moral command, "You shall not covet!," in the Christian's mind. The law's admonishment is specified to the particular temptation of lust for the pretty girl. Then, Luther explained that the Christian "*knows* the law and *perceives sin* in his flesh, against which he fights day and night."[82] Luther used two verbs relevant to the soul's intellectual powers: "to get knowledge of" or to know (*noscere*) and "to perceive" (*intellegere*). This terminological choice is striking in this passage because it suggests an intellectual comprehension of the law to recognize the sin in the flesh prior to action upon it. Next, Luther showed the Christian to act on this knowledge. He showed the Christian to judge against the sin and

---

79. WA 39/1:498.19–21; cf. Lund, "Luther's 'Third Use of the Law,'" 184.

80. WA 39/1:422.11–12.

81. WA 39/1:415.3–4. The Spirit's indwelling of the person leads both to moral increase, but also to a blurring of the moral subjects. Adams describes a similarly agential ambiguity in Scotus and Ockham. See Adams, "Genuine Agency," 23–60.

82. WA 39/1:501.10, 17 (emphasis added).

to declare, "Do not rule flesh!" Thus, we see the salutary law, as it is spoken by the Spirit, as it elevates the *peccator's* intellectual form to negative judgments against sinful inclinations before sin is committed.

Luther operated within the constructs of medieval moral theologies. In those theologies, an intellectual judgment *against* a sinful inclination was not enough to lead to virtue. The intellect must also be able to judge *for* virtuous action toward a lovable object.[83] Here, the positive dimension of John 16:8 comes into view: the Spirit convicts the world of righteousness through the law. The law exhorts the Christian that "once you were Gentiles, now you are sprinkled by Christ's blood.... Offer your bodies to righteousness, put away desires of the flesh, and be imitators of the righteousness of good works!"[84] Once again, the Christian youth narrative demonstrates Luther's thinking. As soon as the admonishment against lust for the girl was complete, Luther depicted a positive formulation of the law to appear in the mind. "[Don't] persuade or incite me to fornication, adultery, ... [or] other shameful acts against my God, but I will wait until God will give a woman to me whom I will love!"[85] Luther's formulation contained both a negative judgment (do not persuade me to fornication) and a positive one (I will wait until God ...). When Luther restated the content of the mind, he assigned the words to Christ and the Spirit, framing the words specifically as an exhortation: "Leave the girl in peace. I will give you another."[86] What we see here is an instantiation of the participatory concept of mind Luther deployed in his instructions to Peter Barber. The Spirit is speaking in the Christian's own thoughts, elevating the intellectual form in judging what is good, righteous, and virtuous to do.

The intellectual judgment comes about in two ways. First, the Spirit speaks the salutary law in the mind, as we have seen in chapter 4. Because the Spirit's pronouncements of law are blurred with the Christian's own thoughts, Luther depicted the Christian youth to respond to those cognitive judgments with action. Second, the Spirit also directs the Christian toward Christ's example (*exemplum Christi*) as an image of righteous action on the law. As we saw in chapter 3, Luther was adamant that Christ

---

83. Saarinen suggests that Luther permits right reason as a functioning power that remains in the human person, but that the will always chooses against reason in sin. See Saarinen, "Einige Themen der spätmittelalterlichen Ethik," 294.

84. WA 39/1:475.1–6.

85. WA 39/1:500.23–25.

86. WA 39/1:501.2.

did not nullify the law but reestablished it through his example of love of the neighbor. Christ's love ultimately culminated with giving of himself for the neighbor, the sinner.[87] Luther positioned Christ's example within the three estates. Christ teaches the Christian "how to be obedient to God, parents, and authorities" and "how to have good works and virtues."[88] Together, the Spirit's pronouncements of the salutary law in the mind and Christ's example clarify the intellect's blurry vision, enabling it to see more clearly what is good and pleasing to God.

Next, Luther repositioned the volitional form in relation to the Spirit to revive volitional consent to the intellect's judgments. As discussed in chapter 3, Luther understood the Spirit to recreate the Christian's soul, her form.[89] One thing Luther assigned to the recreated soul is a new will, which contains new affections that are directed toward love of God. The new will "begins to truly love God and hate sin remaining in the flesh."[90] By faith and with the Spirit, the new will is moved by love of God and hatred against sin. However, something even more interesting occurs when this new will refers back to the judgments now supplied in the intellectual form of the soul by the salutary law and Christ's example. In this moment, Luther described the will as having positive affective responses to the salutary law! The will "delights" in the law, "enjoys" the law, and "loves" the law.[91] The *peccator's* will is now going to consent to the good precept supplied by the law because its new affections, supplied by the Spirit when the Spirit recreated the will, coincide with the law's determinations of goodness. Because of the way salutary law functions in the intellectual form vis-à-vis Christ's example, Luther magnified the intellectual form's strength for guiding the will's desires. The will is "moved by two testimonies in order that it might be well-disposed and more freely obey."[92] The bondage of the will is no more. Instead, with the Spirit and the law guiding the soul's intellectual

---

87. WA 39/1:464.13–15.

88. WA 39/1:464.20–22.

89. WA 39/1:373.2–4. Building on his claim that Luther inverts the love and faith in the formal and material positions, Mannermaa sees Christ as the form in the *forma fidei*. He takes this to mean that Christ is the subject of the Christian's actions, not the Christian herself. Mannermaa, *Christ Present in Faith*, 24–26.

90. WA 39/1:373.2; 395.22–24. Because Mannermaa sees Christ as the formal cause, he excludes the Spirit's effect in elevating the Christian to love of God. See Mannermaa, *Christ Present in Faith*, 29.

91. WA 39/1:373.2; 374.10, 15.

92. WA 39/1:464.2–5.

judgments and moving the soul's volitions, the *peccator* gains a new sense of volitional freedom to obey the law.

The new intellectual capacity for moral judgment comes together with the new volitional freedom to produce a new kind of moral action. Luther no longer insisted that "the will can only consent to erroneous precept," as he did in the *Disputation against Scholastic Theology*. In 1537, he sketched out the little opening he left in 1517 when he said that good works result from justification. Now, he claimed the Christian "takes sin captive"[93] and overcomes the sinful inclinations in the flesh that are generated by the ember of sin. Instead of giving in to the inclination, the *peccator* "obeys God's word and law."[94] "Even though [the Christian] has opportunity, place, and time to fornicate, commit adultery, steal without disgrace or punishment, *still [she] does not do it*."[95] The Christian does not produce just sinful acts but rather incipient righteousness as "good works."[96] Luther laid out these features of good action in order to justify his claim that law fulfillment in the Christian (*in nobis*) begins to occur after justification "in the Spirit" here in the temporal life.[97] This is the moral dynamism of the *partim-partim* aspect of the *simul*.

To summarize, this chapter investigates how Luther expanded his theological anthropology in view of human moral action. The purpose was to accommodate new claims about formal righteousness and moral activity he assigned to the Christian life in relation to the Spirit and salutary law. We clarified how Luther correlated his anthropological construct, *simul iustus et peccator*, to relative and formal righteousness, specifying the *partim-partim* dimension of the *simul* to the Christian's own formal righteousness. This section built on that analysis by examining how Luther assigned the *peccator* as "form" to the anthropological language of the noetic triad (*anima, intellectus, voluntas*). By nuancing the Spirit's work on the soul's powers in the triad, Luther was able to build a theological structure

---

93. WA 39/1:501.5-6.

94. WA 39/1:501.5-10. Saarinen argues that the individual can cooperate with God in the "lower things" in everyday life. Saarinen, *Weakness of Will*, 130.

95. WA 39/1:436.16—437.3 (emphasis added).

96. WA 39/1:434.8-10.

97. WA 39/1:365.3-4. Christe rejects partial law fulfillment because he interprets law fulfillment in terms of a justifying act. Here we see Luther making space for partial law fulfillment as a means for and measure of developing formal righteousness, not justification. Christe, "Gerecht und Sünder zugleich," 79; cf. Dieter, *Der junge Luther und Aristotles*, 330-31.

around the dynamic picture of moral change in the *partim-partim* aspect. He showed how particular benefits of faith given to the Christian through Christ, namely the Spirit, function to elevate the natural form of the soul up and away from the sinful inclination.

Luther brought the Spirit and the salutary law together with the noetic forms of the soul to rehabilitate and support their moral function. The salutary law helps the intellectual form compensate for the *peccator's* "blind reason." The law, spoken by the Spirit, guides the intellectual form in judgments against the sinful inclinations of the flesh and for love of God. In a similar way, Luther made the Spirit work on the *peccator's* weak will by recreating the soul with new affections for the law in the will. The result is a new capacity to *will against*—to "nill" in Ockham's terminology—sinful affections and to *will for* the moral directives supplied to the intellect by the salutary law. Because Luther found a way to calibrate volitional consent with "right reason," he made room for a new kind of free will in the *peccator's* soul in cooperation with the Spirit. However, this will is only "well-disposed" and freely obedient when it is saturated and moved by the Spirit. Consequently, the Spirit's help in moral action actually leads to a blurring of moral subjects. We appear to have a view of the medieval doctrine of *cooperatio* in the justified life. The Christian and the Spirit are both actors when the Spirit comes in and boosts capacity in the Christian's noetic form. The Christian is not passive in moral action after justification but is working in cooperation with the Spirit and with the Spirit's help.

At this juncture, we are able to see how Luther's *partim-partim* concept is not adequately captured by the causal picture depicted in a relational ontology discussed at the start of this chapter. Divine agency as efficient and final causality on the vertical axis comes to bear on the human agent as formal-material cause on the horizontal axis. Justification and the subsequent gift of the Spirit propel the human person as formal and material cause (horizontal axis) closer to the final cause of righteousness in eternal life with God as the *peccator* slowly becomes formally righteous with the Spirit's help. Although the Christian remains *simul iustus et peccator* when viewed from the *totus-totus* perspective with its eschatological vantage point, we now need a new anthropological model for the *partim-partim* aspect in Luther's theology that permits human agency and moral progress after justification with divine help. It is to that new construct that we now turn.

THE HUMAN SUBJECT AFTER JUSTIFICATION

The *Peccator* as Christian Soldier Battling Sin

In this chapter, we are exploring the ways Luther expanded his anthropology to support his claims against Agricola that "in the Spirit" the Christian begins to both fulfill the law and become formally righteous. As we have seen, the picture of moral agency and progress depicted in these claims does not fit with the way scholars typically interpret Luther's theological anthropology. Based on forensic notions of justification and the resulting relational ontology, these interpretations emphasize the radical dialectic in Luther's *simul* construct. Yet, this dialectic is only one aspect of Luther's *simul* formula, namely the *totus-totus* aspect. But Luther also spoke of the human person as *partim-partim* as a way to discuss the dynamic relation of sin and righteousness in the Christian after justification. In this final section, we are going to examine another anthropological construct that Luther wove together with the *partim-partim* aspect of the *simul* to describe the Christian as she works to reign in her sin and obey the law in the Spirit. That construct is the triumphant-militant Christian (*christianus triumphans-militans*).

Luther described the Christian as the "soldier of Christ" (*miles Christi*), a militant Christian (*christianus militans*).[98] This metaphor works in parallel to the Christian youth narrative, and Luther again leveraged that narrative to introduce the concept:

> But there immediately when these things happen, and this law or that carnal nature infected with the poison of Satan shows itself in paradise and tempts the poor Christian either to lust, avarice, despair, or hatred of God, there the Christian [soldier] rouses himself, and with wonder, he says: "Behold, you are still here, you have come well, lord of sin. Where were you? Where did you entertain yourself for so long? Are you still alive? Where do you come from? Hang yourself on the cross. No, [that sin] will not be so. I will keep my virginity and do what is right." Or "I refuse you, and the more you torment me or invite you to spoil, lustful despair and worry, the more I will laugh at you and, relying on the help of my Christ with a great and strong heart, I will despise you and crush your head. What do I have to do with you? I have another master in whose camp I am now a soldier."[99]

---

98. WA 39/1:495.21; 503.20.
99. WA 39/1:504.7; 505.3–14.

The militant Christian is the dimension of the Christian after justification that remains in the flesh where she battles ongoing sinful inclinations. The militant Christian "battles against sin, concupiscence, and the sinful inclination."[100] Luther doubled down on the process from the Christian youth narrative, depicting the Christian soldier as stirring himself up to battle sinful inclinations as soon as he recognized them. Both narratives include affective language (hatred, directed love) and decision-making processes of desire, intellection, and volitional nonconsent to sin. Where Luther depicted Christian youth to obey the Spirit and fulfill the law, he described the Christian soldier's victory in militaristic terms. The Christian soldier "makes a great massacre of the devil's army."[101] The militant Christian is an active anthropological dimension in which the Christian takes her sinful inclination captive and fights for righteousness.

A disturbing and problematic metaphor in the age of racial violence and Christian nationalism, this anthropological image of the Christian soldier has a biblical basis in Paul's Letter to the Ephesians. Drawing to mind the image of the legionnaires of the Imperial Roman Army familiar to his readers, Paul encouraged the Christians at Ephesus to put on the "armor of God" in the fight against evil and spiritual forces of darkness.[102] Akin to Roman soldiers, God's armament equipped the Christian with both defensive and offensive tools. The breastplate of righteousness, shield of faith, and helmet of salvation protected the Christian soldier, deflecting the enemy's flaming arrows. The sword of the Spirit, the word of God, was useful for the offensive, equipping the Christian soldier to conquer. Luther picked up Paul's militaristic language with only slight modification. He named the breastplate of righteousness, the shield of faith, and the helmet of salvation.[103] The militant Christian, in the midst of the enemy, uses the sword of the Spirit to arm herself.[104] Using Paul's imagery, Luther depicted the Christian in the temporal life to employ spiritual weaponry to fight against sin and for righteousness.

---

100. WA 39/1:502.4–5.

101. WA 39/1:505.15.

102. Mattox additionally draws out the Old Testament origins of Luther's association between the Christian life and warfare. However, Old Testament figures are absent in Luther's use of militaristic language in the *Antinomian Disputations*. Mattox, "Warrior Saints," 46.

103. WA 39/1:492.7–11.

104. WA 39/1:502.11.

Luther's use of this militaristic imagery also has a more immediate interpretive context in Luther's own day: the Latin West's violent encounters with Islam in the Crusades. Though the Crusades are often more closely associated with earlier centuries, in 1518, Pope Leo X called for a crusade against the Ottoman Empire to begin in 1523.[105] The Ottoman Turks posed a serious military, political, and cultural threat to Europe at this time. In 1453, Constantinople had fallen to the Ottomans, paving the way for the movement of the Turks into Europe. In 1526, the Ottomans defeated the Hungarians at the Battle of Mohács and advanced as far as the Danube River in Vienna. Fear of expansion into Germanic lands cannot be understated. Tales of forced marriage, forced conversion, and enslavement circulated rapidly as so-called escaped slaves told tales of survival.[106]

Unsurprisingly, Luther weighed in on the topic in his 1529 treatise, *On War against the Turks*. In this text, Luther used his Two Kingdoms doctrine to position responsibility of military resistance to political authorities. He called on the Holy Roman Emperor, Charles V, to resist an Ottoman invasion, rejecting a straightforward notion of holy war or Crusade.[107] However, Luther also called on Christians to fight the Ottomans, who he saw as the devil's proxy. Their weaponry would be repentance and prayer.[108] For Luther, the Christian soldier was in fact in a holy war, but this war was spiritual, not political. A new Ottoman campaign into Hungary materialized in 1540, which Luther addressed in a number of writings on the subject in the late 1530s and early 1540s. In an era of increasing militarization of German society, the Christian soldier was a theme on Luther's mind at the time of the *Antinomian Disputations* as well.

The tradition of linking the Christian's spiritual battle to the Crusades had a precedent in Bernard of Clairvaux. Bernard was a twelfth-century Cistercian monk and mystic from whom Luther had previously borrowed bridal metaphors to articulate his doctrine of justification. Bernard is one of only a few theologians Luther mentioned by name in the *Antinomian Disputations*.[109] We know fundamental contours of Luther's theology came from Bernard, including the bridal metaphor for justification and the theology of the cross. In Bernard's letters and writings on the monastic

---

105. Madden, *New Concise History*, 204–11.
106. Miller, *Turks and Islam*, 2.
107. WA 30/2:129–30; cf. Miller, "Fighting Like a Christian," 41–57.
108. WA 30/2:121.
109. WA 39/1:400.21.

life, he developed the theme of obedience to the divine will and spiritual warfare as works that extend out of conversion. Bernard used phrases in his letters linking the Christian soldier concept to the moral life that are echoed in Luther. Writing to the abbot of St. Denis, Bernard claimed that he was a "resolute soldier" in reforming his way of life, a phrase Luther used repeatedly.[110] In another letter, Bernard asked, "Where is your shield of faith, your helmet of salvation, your breastplate of patience?" naming the same Pauline armament we find in Luther. Similarly, Bernard called on the soldier of Christ to "arise."[111] Luther often asserted the Christian must "awaken" or "stir himself up" against sin.[112]

Bernard's militaristic imagery came from the Knights of Templar. G. R. Evans reports that Bernard saw the Knights of Templar as "soldier-monks of the Holy Land, perpetually engaged in that holy war . . . acting out in the external world of the spiritual warfare in every Christian soul."[113] The Knights Templar reflected the spiritual battle between good and evil, virtue and vice, in which every Christian was called to engage. Luther followed Bernard in the *Antinomian Disputations* by layering Crusader history with biblical language. He applied it to the Christian's task of overcoming sin and evil. The Ottomans poised at the Danube were God's terrifying call to every Christian to live a moral life.

Against the backdrop of this inheritance from Paul, the Crusades, Bernard, and now the Ottomans, Luther developed the Christian soldier theme in the *Antinomian Disputations* to describe the Christian battling and overcoming sin in her temporal life.[114] He layered this new anthro-

---

110. Bernard of Clairvaux (Letter 78, 1. LTR VII. 201.15-18) in Evans, *Mind of St. Bernard of Clairvaux*, 24. Erasmus of Rotterdam, Luther's adversary in 1525 over the freedom of the will, also wrote a book linking morality to the Christian soldier theme titled *Enchiridion militis christiani* (1501). Erasmus was motivated "to counteract the error of those who make religion in general consist in rituals and observances of an almost more than Jewish formality, but who are astonishingly indifferent to matters that have to do with true goodness" (Ep 181:53-9 in Rummel, *Erasmus Reader*, 138). Although Luther likely knew of Erasmus's text, Erasmus's text does not appear to have been a direct influence here. Erasmus's title was derived, in part, from his audience, a military officer, rather than the Pauline imagery.

111. Bernard of Clairvaux (Letter 1, 13. LTR VII. 10.17-18) in Evans, *Mind of St. Bernard of Clairvaux*, 24.

112. Bernard of Clairvaux (Letter 2, 12. LTR VII. 22) in Evans, *Mind of St. Bernard of Clairvaux*, 24.

113. Evans, *Bernard of Clairvaux*, 25.

114. Vind points toward the importance of practical theology for Luther's theological

pological construct, the triumphant and militant Christian (*christianus triumphans et militans*), onto the *simul*.

Luther aligned the triumphant part of the Christian with the Christian's just dimension. Relative righteousness received from Christ grounded the connection. Discussing the ongoing relevance of law in the Christian life, Luther observed that law belongs to the militant part, not the triumphant part.[115] The reason is that the triumphant part "dwells under the shadow of the wings of his lord."[116] One of Luther's favorite metaphors for describing imputed righteousness depicted Christ as the protective hen covering the sinner with his (her) wings.[117] Deploying biblical language, this phrase, "the shadow of the wings," meant that the Christian's sins are not imputed to her. Christ hides her from the law's accusations. Before the accusing law, the Christian is "just by a just reputation," which is made available by faith in Christ.[118] In the Christian's triumphant part, sin is ruled.

The militant part of the Christian has to do with the Christian as sinner, the dimension of her being in which she must work to become formally righteous. While the triumphant Christian is free from law, law remains for the militant part of the Christian because "in this life" she "still dwells in the flesh."[119] Like Paul's struggle in Romans 7, the "carnal flesh infected by Satan's venom," the ember of sin, "displays itself and agitates the poor Christian either to lust, or to greed, or to despair or hatred of God."[120] However, the Christian soldier does not consent to these sinful affections but battles them, scorns them, and overcomes them. Luther described the Christian soldier to act justly against his vicious will and "wins gloriously."[121] Luther

---

anthropology. In both the Christian soldier image and in his discussion of prayer and temptation, Vind's observation holds true in the *Antinomian Disputations*. Vind, "Human Being According to Luther," 84.

115. WA 39/1:503.19—504.1.

116. WA 39/1:504.6-7.

117. WA 8:142.9.

118. WA 39/1:504.16-18.

119. WA 39/1:496.16; 504.21-22. Luther also described the church to be militant (drawing on the Crusader history) because the church consists of Christian soldiers. Mannermaa positions the battle against sin in relation to the *partim-partim simul* construct. Mannermaa, *Christ Present in Faith*, 58.

120. WA 39/1:505.4-6.

121. WA 39/1:505.9-16. Luther's "glorious soldier and strong George" reference has a double referent: St. George, the patron saint of soldiers and slayer of the devil who became popular during the Crusades, and Luther himself, who, dressed as Knight George, "slayed" the Pope, the Antichrist.

linked this battle against sin to formal righteousness: when the Christian begins to battle sin by means of the Holy Spirit, he claimed, she begins to become formally just.[122] This Christian soldier is the *peccator* fighting for formal righteousness in this life. The triumphant Christian correlates to the *iustus* dimension that is relatively righteous. The militant Christian has to do with the *peccator* dimension working toward formal righteousness.

Here, Luther resisted scholarly restrictions positing his primary interest in the just-triumphant part of the Christian. Instead, he refocused his attention on expanding his descriptions of the sinful-militant part. This focus allowed him to clarify how the Christian reigns in her sin and works to obey the law in herself, her formal dimension. To justify this emphasis, Luther claimed that the triumphant-just part sends the Christian into military battle against sin. He says:

> Nevertheless on account of [remission of sins], you are not to be secure and deafly asleep. But this divine reputation, by which your sins are freely remitted on account of Christ, sends you as if into military service and into battles in order that you fight and combat sin the world, the devil, and your flesh without ceasing for the entire life.[123]

The Christian's righteous reputation incites her militant part to battle sin for the duration of her temporal life. The goal of this battle is to "fight night and day" "to purge sin in the flesh . . . until it will be finally totally purged out,"[124] to "purge what is left of sin until I become totally pure."[125] This battle has an eschatological vision of perfection, but that vision is not realized. The battle to scorn and mock sin must still be fought.[126]

The reason is ongoing sin threatens the Christian's faith with despair. Luther built the argument over the course of the introduction and first argument of the third disputation. The Antinomians are a threat to justification because they make Christians secure about ongoing sin.[127] The impact is that Christians "fall asleep" in their sin, where the devil can more

---

122. WA 39/1:494.1–3.
123. WA 39/1:494.5–9.
124. WA 39/1:474.20, 18.
125. WA 39/1:434.10–11.
126. WA 39/1:505.9–13. Christe interprets this as an ontological battle between two wills, however, I located no instance where Luther identified the recreated will as distinct from the natural one. Christe, "Gerecht und Sünder zugleich," 77.
127. WA 39/1:489.14–15.

easily overtake them.[128] Luther contrasted the sleeping, secure Christian with the Christian soldier, who is vigilant and alert to her sin. This is why, Luther said, "God wants us to be strong soldiers against the sin which is still present"—so we can "fight the remaining sin."[129] Luther stated clearly that he was "not speaking about bodily struggles and tribulations alone, but about every sort, both inner and outer . . . so that we might be armed not only against bodily evils, but also against despair, mistrust, presumption and hatred and contempt of God."[130] The danger of false security is despair, but this goes together with "body struggles and tribulations." The inner and outer struggles are connected. The Christian soldier needs to be armed against sin so she does not fall asleep and lose her faith.

The Spirit plays a central role in arming the Christian. We are formally righteous, Luther claimed, "as soon as I, in faith, begin to struggle and battle sin and blasphemy by virtue of these first fruits and the Holy Spirit given me from heaven."[131] Here, the Spirit is positioned after faith as one of the first fruits of justification but also as the means for the battle. This placement of the Spirit is intentional—and strategic. Making a play on words, Luther made clear the Spirit's central role by upending one of his common tropes for justification: Christ as a protective mother hen. The Latin term for hen is *gallina*, which can also be translated as gladiator. Luther made nimble use of both meanings to clarify Christ and the Spirit's roles in the Christian soldier's fight against sin.

Christ is both a protective mother hen, who flaps and spurs and seizes threats to her chicks, and a confident, powerful gladiator, leading into battle. Christ as *gallina* "does not allow anyone to be sound asleep in this narrow bed."[132] Here, Christ is a hen who crows his chicks awake. Then, Luther switched into militaristic connotations of the term. Christ as *gallina* also "wishes to rein and be king alone." He is "exceedingly impatient" with the flesh and wishes that it be "*admonished, exhorted,* and *exposed.*" "This is why the law needs to be sharpened carefully in the militant part," Luther said, because "we live and act here in the flesh."[133] The law finds our blemishes.

---

128. WA 39/1:489.18.
129. WA 39/1:492.6.
130. WA 39/1:494.10–13.
131. WA 39/1:494.1–3.
132. WA 39/1:498.17.
133. WA 39/1:498.10–11.

How does the law accomplish this? For this, Luther returned to his play on words. Christ as *gallina* "can lead into battle . . . but he himself wants to console the conscience." Yet, Luther made an interjection here. Christ, as gladiator, leads into battle "having given for this purpose the Holy Spirit who sufficiently arms those who are his."[134] We have here a deployment of the sequential categories "under Christ" and "in the Spirit" in conjunction with a reference to the law's three functions to reveal sin, admonish against it, and exhort to the good. The Christian soldier's armament for battle is the Spirit, who is given by Christ in justification and who brings with it the law "to convict of righteousness."

Just as we saw in chapter 3, the law plays a crucial role in the Christian soldier's battle. Luther specified that here we are talking about a different part (than the triumphant part); we are talking about the "militant Christian." As soon as the Christian sees "the carnal nature" rearing its head and inciting him to greed, lust, and despair, the Christian "stirs herself up for battle."[135] Like a strong soldier confident in her skill, she mocks the sinful inclination and speaks formulations of law against it and for righteous works:

> Aha! You are still here! . . . It will absolutely not be so. I will protect my virgin and will do what is just, even against your will. . . . The more you torture me, even challenge and incite me to dishonor . . . the more I will laugh at you with a spirit that is both confident and strong![136]

Luther then stated something similar to the Christian youth narrative: "This one is that glorious soldier and strong George who makes a great massacre in the army of the devil and wins gloriously. . . . He does not permit sin to devour his flesh."[137] The law functions in this narrative to help stir the Christian up, providing an admonishment as negative judgment against an inclination and an exhortation as positive consent to a righteous alternative.

The use of law, therefore, has to do with the Christian soldier's moral functions. The militant Christian "knows the law and considers the sin in the flesh, against which she fights day and night."[138] Because she knows the law's moral directives and uses it to recognize sin in her flesh, she

134. WA 39/1:498.20-21.
135. WA 39/1:505.6; 495.21.
136. WA 39/1:505.7-13.
137. WA 39/1:505.14-16.
138. WA 39/1:501.17.

then also becomes able to will against the sin using the recreated and redirected will from the Spirit, crushing sin's head.[139] Law is the Christian's battle cry that arouses her aggression against sin, arming her with the intellectual powers to see sin as her mortal enemy and the volitional direction to slash it with the Spirit.

The Christian soldier's battle gives explanatory force to Luther's earlier claims about sin and righteousness in the Christian life from the first and second disputations. He depicts the Christian soldier to be taking sin captive (*peccatum captivare*) as she wills against or does not consent to the sinful inclination.[140] Here, Luther's earlier claim that the Christian "drives sin back" is clarified by his explanation that the Christian soldier "purges it with the help of the Holy Spirit," obeying the Spirit and the law.[141] The Christian soldier and Christian youth narratives in the third disputation provided narrative structure to demonstrate what Luther meant when he talked about sin being formally removed and purged.[142] The result of the process is that the Christian soldier begins to become "formally righteous" because "[she] begins to battle sin with the help of the Holy Spirit."[143] This change from the form of sin to the form of righteousness displays itself in the Christian's actions:

> Even though I have the occasion, place, and time to fornicate, commit adultery, steal, etc. without any disgrace or punishment [because of Christ's righteousness], still I do not do it. Here, I experience truly and in myself that the Holy Spirit dwells in my heart and is efficacious.[144]

The battle against sin and for formal righteousness actually accomplishes something; it insulates the Christian's faith against despair where the devil lurks to destroy her.

The Christian soldier metaphor gave language to the movement between victory over sin and being overcome by it in Luther's *partim-partim* concept. The Christian soldier must fight "day by day," "day and night" until her "old person," her carnal flesh, is completely removed and her

---

139. WA 39/1:505.9–10; 501.15–18.
140. WA 39/1:500.21—501.1, 4–5; 436.11.
141. WA 39/1:436.10–11; 501.9–11.
142. WA 39/1:432.7–8.
143. WA 39/1:494.1–3.
144. WA 39/1:436.16—437.3.

"new person," her just person, emerges.[145] Luther was clear: this battle is won "more and more" every day as the Christian purges sin in her flesh.[146] Luther used another narrative example to give shape to this picture. Referencing Tertullian, Luther wrote of a Christian soldier who "performed heroic acts." He resisted prostitutes, bit off his tongue, and "could not be overcome and pushed into love by his flesh raging . . . but like a bronze wall stood firm in faith in Christ."[147] However, Luther conceded that this war is never fully won in this life.[148] Here, Luther detailed the other side of the battle, asking what would be the victory for a Christian soldier who allowed himself to be overcome by desire for the prostitute. "Is he not a Christian?" Luther asked, replying, "I deny this. . . . In that part you are not a Christian. But the one who fights and does not allow himself to be overcome by sin and to be ruled by sin is called a Christian." Here Luther drew out the tension in the militant part of the Christian. She is simultaneously becoming formally righteous and still sinful. There is movement between the moral polarities. Thus, the Christian soldier fights to take sin captive every day and slowly wins the battle on her last day.

In conclusion, this section has examined Luther's Christian soldier motif as a new anthropological possibility for understanding the Christian's agency and action vis-à-vis the law after justification in the Spirit. Luther layered the triumphant-militant construct onto the *partim-partim* aspect of the *simul iustus et peccator* construct. These two constructs are then aligned with the moral dimension of relative and formal righteousness. The result is that the Christian's *iustus* dimension is the triumphant Christian through relative righteousness. The Christian's *peccator* dimension is the militant Christian who continues to work toward formal righteousness in herself. The emphasis Luther placed on the Christian soldier reflects his interest in further nuancing the *peccator* dimension of the Christian person. While he discussed the triumphant-just dimension of the Christian, he did so only to show how justification should instigate moral improvement in the temporal Christian herself as militant *peccator*.

When Luther attended to the *peccator* as the Christian soldier, he depicted the Christian as she is empowered by the Spirit and the law in her pursuit of formal righteousness. Because the Christian must first fight

---

145. WA 39/1:432.7–11.
146. Cf. Anderas, *Renovatio*, 106.
147. WA 39/1:506.20—507.7.
148. WA 39/1:510.3–4.

against her sinful inclinations, she protects herself using the benefits of faith that she received from Christ. Though she may stumble in battle and give in to sin, she is protected by Christ's righteousness, by salvation, and by faith. She will not die. The Christian is armed against the sinful inclinations with the Spirit who gives her the law. The Christian uses the law to stir herself up, to awaken herself to battle sin. Law helps her to recognize sinful inclinations so that she is always prepared to attack it and, instead, do what is right and just. The result of the Christian's battle is that she begins to overcome her sinful inclinations by using these spiritual weapons and she begins to become righteous in herself in the form of her soul.

Luther's Christian soldier construct allows us to attend more carefully to the way Luther nuanced moral agency and moral progress in the Christian as *peccator*. The Christian as sinner is not simply a static moral condition nor is the Christian as *peccator* morally passive, as Luther scholars have supposed. Rather, the Christian as *peccator* is morally engaged and active, empowered by the Spirit. She is vigilant and on the attack against sin. As she uses her spiritual weapons, she makes moral progress even if this is not complete until her death.

Another benefit of Luther's Christian soldier construct is that it provides us with a new angle from which to view the Christian's moral functioning. When we examined the Christian's intellectual and volitional capacities as *peccator*, we saw these noetic forms to remain hindered by sin and then to be elevated to new moral strength by the Spirit and the law. The result was a blurred subjectivity in which the Christian and the Spirit were mutual actors. The Christian soldier, however, reflects more of the Christian's own intellectual and volitional acts as she puts these forms to use in moral action. Gone is the problem of blurred subjectivity that we saw in the Christian youth narrative. Now, we see the Christian as the active agent. She uses the law, given by the Spirit, as a spiritual weapon or tool in her fight against sin and pursuit of formal righteousness. Though we know from the "internal" examination of the Christian's form that the Spirit is indwelling the Christian to make possible her use of these renewed moral forms, the Christian soldier presents a kind of external perspective. The Christian soldier presents an image of the Christian as a moral agent resulting from the Spirit's regenerative and sanctifying activity.

Chapter Conclusions

This chapter has examined how Luther developed his theological anthropology of the Christian person to support his picture of moral progress in the temporal life in the Spirit. This investigation counters the way Luther scholars have typically interpreted Luther's theological anthropology as undermining human moral agency and moral progress. The dominant scholarly focus is on Luther's anthropological construct, *simul iustus et peccator*. Scholars interpret this formula to mean that the person is just eschatologically but remains unchanged as sinner in the temporal life. Because the effects of justification are only eschatological, human reason remains blind and the will is totally bound. Possibilities for moral agency in this picture are bleak.

However, in this chapter, we found that Luther was actually very interested in human moral reasoning in the anthropological dimension of the *peccator*. He correlated the two parts of the *simul* formula, *iustus* and *peccator*, to a two-part moral determination, relative and formal righteousness. Then, he added a third layer onto this in relation to the *partim-partim* aspect to describe human action, the triumphant-militant Christian. Because formal righteousness has to do with the person's formal cause, the shape of the soul, we saw Luther to specify particular noetic forms required for moral reasoning and moral agency in the *peccator* dimension. The Christian as *peccator* has intellection and volition for moral action as these are enlivened and supported by the Spirit. The challenge was that the moral determination Luther overlaid onto the *peccator* dimension was formal righteousness, or righteousness as the shape of the *peccator*'s soul. This righteous condition is clearly paradoxical to the *peccator* and not yet realized.

In order to reconcile the *peccator* dimension with the moral determination of formal righteousness, Luther introduced the Spirit and the law into his anthropology. Because the human form itself has sinful affections leftover from the *fomes peccati*, the Spirit and the law elevate the moral processes that control action on or resistance of a particular affection. The Spirit and law must recover human intellection and volition for moral action. Therefore, Luther shows the Spirit to give the law in order to compensate for intellectual deficiencies in the *peccator*. The law supplies intellectual judgments about the moral goodness of a particular affection or inclination. When this judgment moves on to volitional acts of consent or nonconsent to an affection, the Spirit elevates the volitional capacities to will/not will in accord with the intellectual judgment. In this way, Luther carved out a new type of freedom of the will in the *peccator* using a more robust pneumatology. Freedom of the will requires that the intellect and will work together for moral action. While Luther's early writings permitted neither good precept in the intellect nor the volitional capacities to consent to a good precept, now Luther brought the Spirit and the law together to rehabilitate this functionality.

The consequence of this new mode of moral reasoning in the *peccator*, however, is that Luther blurred the subjective boundaries between the Spirit and the human person. While he attributed the actions themselves to the human person, he also described the Spirit as taking over the human's intellectual and volitional movements, suggesting a type of *cooperatio*. Viewed from the outside, Christian soldier's moral activity builds a view of the Christian as an active agent in her righteousness insofar as she relies on the Spirit and law as weapons in her battle against sin. Were one to open up the Christian soldier and peek inside her soul, one would see the law and the Spirit compensating for her intellectual and volitional deficiencies. However, the image of the Christian soldier itself is an image of the Christian as the agent of the moral activity. The Christian uses the law to incite herself to moral improvement. She uses it to recognize her sin and to guide her action with the result that she makes a degree of moral progress toward formal righteousness in her temporal life. This progress is itself proof that the Spirit indwells the soul and is efficacious in vivifying and sanctifying her soul, her formal cause as *peccator*.

If we place the Christian soldier back onto the Aristotelian causal diagram used in Luther scholarship to outline Luther's theological anthropology, we see a new interplay between the vertical and horizontal axis. The eschatological person depicted through the vertical axis affects the temporal person viewed through horizontal axis. The Spirit properly belongs to the vertical axis representing divine efficient causality of the eschatological person. However, the Spirit works on and elevates the formal cause, the soul, that sits on the horizontal axis of the temporal person. When the Spirit elevates the temporal person's formal cause, the entire horizontal axis—form and matter, soul and body—are moved closer to the final end of righteousness in eternal life. The movement of the horizontal axis is measured according to the moral determination that Luther associated with the *peccator* on the horizontal axis, namely formal righteousness. This suggests more than a relational ontology. Divine agency in making the eschatological person just has a real effect on the temporal human person in herself as sinner. Because of Christ's gift of the Spirit in justification and the Spirit's regenerative and sanctifying activities, the Christian is able to produce moral change after justification in the temporal life. The expansion in Luther's pneumatology that we saw in chapters 3 and 4 now involves a real anthropological effect that creates human moral agency and stimulates temporal moral progress.

Chapter 6

Conclusions: Human Agency in the Spirit

THIS STUDY HAS SOUGHT to retrieve a cohesive theological picture of the human person in herself, in the interplay between inner and outer person, in light of her relation to God. To do so, we examined the complex anthropological picture Luther painted when he parsed human personhood vis-à-vis the Holy Spirit. I have argued that the 1537–1540 controversy with Johann Agricola over law and gospel led Luther to narrate a new theological anthropology in the *Antinomian Disputations*. Agricola's antinomianism was premised on Luther's doctrine of justification. Established in Luther's early polemics against Scholastic theology, Luther understood justification to require total human passivity and total divine agency to guarantee the God-human relationship. However, beginning in 1537, Luther worked to revive and renew human moral agency *after* justification by maximizing another divine agent whose work did not compete with but actually bolstered human agency. The vivifying and sanctifying Holy Spirit recreates and sustains human moral agency after justification by elevating the person's moral powers in the soul. Most interestingly, Luther depicted the Spirit's connection to law as the key to sustaining the Spirit's activity to elevate the Christian's moral powers. In presenting human agency in this way, Luther demonstrated that divine grace has a real, temporal effect on the human person, her moral capacity, and her temporal life and experiences. God does everything in justification, but God and the human person work together for moral action as a result.

Luther's new insights about human moral agency after justification emerged within the *Antinomian Disputations* as Luther clarified connections between the person, the Spirit, and the law he saw in the gospel of John. As I discussed in chapters 2 and 3, Agricola distorted Luther's law/gospel principle on the basis of a problematic pneumatology. Agricola linked the Spirit to the accusing function of law while maintaining the traditional theological view that the Spirit is God's gift in justification. From this, Agricola conflated law into gospel. He concluded that the gospel must both convict of sins and announce remission of sins in Christ because the Spirit was only given in the gospel. With the emerging antinomian controversy percolating in the background, Luther fleshed out the connection of the Spirit to the law in his sermonic expositions on John 16:8. In this passage, Luther discovered that Christ assigns two operations to the Spirit: (1) to convict of sins, which was a function of law; and (2) to convict of righteousness, a function of gospel. Chapter 3 clarified Luther's contextual problem as a need to separate law from gospel while also maintaining the Spirit's connection to both law and gospel based on John 16:8.

Luther's solution to this problem required developments to his pneumatology, conception of law, and theological anthropology. Luther's first task was to resolve his pneumatological problem. How could the Spirit both convict of sins and righteousness and relate to both law and gospel? Luther decided the Spirit must be the divine agent of the law, the "author of the law." This pneumatological expansion increased the Spirit's relation to the accusing law prior to justification. Because the Spirit was connected to the accusing law, Luther's expansion also meant the law could have a role in the Christian life after justification when the Spirit was given to the Christian as Christ's gift. Before justification, the Spirit used the law to accuse. After justification, Luther determined that the Spirit speaks the law to the Christian to admonish against sin and to exhort her toward the good. This was a sanctifying use of law under gospel.

The Spirit's new relation to law allowed Luther to develop a more robust view of human experience under law and gospel. His first insight had to do with human affective experience. The way the Spirit speaks the law to accuse, admonish, and exhort elicits two different emotional responses, which Luther cloaked in medieval penitential language. Sorrow is the human response to the Spirit's accusing use of law to convict of sins. A good intention is the human response to the Spirit's sanctifying use of law to convict of righteousness. However, for the human person to have any capacity to stand before the law without accusation and condemnation, Luther had to position these new relations to law in relation to justification.

The new law relation required that Luther plot particular moments in the changing human relation to the Spirit and the law in parallel to law/gospel. Luther articulated this order using four categories: before Christ, under Christ, in the Spirit, and after Christ. We focused on the first three temporal categories. Before Christ and under Christ expressed the human dimension of law/gospel. The law accuses before Christ, but the law's accusing power is removed through the remission of sins and imputation of Christ's righteousness under Christ. The third category, in the Spirit, opened the Christian up to the sanctifying use of law because Christ had removed the accusing power of the law and given over the Spirit, who is the divine agent of law. Christ's gifts—both his righteousness and the Spirit—transformed the human relation to the Spirit. This new relation between the Christian and the Spirit opened up a new relation to law: in the Spirit, Luther claimed, the Christian begins to fulfill the law. The fourth stage, after Christ, is eschatological and speaks to a final abrogation of law. Because this stage had to do with the eschatological picture, not the temporal one, we did not analyze this category in this study.

Luther made a surprising claim when he said that the Christian begins to fulfill the law in the Spirit because Luther supposedly problematized human law fulfillment based on human sin. Chapter 4 saw Luther clarify how law relates to human sin alongside of distinct processes in which sin is separated from the human person in relation to law and divine persons. Luther reintroduced medieval hamartiological categories of original and actual sin that distinguished sin in human nature universally from the actual sin of individuals. Before Christ, law accused original sin and all resulting sin, but Christ redeemed and covered all sins spurred by the sinful inclination in human nature. In the process of imputation, guilt for original sin was forgiven in Christ and the Christian was imputed with Christ's relative righteousness. The problem was, under Christ, Christ's imputed righteousness did not effect substantial change in individual persons. The Christian remained subject to sinful inclinations, leading to ongoing, actual sin. Here, Luther looked to the Spirit and the sanctifying law for solutions. Sanctifying law reveals the Christian's ongoing sin, but without accusation. Instead, with the Spirit's help, the sanctifying law supports the Christian through the process of purgation—of purging her actual sin and developing formal righteousness in herself.

Purgation has to do with the Christian's temporal life, with fighting sin and becoming righteous in herself from justification-to-grave. To articulate the Spirit's role in aiding purgation, Luther turned to practical theology. He wanted to clarify in experiential terms how the Christian goes about purging sin through prayer and temptation. Prayer concentrates the Christian's experience of and relation to the Spirit and the sanctifying law. With reference to meditative prayer practices birthed in medieval mysticism, Luther maintained that the Christian speaks the law to herself in an admonishing and exhortative way by repeating the petitions of the Lord's Prayer.

These prayerful reiterations of law heightened the Christian's connection to the law's divine agent, the Spirit. Luther described the Christian's repetitive petitions in prayer to spur a mystical moment in which the Spirit speaks within the Christian's own thoughts and specifies the law to the Christian's immediate experience. In particular, Luther depicted the Spirit to apply the law to a particular temptation the Christian was facing. In an act of shared intellectual agency, the Spirit admonishes the Christian who is lusting after a pretty girl to leave the girl in peace and instead to wait on a wife. These cognitive processes reflected both a positive judgment against an act and a positive intention on what to do instead. Luther depicted these shared judgments as an expansion on the command, "Thou shall not covet." With the Spirit speaking in the Christian's thoughts, Luther described the Christian as moving to a volitional act to love God's law and hate the temptation. Even this volitional act is elevated by the Spirit. The Spirit recreates the will and aligns it to the law's admonitions, leading to the Christian's decision to obey the law. Luther concluded that prayer in temptation led to the ability to resist these sinful urges in temptation, to purge sinful inclinations. This, Luther firmly asserted, is how the Christian overcomes sin, obeys the law, and begins to become formally righteous in herself.

Questioning relational ontology interpretations of Luther's *simul iustus et peccator* concept, chapter 5 examined Luther's use of philosophical terms to describe the effect of justification on the human herself as human. Luther rehearsed Ockham's specification of the formal cause of the human personhood in terms of the moral powers of the soul: intellection, volition, and affection. Here, Luther looked beyond Christ's agency in justification to see the Holy Spirit's effect on the Christian's temporal being. What Luther discovered was the gift of the Spirit, not Christ, works specifically on the formal cause of the Christian's being in order to elevate her intellectual and volitional powers to righteousness. The Spirit speaks the law in the mind to improve the soul's intellectual capacities to judge rightly about the divine will and to perceive sinful inclinations presented to the human will as sinful. The Spirit also affects human volition because the Spirit recreates and orients the human will to the law by filling the will with new affections for God. Luther admitted, however, the Christian's new moral powers do not always function perfectly. Sometimes sins break in and the person becomes weak-willed. When this occurs, the consolation of the gospel brings comfort, reminding her that she is justified by the deeds of another; she need only stir herself up anew for the next battle.

So, how does the person resist sin in the Spirit sometimes and not others? Here, Luther's anthropological construct of the triumphant and militant Christian lends insight. Luther layered this construct on top of the *simul* formula through the *partim-partim* aspect. Triumphant and militant also map onto the moral determinations of relative and formal righteousness developed in chapters 4 and 5. The triumphant Christian is the just, relatively-righteous dimension of the person that sees eschatological realization. The militant Christian is the sinner who is fighting to become formally righteous in her temporal life with the help of the Spirit. When the Christian is militant against sin, she stirs herself up for the battle against sin by the law and the Spirit. Then, the Spirit helps her to resist elevating her moral functions. What is key is that she must be mindful and alert, prepared for the fight. When she lets her guard down and becomes complacent, as Luther feared would be the case without the law, sin creeps in and overtakes her.

Increasing Human Agency and Law in Luther Research

Luther escalated human moral agency after justification to address antinomian readings of his early theology. He needed to separate law from gospel contra Agricola while simultaneously upholding his exegetical insight that linked the Spirit to the law. The sustained development of the three interrelated dogmatic positions across the four-year span of the disputations casts serious doubt on the forgery thesis maintained by Elert, Ebeling, and more recently in American scholarship, Timothy Wengert. This study works alongside earlier analysis by Norman Lund and Phil Anderas to chart the constellations of major developments in Luther's theology in this period. Lund showed the development and crystallization of a new, theologically coherent use of law across the series of disputations. Anderas contextualized these developments as part of Luther's interest in Augustinian notions of holiness and sanctification and were evident across multiple genres of Luther's writings beginning in the 1530s.

The present study's further investigation into the historical context and theological and philosophical developments across the entirety of the disputations reveals that Luther was working out the systematic ramifications in other dogmatic regions of pneumatological insights from his study of the gospel of John. The Spirit was the key that he was missing in 1517's *Disputation against Scholastic Theology* or the 1522 *Church Postilles* (à la Ebeling) to make sense of human moral action on the law. Because the Spirit is given over to the Christian *after* justification, Luther found a way in 1537 to include law fulfillment in the Christian life as moral improvement after justification. He was developing a coherent doctrine of sanctification. Luther's new emphasis on the Spirit for formal righteousness enabled him to maintain Christ's agency in justification while opening up what Marilyn Adams would have called a type of "shared agency"[1] between the Christian and the Spirit. This shared agency made possible action on a kind of "third use" of law after justification.

This study makes a strong set of claims in light of the emphasis in Luther research on a forensic notion of justification and its deferred eschatological fulfillment in the human person. These assumptions generate pressing yet unanswerable questions about human experience of God's presence in justification. Anna Vind asks this type of question in her article "The Human Being According to Luther," when she asks what is the relation between the epistemic and experiential (i.e., the temporal/sensory) dimensions of human personhood and faith in Luther's theological anthropology.[2] Her question rests on an assumption that faith is the only viable anthropological category in the God-human relationship in Luther's theology, leaving human temporal experience unexplained. This study contributes additional answers from Luther's abiding interest in the temporal effect of justification on the person's sensory and cognitive experience. Without attention to Luther's pneumatological impulses in his late anthropological writings, it is not possible to resolve Vind's question. Attention to the Holy Spirit brings to light the way Luther integrated

---

1. Adams, "Genuine Agency," 23.
2. Vind, "Human Being According to Luther," 77.

theological concepts, like justification, with the so-called philosophical anthropological categories he supposedly denigrated, like human reason and volition. The way Luther pulled the Spirit together with the "philosophical determination" of the human person gives voice to the epistemic and experiential dimensions of the person in view of faith.

In light of the Spirit's temporal effects, the boldest claim made in this study is that Luther was not just interested in how God compensates for human moral incapacity but actively sought to clarify how the God-human relationship recreates and sustains human moral agency. This argument maintains the scholarly consensus that divine and human agency are in inverse linear proportions in Luther's doctrine of justification. This remains uncontested. But this consensus highlights the agency of only one divine person in the economic Trinity, Christ. I am adding to this the claim that Luther also explored the agency of another divine person implicated in the economic Trinity in relation to human agency: the Spirit. What he found was that the Holy Spirit is not in competition with human agency as was the case for Christ's work in justification. Instead, the Spirit *creates* and *sustains* human agency by vivifying and elevating the human actor to moral action and progress. Luther was making the case for sanctification. In light of this, it appears that Luther's critique of human agency was not a refutation of works per se, but of their placement before justification and as contributing to justification.

Luther's Contributions to Broader Theological Anthropology and Theological Ethics

Luther sustained his claims about the Spirit's temporal effects on the human person after justification by looking to experiential categories in practical theology and philosophical anthropology pertaining to the emotions or affect. It is here where Luther's contribution to contemporary theological anthropology, ethics, and spiritual practice most clearly emerges. Yet, as feminist, womanist, and mujerista theologians have shown, these experiential categories are all too often missing from Protestant theological anthropologies, which have emphasized the Christological connections in the *imago Dei* since the dialectical turn popularized by Karl Barth. The problem is the Christological reading of the *imago Dei* reduces human personhood to soteriological concepts—original sin, redemption, and eschatological fulfillment. The human person as she is here and now, as she experiences God and herself in relation to God, struggles to find a voice.

Theological anthropologies that emphasize the *imago Dei* and, thus, Christology leave experiential questions at the heart of human life unanswered. How do individual persons relate back to God and experience that relational reciprocation? How are we to account for an individual's daily experience of being human when this threefold relational structure is not an experiential part of normal daily life with joys, fears, and struggles? When our theological anthropologies attend solely to diagnostic categories for the human condition and the arc of human reconciliation to God, real human experience of being human and of being in relation to God get left behind.

Here, Luther beckons theologians back to persons as persons and their subjective capacities that both make them in the image of God and make the relationship with God anthropologically possible. Luther's use of philosophical anthropological categories indicates the necessity and possibility for probing how the all-encompassing scope of economic trinitarian activity meets individual experience of God and the self—how human persons think and feel in relation to God, how persons see themselves to change over time in response to God, and activities human persons initiate to invoke religious experiences of God. Luther reminds theologians that human self-experience changes as a result of justification: the Christian gains moral strength, sees moral progress in herself, and finds assurance that the Spirit is in her. Luther also points to possibilities for better articulating the person as an ethical agent by employing philosophical categories like intellection, volition, and affection. He elevates human activities that foster and heighten the God-human relationship, such as meditation and prayer, temptation and moral struggle, and emotional responses to God. The legacy of Luther's *Antinomian Disputations* is his call to more robustly explore the dual aspects of theological anthropology: the theological as the dimension having to do with the *entire* economic Godhead in relation to persons and the anthropological as the aspect of personhood that centers on the person as person, her ontology, her experience, her actions. To attend to the former at the expense of the latter is to miss what makes the human relation to God human and the human ethical relation to the world theological.

Bibliography

Abelard, Peter. *Ethics*. In *Ethical Writings*, translated by Paul Vincent Spade, 1–58. Indianapolis, IN: Hackett, 1995.
———. *Scito te ipsum*. Vol. 4 of *Opera Theologica*. Edited by R. M. Illgner. Corpus Christianorum 190. Turnhout: Brepols, 2001.
Aberth, John. *From the Brink of the Apocalypse: Confronting Famine, War, Plague, and Death in the Later Middle Ages*. New York: Routledge, 2001.
———. *Plagues in World History*. Exploring World History. New York: Rowman & Littlefield, 2011.
Adams, Marilyn McCord. "Genuine Agency, Somehow Shared? The Holy Spirit and Other Gifts." In vol. 1 of *Oxford Studies in Medieval Philosophy*, edited by Robert Pasnau, 23–60. Oxford: Oxford University Press, 2013.
———. "Ockham on Will, Nature, and Morality." In *Cambridge Companion to Ockham*, edited by Paul Spade, 245–72. Cambridge: Cambridge University Press, 1999.
———. "The Structure of Ockham's Moral Theory." *Franciscan Studies* 46.3 (1986) 1–35.
———. *William Ockham*. 2 vols. Notre Dame, IN: University of Notre Dame Press, 1987.
Agricola, Johann. *Die Sprichwörtersammlungen*. Edited by Sander L. Gilman. 2 vols. Berlin: de Gruyter, 1971.
Alfsvaag, Knut. "Virtue, Reason and Tradition: A Discussion of Alasdair MacIntyre's and Martin Luther's Views on the Foundations of Ethics." *Neue Zeitschrift für systematische Theologie und Religionsphilosophie* 47 (2005) 288–305.
Althaus, Paul. *Die Ethik Martin Luthers*. Gütersloh: Gütersloher Verlagshaus, 1965.
———. *Gebot und Gesetz: Zum Thema "Gesetz und Evangelium."* Gütersloh: Bertelsmann, 1952.
———. *Die Theologie Martin Luthers*. 6th ed. Gütersloh: Gütersloher Verlagshaus Mohn, 1983.
———. *The Theology of Martin Luther*. Translated by Robert C. Schultz. Philadelphia: Fortress, 1966.
Anderas, Phil. *Renovatio: Martin Luther's Augustinian Theology of Sin, Grace, and Holiness*. Refo500 Academic Studies 57. Göttingen: Vandenhoeck & Ruprecht, 2019.
Angelelli, Ignacio. "The Techniques of Disputation in the History of Logic." *The Journal of Philosophy* 67 (1970) 800–815.

BIBLIOGRAPHY

Anselm of Canterbury. *On the Virgin Conception and Original Sin.* In *Anselm of Canterbury: The Major Works*, edited by Brian Davies and G. R. Evans, translated by Camilla McNab, 357–89. Oxford: Oxford University Press, 2008.

Aquinas, Thomas. *Summa Theologiae.* Translated by Fathers of the English Dominican Province. New York: Benziger Brothers, 1947.

Arbesmann, Rudolph. "The Concept of 'Christus Medicus' in St. Augustine." *Traditio* 10 (1954) 1–28.

Aristotle. *Metaphysics.* In *A New Aristotle Reader*, edited by J. L. Ackrill, 253–360. Princeton: Princeton University Press, 1987.

———. *Nicomachean Ethics.* Translated by Terence Irwin. 2nd ed. Cambridge: Hackett, 1999.

Asendorf, Ulrich. *Heiliger Geist und Rechtfertigung.* Göttingen: Vandenhoeck & Ruprecht Unipress, 2004.

———. "Luthers Theologie nach seinen Katechismuspredigten." *Kerygma und Dogma: Zeitschrift für theologische Forschung und kirchliche Lehre* 38 (1992) 2–19.

———. *Die Theologie Martin Luthers nach seinen Predigten.* Göttingen: Vandenhoeck & Ruprecht, 1988.

Asheim, Ivar. "Lutherische Tugendethik?" *Neue Zeitschrift für systematische Theologie und Religionsphilosophie* 40 (1998) 239–60.

Assel, Heinrich, ed. *Karl Holl: Leben—Werk—Briefe.* Tübingen: Mohr/Siebeck, 2021.

———. "The Luther Renaissance." *Oxford Research Encyclopedia of Religion*, March 29, 2017. https://doi.org/10.1093/acrefore/9780199340378.013.297.

Atkins, Anne. *Split Image: Male and Female after God's Likeness.* Grand Rapids: Eerdmans, 1987.

Augustine. *The City of God.* Translated by Markus Dods. New York: Penguin, 1950.

———. *On the Holy Trinity.* In vol. 3 of *The Nicene and Post-Nicene Fathers*, Series 1. Edited by Philip Schaff. Translated by Arthur West Haddan. Peabody, MA: Hendrickson, 1994.

———. *On the Spirit and the Letter.* In vol. 5 of *The Nicene and Post-Nicene Fathers*, Series 1. Edited by Philip Schaff. Translated by Peter Holmes and Robert Ernest Wallis. Revised by Benjamin B. Warfield. Grand Rapids: Eerdmans, 1956.

Barth, Karl. *Evangelium und Gesetz.* Theologische Existenz Heute 32. Munich: Chr. Kaiser, 1935.

Bayer, Oswald. "Being in the Image of God." *Lutheran Quarterly* 27 (2013) 76–88.

———. "Ethik der Gabe." In *Die Gabe: Ein "Urwort" der Theologie?*, edited by Veronika Hoffmann, 115–66. Frankfurt am Main: Verlag Otto Lembeck, 2009.

———. *Freedom in Response: Lutheran Ethics: Sources and Controversies.* Translated by Jeff Cayzer. Oxford: Oxford University Press, 2007.

———. *Living by Faith: Justification and Sanctification.* Translated by Geoffrey W. Bromiley. Grand Rapids: Eerdmans, 2003.

———. "Luthers Verständnis der Menschenwürde." *Kerygma und Dogma: Zeitschrift für theologische Forschung und kirchliche Lehre* 59 (2013) 186–92.

———. *Martin Luthers Theologie.* 2nd ed. Tübingen: Mohr/Siebeck, 2004.

———. "Oratio, Meditatio, Tentatio: Eine Besinnung auf Luthers Theologieverständnis." *Lutherjahrbuch* 55 (1988) 7–59.

———. *Promissio: Geschichte der reformatorischen Wende in Luthers Theologie.* Göttingen: Vandenhoeck & Ruprecht, 1971.

BIBLIOGRAPHY

Baylor, Michael G. *Action and Person: Conscience in Late Scholasticism and the Young Luther*. Studies in Medieval and Reformation Thought 20. Leiden: Brill, 1977.

Beintker, Horst. "Zu Luthers Verständnis vom geistlichen Leben des Christen im Gebet." *Lutherjahrbuch* 31 (1964) 47–68.

Biel, Gabrielis. *Canonis Misse Expositio*. Edited by Heiko A. Oberman and William J. Courtenay. 3 vols. Veröffentlichungen des Instituts für Europäische Geschichte Mainz 31–33. Wiesbaden: Franz Steiner GMBH, 1963–1966.

———. *Collectorium circa quattuor libros Sententiarum*. Edited by Hans Rückert. 3 vols. Tübingen: Mohr/Siebeck, 1973.

Bielfeldt, Dennis. "The Ontology of Deification." In *Caritas Dei: Beiträge zum Verständnis Luthers und der gegenwärtigen Ökumene*, edited by Oswald Bayer et al., 90–113. Helsinki: Luther-Agricola-Society, 1997.

Bornkamm, Karin. *Luthers Auslegungen Des Galaterbriefs von 1519 und 1531: Ein Vergleich*. Arbeiten Zur Kirchengeschichte 35. Berlin: de Gruyter, 1963.

Bossy, John. *Christianity in the West 1400–1700*. Oxford: Oxford University Press, 1985.

Brecht, Martin. *Martin Luther*. Translated by James Schaaf. Vols. 2–3. Minneapolis: Fortress, 1993–1994.

———. "'Und willst das Beten von uns han': Zum Gebet und seiner Praxis bei Martin Luther." In *Die frühe Reformation in Deutschland als Umbruch: Wissenschaftliches Symposion des Vereins für Reformationsgeschichte 1996*, edited by Bernd Moeller, 268–88. Gütersloh: Gütersloher Verlaghaus, 1998.

Brock, Brian. *Wondrously Wounded: Theology, Disability, and the Body of Christ*. Waco, TX: Baylor University Press, 2019.

Buchanan, Harvey. "Luther and the Turks 1519–1529." *Archiv für Reformationsgeschichte* 47.2 (1956) 145–59.

Bühler, Pierre. "Der Mensch vor der Aufgabe ethischer Verantwortung: Anthropologie und Ethik in Luthers Genesisvorlesung." In *Luthers Ethik: Christliches Leben in Ecclesia, Oeconomia, Politia=Luther's Ethics in the Realms of Church, Household, Politics: Referate und Berichte des Elften Internationalen Kongresses für Lutherforschung Canoas/RS 21.-27. Juli 2007*, edited by Helmar Junghans, 57–76. Göttingen: Vandenhoeck & Ruprecht, 2009.

Burger, Christoph. "Luthers Gebetsvorschlag für Herzog Johann Friedrich von Sachsen: Zur Bedeutung des Gebets in christlicher Theologie und zu Luthers Wertschätzung des Gebets." In *Oratio: Das Gebet in patristischer und reformatorischer Sicht*, edited by Emidio Campi et al., 185–96. Forschungen zur Kirchen- und Dogmengeschichte 76. Göttingen: Vandenhoeck & Ruprecht, 1999.

Byrne, Joseph Patrick. *Encyclopedia of Pestilence, Pandemics, and Plagues*. Westport, CT: Greenwood, 2008.

Cary, Phillip. *Augustine's Invention of the Inner Self: The Legacy of a Christian Platonist*. Oxford: Oxford University Press, 2000.

Christe, Wilhelm. "'Gerecht und Sünder zugleich': Zur Ontologie des homo christianus nach Martin Luther." In *Niemand ist eine Insel: Menschen im Schnittpunkt von Anthropologie, Theologie und Ethik; Festschrift für Wilfried Härle zum 70. Geburtstag*, edited by Christian Polke et al., 65–85. Berlin: de Gruyter, 2011.

———. *Gerechte Sünder: Eine Untersuchung zu Martin Luthers "simul iustus et peccator."* Leipzig: Evangelische Verlagsanstalt, 2014.

Colish, Marcia. *Peter Lombard*. 2 vols. Leiden: Brill, 1994.

Corrigan, John. "Introduction: The Study of Religion and Emotion." In *The Oxford Handbook of Religion and Emotion*, edited by John Corrigan, 3–16. Oxford: Oxford University Press, 2008.

d'Ailly, Pierre. *Quaestiones super libros Sententiarum cum quibusdam in fine adjunctis*. 1490. Reprint, Frankfurt am Main: Minerva, 1968.

Davis, Natalie Zemon. *The Gift in Sixteenth-Century France*. Madison: University of Wisconsin Press, 2000.

Dieter, Theodor. "'Du mußt den Geist Haben': Anthropologie und Pneumatologie bei Luther." In *Der Heilige Geist: Ökumenische und reformatorische Untersuchungen*, edited by J. Heubach, 65–88. Erlangen: Martin-Luther, 1996.

———. *Der junge Luther und Aristotles: Eine historisch-systematische Untersuchung zum Verhältnis von Theologie und Philosophie*. Berlin: de Gruyter, 2001.

Dörnemann, Michael. *Krankheit und Heilung in der Theologie der frühen Kirchenväter*. Studien und Texte zu Antike und Christentum 20. Tübingen: Mohr/Siebeck, 2003.

Dragseth, Jennifer Hockenbery. *The Devil's Whore: Reason and Philosophy in the Lutheran Tradition*. Minneapolis: Fortress, 2011.

———. "Introduction: Augustine and Luther on Human Agency." In *On the Apocalyptic and Human Agency: Conversations with Augustine of Hippo and Martin Luther*, edited by Jennifer Hockenbery Dragseth and Kirsi Stjerna, 69–80. Newcastle upon Tyne, UK: Cambridge Scholars, 2014.

Ebeling, Gerhard. *Luther: An Introduction to His Thought*. Translated by R. A. Wilson. Philadelphia: Fortress, 1970.

———. *Luthers Seelsorge: Theologie in der Vielfalt der Lebenssituationen, an seinen Briefen Dargestellt*. Tübingen: Mohr/Siebeck, 1997.

———. "Luthers Wirklichkeitsverständnis." *Zeitschrift für Theologie und Kirche* 90 (1993) 409–24.

———. *Lutherstudien: Disputatio de homine*. 3 vols. Tübingen: Mohr/Siebeck, 1977–1989.

———. *Wort und Glaube*. Vol. 1. Tübingen: Mohr/Siebeck, 1975.

———. *Die Zehn Gebote in Predigten ausgelegt*. Tübingen: Mohr/Siebeck, 1973.

———. *Zum Gebet: Predigten über das Unser-Vater*. Tübingen: Mohr/Siebeck, 1963.

Edwards, Mark U. *Luther and the False Brethren*. Stanford: Stanford University Press, 1975.

Elert, Werner. "Eine theologische Fälschung zur Lehre vom tertius usus legis." *Zeitschrift für Religions-und Geistesgeschichte* 1.2 (1948) 168–70.

———. "Gesetz und Evangelium." In *Zwischen Gnade und Ungnade: Abwandlungen des Themas Gesetz und Evangelium*, by Elert Werner, 132–69. Munich: Evangelischer Preßeverband, 1948.

———. *The Structure of Lutheranism*. Translated by Walter A. Hansen. Foreword by Jaroslav Pelikan. Vol. 1 of *The Theology and Philosophy of Life of Lutheranism Especially in the Sixteenth and Seventeenth Centuries*. Saint Louis: Concordia, 1962.

Ernst, Wilhelm. *Gott und Mensch am Vorabend der Reformation: Eine Untersuchung zur Moralphilosophie und-Theologie bei Gabriel Biel*. Leipzig: St. Benno, 1972.

Etzelmüller, Gregor, and Annette Weissenrieder, eds. *Religion und Krankheit*. Darmstadt: Wissenschaftliche Buchgesellschaft, 2010.

Evans, G. R. *Bernard of Clairvaux*. Oxford: Oxford University Press, 2000.

———. *Law and Theology in the Middle Ages*. London: Routledge, 2002.

———. *The Mind of St. Bernard of Clairvaux*. Oxford: Clarendon, 1983.

BIBLIOGRAPHY

———. *The Roots of the Reformation: Tradition, Emergence and Rupture*. 2nd ed. Downers Grove, IL: IVP Academic, 2012.

Falcon, Andrea. "Aristotle on Causality." *Stanford Encyclopedia of Philosophy*, March 7, 2023. Edited by Edward N. Zalta and Uri Nodelman. https://plato.stanford.edu/entries/aristotle-causality.

Farthing, John. *Thomas Aquinas and Gabriel Biel: Interpretations of St. Thomas Aquinas in German Nominalism on the Eve of the Reformation*. Duke Monographs in Medieval and Renaissance Studies 9. Durham: Duke University Press, 1988.

Feckes, Carl. *Die Rechtfertigungslehre des Gabriel Biel und ihre Stellung innerhalb der nominalistischen Schule*. Münster: Aschendorffschen, 1925.

Fisher, Jeffrey. "Gerson's Mystical Theology: A New Profile of Its Evolution." In *A Companion to Jean Gerson*, edited by Brian Patrick McGuire, 205–48. Brill's Companions to the Christian Tradition. Leiden: Brill, 2006.

Flogaus, Reinhard. *Theosis bei Palamas und Luther: Ein Beitrag zum ökumenischen Gespräch*. Göttingen: Vandenhoeck & Ruprecht, 1997.

Gaebler, Mary. *The Courage of Faith: Martin Luther and the Theonomous Self*. Minneapolis: Fortress, 2013.

Garza, Randal Paul. *Understanding Plague: The Medical and Imaginative Texts of Medieval Spain*. New York: Lang, 2008.

"Gaslight." *APA Dictionary of Psychology*, November 15, 2023. https://dictionary.apa.org/gaslight.

Geerlings, Wilhelm. *Christus Exemplum: Studien zur Christologie und Christusverkündigung Augustins*. Mainz: Matthias-Grünewald, 1978.

Gerber, Chad. *The Spirit of Augustine's Early Theology: Contextualizing Augustine's Pneumatology*. Farnham: Ashgate, 2012.

Gilman, Ernest B. *Plague Writing in Early Modern England*. Chicago: University of Chicago Press, 2009.

Gottfried, Robert S. *The Black Death: Natural and Human Disaster in Medieval Europe*. London: Collier MacMillan, 1983.

Grane, Leif. *Contra Gabrielem: Luthers Auseinandersetzung mit Gabriel Biel in der Disputatio contra Scholasticam Theologiam*. Copenhagen: Gyldendal, 1962.

Haemig, Mary Jane. "Praying Amid Life's Perils: How Luther Used Biblical Examples to Teach Prayer." In *Encounters with Luther: New Directions for Critical Studies*, edited by Kirsi Stjerna and Brooks Schramm, 177–88. Louisville, KY: Westminster John Knox, 2016.

Hägglund, Bengt. "Luthers Anthropologie." In vol. 1 of *Leben und Werk Martin Luthers von 1526 bis 1546: Festgabe zu seinem 500. Geburtstag*, edited by Helmar Junghans, 63–76. Göttingen: Vandenhoeck & Ruprecht, 1983.

———. "Theologische und philosophische Anthropologie bei Luther." *Studia Theologica* 37 (1983) 101–24.

Hamm, Berndt. *The Early Luther: Stages in a Reformation Reorientation*. Translated by Martin Lohrmann. Grand Rapids: Eerdmans, 2014.

———. *Promissio, Pactum, Ordinatio: Freiheit und Selbstbindung Gottes in die scholastische Gnadenlehre*. Tübingen: Mohr/Siebeck, 1977.

———. "Pure Gabe ohne Gegengabe: die religions-geschichtliche Revolution der Reformation." *Jahrbuch für Biblische Theologie* 27 (2012) 241–76.

———. *The Reformation of Faith in the Context of Late Medieval Theology and Piety: Essays by Berndt Hamm*. Edited by Robert J. Bast. Leiden: Brill, 2004.

———. "Wie mystisch war der Glaube Luthers?" In *Gottes Nähe unmittelbar erfahren: Mystik im Mittelalter und bei Martin Luther*, edited by Berndt Hamm and Volker Leppin, 237–88. Tübingen: Mohr/Siebeck, 2007.

Harnack, Adolf von. *Medicinisches aus der ältesten Kirchengeschichte*. Leipzig: Hinrichs'sche, 1892.

Harned, David Baily. *Images for Self-Recognition: The Christian as Player, Sufferer and Vandal*. New York: Seabury, 1977.

Helmer, Christine. "Does Luther Have a 'Waxen Nose?' Historical and Philosophical Contextualizations of Luther." In *The Devil's Whore: Reason and Philosophy in the Lutheran Tradition*, edited by Jennifer Hockenbery Dragseth, 23–30. Minneapolis: Fortress, 2011.

———. *How Luther Became the Reformer*. Louisville: Westminster John Knox, 2019.

———. "Introduction." In *The Medieval Luther*, edited by Christine Helmer, 1–12. Tübingen: Mohr/Siebeck, 2020.

———. "Luther's Trinitarian Hermeneutic and the Old Testament." *Modern Theology* 18.1 (2002) 49–73.

———. *The Trinity and Martin Luther: A Study on the Relationship between Genre, Language and the Trinity in Luther's Works (1523–1546)*. Veröffentlichungen des Instituts für Europäische Geschichte Mainz: Abteilung abendländische Religionsgeschichte 174. Mainz: Philipp von Zabern, 1999.

Helmer, Christine, and Bo Kristian Holm, eds. *Lutherrenaissance: Past and Present*. Forschungen zur Kirchen- und Dogmengeschichte 106. Göttingen: Vandenhoeck & Ruprecht, 2014.

Helmrath, Johannes. "German *Reichstage* and the Crusade." In *Crusading in the Fifteenth Century: Message and Impact*, edited by Norman Housley, 53–69. New York: Palgrave MacMillan, 2004.

Heng, Geraldine. *The Invention of Race in the European Middle Ages*. Cambridge: Cambridge University Press, 2018.

Henry, Michael. *Incarnation: Une Philosophie de la Chair*. Paris: Seuil, 2000.

Herdt, Jennifer. "Virtue's Semblance: Erasmus and Luther on Pagan Virtue and the Christian Life." *Journal for the Society of Christian Ethics* 25.2 (2005) 137–62.

Herms, Eilert. "Opus Dei Gratiae: Cooperatio Dei et Hominum." *Lutherjahrbuch* 78 (2011) 61–136.

Herzog, Markwart. "Christus Medicus, Apothecarius, Samarituanus, Balneator: Motiv einer 'medizinisch-pharmazeutischen Soteriologie.'" *Geist und Leben: Zeitschrift für christliche Spiritualität* 67 (1994) 414–34.

Heschel, Susannah. *The Aryan Jesus: Christian Theologians and the Bible in Nazi Germany*. Princeton: Princeton University Press, 2008.

Hirvonen, Vesa. "William Ockham on Human Being." *Studia Theologica* 53 (1999) 40–49.

Holl, Karl. "Der Neubau der Sittlichkeit." In *Luther*, by Karl Holl, 155–287. Vol. 1 of *Gesammelte Aufsätze zur Kirchengeschichte*. Tübingen: Mohr/Siebeck, 1948.

———. "Was Verstand Luther unter Religion?" In *Luther*, by Karl Holl, 1–110. Vol. 1 of *Gesammelte Aufsätze zur Kirchengeschichte*. Tübingen: Mohr/Siebeck, 1948.

Holm, Bo. "Dynamic Tensions in the Social Imaginaries of the Lutheran Reformation." In *Lutheran Theology and the Shaping of Society: The Danish Monarchy as Example*, edited by Bo Holm and Nina Koefed, 85–106. Göttingen: Vandenhoeck & Ruprecht, 2018.

BIBLIOGRAPHY

———. *Gabe und Geben bei Luther: Das Verhältnis zwischen Reziprozität und reformatorischer Rechtfertigungslehre*. Berlin: de Gruyter, 2006.

———. "Rechtfertigung und Gabe: Ein Beitrag zur 'Resozialisierung' der Rechtfertigungslehre." *Ökumensiche Rundschau* 60.2 (2011) 178–90.

Honecker, Martin. "Christus medicus." *Kerygma und Dogma: Zeitschrift für theologische Forschung und kirchliche Lehre* 31.4 (1985) 307–23.

Hordern, Joshua. *Political Affections: Civic Participation and Moral Theology*. Oxford: Oxford University Press, 2013.

Housley, Norman. *Crusading and the Ottoman Threat, 1453–1505*. Oxford: Oxford University Press, 2012.

Hübner, Jorg. "Christus Medicus: Ein Symbol des Erlösungsgeschehens und ein Modell ärztlichen Handelns." *Kerygma Und Dogma: Zeitschrift für theologische Forschung und kirchliche Lehre* 31.4 (1985) 324–35.

Huovinen, Eero. "The Infusio-Gedanke als Problem der Lutherforschung." In *Caritas Dei: Beiträge zum Verständnis Luthers und der gegenwärtigen Ökumene*, edited by Oswald Bayer et al., 193–204. Helsinki: Luther-Agricola-Society, 1997.

Irwin, Terence. *From Socrates to the Reformation*. Vol. 1 of *The Development of Ethics: A Historical and Critical Study*. Oxford: Oxford University Press, 2007.

Iserloh, Erwin. "Gratia und Donum, Rechtfertigung und Heiligung nach Luthers Schrift 'Wider den Löwener Theologen Latomus' (1521)." *Catholica* 24.1 (1970) 67–83.

———. "Sacramentum et Exemplum: Ein augustinisches Thema lutherischer Theologie." In *Reformata Reformanda: Festgabe für Hubert Jedin zum 17. Juni 1965*, edited by Erwin Iserloh and Konrad Repgen, 247–64. Münster: Aschendorff, 1965.

Janz, Denis. *Luther and Late Medieval Thomism: A Study in Theological Anthropology*. Waterloo: Wilfrid Laurier University Press, 1983.

———. *Luther on Thomas Aquinas: The Angelic Doctor in the Thought of the Reformer*. Veröfftentlichungen des Instituts für Europäische Geschichte Mainz: Abteilung für abendländische Religionsgeschichte 140. Stuttgart: Franz Steiner Wiesbaden GMBH, 1989.

———. "A Reinterpretation of Gabriel Biel on Nature and Grace." *The Sixteenth-Century Journal* 8.1 (1977) 104–8.

Joest, Wilfried. *Gesetz und Freiheit: Das Problem des Tertius usus legis bei Luther und die neutestamentliche Parainese*. Göttingen: Vandenhoeck & Ruprecht, 1961.

———. *Ontologie der Person bei Luther*. Göttingen: Vandenhoeck & Ruprecht, 1967.

Jung, Martin H. *Frömmigkeit und Theologie bei Philipp Melanchthon*. Beiträge zur historischen Theologie 102. Tübingen: Mohr/Siebeck, 1998.

Jüngel, Eberhard. "Humanity in Correspondence to God." In *Theological Essays*, edited by J. B. Webster, 124–53. Edinburgh: T&T Clark, 1989.

Kang, Chi-Won. "Die Lectio Divina in der Evangelischen Kirche: Untersuchungen über die Rezeption und den Gebrauch der Lectio Divina in der lutherischen Kirche von der Reformation bis zum Pietismus." 한국기독교신학논총 72 (2010) 109–27.

Karant-Nunn, Susan. *The Reformation of Feeling: Shaping the Religious Emotions in Early Modern Germany*. Oxford: Oxford University Press, 2010.

Kärkkäinen, Pekka. "Interpretations of the Psychological Analogy from Aquinas to Biel." In *Trinitarian Theology in the Medieval West*, edited by Pekka Kärkkäinen, 256–79. Helsinki: Luther-Agricola-Society, 2008.

———. "Jodocus Trutfetter (c. 1460–1519) on Internal Senses." In *The Internal Senses in the Aristotelian Tradition*, edited by Seyed Mousavian and Jakob L. Fink, 69–81. Studies in the History of Philosophy of Mind 22. Cham, Switzerland: Springer, 2020.

———. "Luther's Theological Psychology and the Spirit." *Lutherjahrbuch* 85 (2018) 154–71.

———. *Luthers trinitarische Theologie des Heiligen Geistes*. Veröffentlichungen des Instituts für Europäische Geschichte Mainz: Abteilung für abendländische Religionsgeschichte 208. Mainz: Philipp von Zabern, 2005.

———. "Nominalist Psychology and the Limits of Canon Law in Late Medieval Erfurt." In *Lutheran Reformations and the Law*, edited by Virpi Mäkinen, 93–110. Studies in Medieval and Reformation Traditions. Leiden: Brill, 2006.

———. "Synderesis in Late Medieval Philosophy and the Wittenberg Reformers." *British Journal for the History of Philosophy* 20.5 (2012) 881–901.

———. "Theology, Philosophy, and Immortality of the Soul in the Late Via Moderna of Erfurt." *Vivarium* 43.2 (2005) 337–60.

Kawerau, Gustav. *Johann Agricola von Eisleben: Ein Beitrag zur Reformationsgeschichte*. Berlin: W. Hertz, 1881.

Kelsey, David. *Eccentric Existence: A Theological Anthropology*. 2 vols. Louisville, KY: Westminster John Knox, 2009.

Kent, Bonnie. "The Moral Life." In *The Cambridge Companion to Medieval Philosophy*, edited by A. S. McGrade, 231–53. Cambridge: Cambridge University Press, 2003.

Kieckhefer, Richard. "The Notion of Passivity in the Sermons of John Tauler." *Recherches de theologie ancienne et medievale* 48 (1981) 198–211.

Kim, Sun Young. *Luther on Faith and Love: Christ and the Law in the 1535 Galatians Commentary*. Minneapolis: Fortress, 2014.

Kirjavainen, Heikki. "Die Paradoxie des Simul-Prinzips." *Neue Zeitschrift für systematische Theologie und Religionsphilosophie* 28 (1986) 29–50.

Kitamori, Kazoh. *Theology of the Pain of God*. Eugene, OR: Wipf & Stock, 1965.

Kjeldgaard-Pedersen, Stefan. *Gesetz, Evangelium, und Busse: Theologiegeschichtliche Studien zum Verhältnis zwischen dem jungen Johann Agricola (Eisleben) und Martin Luther*. Leiden: Brill, 1983.

Kleffmann, Tom. *Die Erbsündenlehre in sprachtheologischem Horizont: Eine Interpretation Augustins, Luthers und Hamanns*. Beiträge zur Historischen Theologie 86. Tübingen: Mohr/Siebeck, 1994.

Koch, Ernst. "Johann Agricola neben Luther: Schülerschaft und theologische Eigenart." In *Lutheriana: Zum 500. Geburtstag Martin Luthers von den Mitarbeitern der Weimarer Ausgabe*, edited by Gerhard Hammer, 131–50. Cologne: Böhlau Verlag, 1984.

Kolb, Robert. "Gesetz und Evangelium." In *Das Luther-Lexikon*, edited by Volker Leppin and Gury Schneider-Ludorff, 252–53. Translated by Volker Leppin. Regensburg: Bückle & Böhm, 2014.

———. "Human Nature, the Fall, and the Will." In *T&T Clark Companion to Reformation Theology*, edited by David Whitford, 14–31. London: T&T Clark, 2012.

Kolb, Robert, and Timothy Wengert, eds. *The Book of Concord: The Confessions of the Evangelical Lutheran Church*. Translated by Charles Arand et al. Minneapolis: Fortress, 2000.

Korsgaarad, Christine. *The Constitution of Agency: Essays on Practical Reason and Moral Psychology*. Oxford: Oxford University Press, 2008.

Largier, Miklaus. "Medieval Mysticism." In *The Oxford Handbook of Religion and Emotion*, edited by John Corrigan, 364–79. Oxford: Oxford University Press, 2008.

Leppin, Volker. *Die fremde Reformation: Luthers mystische Wurzeln*. München: C. H. Beck, 2016.

BIBLIOGRAPHY

———. "Luther's Roots in Monastic-Mystical Piety." In *Oxford Handbook of Martin Luther's Theology*, edited by Robert Kolb et al., 49–61. Oxford: Oxford University Press, 2014.

———. *Martin Luther*. 2nd ed. Darmstadt: Wissenschaftliche Buchgesellschaft, 2006.

———. "Transformationen spätmittelalterlicher Mystik bei Luther." In *Gottes Nähe unmittelbar erfahren: Mystik im Mittelalter und bei Martin Luther*, edited by Volker Leppin and Berndt Hamm, 165–86. Tübingen: Mohr/Siebeck, 2007.

Leppin, Volker, and Gury Schneider-Ludorff, eds. *Das Luther-Lexikon*. Regensburg: Bückle und Böhm, 2014.

Lim, Hyeyoung, et al. "COVID-19 Pandemic and Anti-Asian Racism and Violence in the Twenty-First Century." *Race and Justice*, 13.1 (2023) 3–8.

Lindbeck, George. "Martin Luther and the Rabbinic Mind." In *Understanding the Rabbinic Mind: Essays on the Hermeneutic of Max Kadushin*, edited by Peter Ochs, 141–64. Atlanta: Scholars, 1990.

Lindberg, Carter. "Do Lutherans Shout Justification but Whisper Sanctification?" *Lutheran Quarterly* 13 (1999) 1–20.

Löhrer, Magnus. "Das augustinische Binom 'Sacramentum et Exemplum' und die Unterscheidung des christlichen bei G. Ebeling und E. Jüngel." In *Mysterium Christi: Symbolgegenwart und theologische Bedeutung: Festschrift für Basil Studer*, edited by Elmar Salmann, 377–403. Studia Anselmiana 116. Rome: Pontificio Ateneo S. Anselmo, 1995.

Lohse, Bernhard. "Luther als Disputator." In *Evangelium in der Geschichte: Studien zu Luther und der Reformation*, edited by Leif Grane et al., 250–64. Göttingen, Vandenhoeck & Ruprecht, 1988.

———. *Martin Luther's Theology: Its Historical and Systematic Development*. Translated by Roy Harrisville. Minneapolis: Fortress, 1999.

Lombard, Peter. *The Sentences*. Translated by Guilio Silano. 4 vols. Toronto: Pontifical Institute of Mediaeval Studies, 2007–2010.

Luhrmann, Tanya. *When God Talks Back: Understanding the American Evangelical Relationship with God*. New York: Vintage, 2012.

Lund, Norman. "Luther's 'Third Use of the Law' and Melanchthon's Tertius Usus Legis in the Antinomian Controversy with Agricola (1537–1540)." PhD diss., University of St. Michael's College, 1985.

Luther, Martin. *Martin Luthers Werke: Kritische Gesamtausgabe*. Edited by Karl Drescher et al. 73 vols. Weimar: Hermann Böhlau Nachfolger, 1883–2009.

Vol. 1. Edited by J. R. F. Knaake.
   Disputatio contra schalsticam theologiam (1517), 221–28.
   Disputatio pro declaration virtutis indulgentiarum (1517), 229–39.
   Disputatio Heidelbergae habita (1518), 353–74.
   Resolutiones disputationum de indulgentiarum virtute (1518), 522–629.

Vol. 2. Edited by J. R. F. Knaake.
   Sermo de duplici iustitia (1519), 143–53.
   Disputatio Johannis Eccii et Martini Lutheri Lipsiae habita (1519), 250–383.

Vol. 7. Edited by Paul Pietsch.
   Tractatus de libertate christiana (1520), 39–74.

Vol. 8. Edited by Gustav Kawerau.
   Rationis Latomianae confutatio (1521), 36–128.

Vol. 18. Edited by Karl Drescher.
: *De servo arbitrio* (1525), 551–787.
Vol. 30/1. Edited by Karl Drescher.
: *Deutsch Catechismus (Der Große Katechismus)* (1529), 123–238.
: *Der Kleine Katechismus* (1529), 239–425.
Vol. 30/2. Edited by Karl Drescher.
: *Vom Kriege wider die Türken* (1529), 81–148.
Vol. 38. Edited by Karl Drescher.
: *Eine einfältige Weise zu beten für einen guten Freund* (1535), 351–75.
Vol. 39/1. Edited by Karl Drescher.
: *Die Disputation de homine* (1536), 174–80.
: *Die Thesen gegen die Antinomer* (1537–1540), 334–58.
: *Die erste Disputation gegen die Antinomer. 18. Dezember 1537*, 359–417.
: *Die zweite Disputation gegen die Antinomer. 12. Januar 1538*, 418–85.
: *Die dritte Disputation gegen die Antinomer (Promotionsdisputation von Cyriakus Gerich?) 6. September 1538*, 486–584.
Vol. 39/2. Edited by Georg Bebermeyer.
: *Die Promotionsdisputation von Georg Major und Johannes Faber. 12. Dezember 1544*, 284–336.
Vol. 40/1. Edited by Karl Drescher.
: *In epistolam S. Pauli ad Galalas Commentarius ex praelectione D. Martini Luther 1531 collectus* (1535), 1–688.
Vol. 40/2. Edited by Karl Drescher.
: *In epistolam S. Pauli ad Galatas Commentarius 1531* (1535), 1–184.
Vol. 42. Edited by Karl Drescher.
: *Text der Genesisvorlesung* (1535–1538), 1–673.
Vol. 45. Edited by Georg Buchwald et al.
: *Eine Predigt über das Evangelium* (1537), 145–56.
: *Das XIV. und XV. Capital S. Johannis gepredigt und ausgelegt* (1537), 465–733.
Vol. 46. Edited by Georg Buchwald and Oskar Brenner.
: *Das XVI. Kapitel S. Johannis gepredigt und ausgelegt*, 1–113.
Vol. 50. Edited by Karl Drescher.
: *Nachwort zu Johann Agricolas Übersetzung davon: Etliche Briefe Johannis Huß aus dem Gefängnis zu Konstanz an die Böhmen geschrieben* (1537), 34–39.
: *Wider der Antinomer* (1539), 461–77.
: *Von den Konziliis und Kirchen* (1539), 488–653.
: *Luthers Randbemerkungen zu den Summarien des Agricola* (1539), 674–75.
Vol. 51. Edited by Karl Drescher.
: *Wider den Eisleben* (1540), 425–44.
: *Ein kurzer Trostzettel für die Christen, daß sie sich im Gebet nicht irren lassen* (1540), 454–57.
Vol. 56. Edited by Georg Bebermeyer.
: *Diui Pauli apostolic ad Romanos Epistola, Die Glossen, Die Scholien* (1515/1516), 3–528.

Madden, Thomas. *The New Concise History of the Crusades.* Lanham, MD: Rowman and Littlefield, 2006.

Mannermaa, Tuomo. *Christ Present in Faith: Luther's View of Justification.* Translated by Kirsi Stjerna. Minneapolis: Fortress, 2005.

BIBLIOGRAPHY

———. "Hat Luther eine trinitarische Ontologie?" In *Luther und Ontologie: Das Sein Christi im Glauben als strukturierendes Prinzip der Theologie Luthers*, edited by Anja Ghiselli et al., 9–28. Helsinki: Luther-Agricola-Gesellschaft, 1993.

Mattox, Mickey. "Warrior Saints: Warfare and Violence in Martin Luther's Readings of Some Old Testament Texts." In *Encounters with Luther: New Directions for Critical Studies*, edited by Kirsi Stjerna and Brooks Schramm, 42–58. Louisville, KY: Westminster John Knox, 2016.

Mau, Rudolf. "Luthers Stellung zu den Türken." In vol. 1 of *Leben und Werk Martin Luthers von 1526 bis 1546: Festgabe zu seinem 500. Geburtstag*, edited by Helmar Junghans, 647–62. Göttingen: Vandenhoeck & Ruprecht, 1983.

McCue, James. "'Simul iustus et peccator' in Augustine, Aquinas, and Luther: Toward Putting the Debate in Context." *Journal of the American Academy of Religion* 48.1 (1980) 81–96.

McDougall, Joy Ann. "A Trinitarian Grammar of Sin." In *The Theological Anthropology of David Kelsey: Responses to Eccentric Existence*, edited by Gene Outka, 107–26. Grand Rapids: Eerdmans, 2016.

McFarland, Ian. *Difference and Identity: A Theological Anthropology*. Cleveland: Pilgrim, 2001.

McGinn, Bernard. "Love, Knowledge, and Mystical Union in Western Christianity: Twelfth to Sixteenth Centuries." *Church History* 56.1 (1987) 7–24.

McLeod, Frederick G. *The Image of God in the Antiochene Tradition*. Washington, DC: Catholic University of America Press, 1999.

Mikoteit, Matthias. *Theologie und Gebet bei Luther: Untersuchungen zur Psalmenvorlesung 1532–1535*. Berlin: de Gruyter, 2004.

Miller, Gregory. "Fighting Like a Christian: The Ottoman Advance and the Development of Luther's Doctrine of Just War." In *Caritas et Reformatio: Essays on Church and Society in Honor of Carter Lindberg*, edited by David Whitford, 41–57. St. Louis: Concordia Academic, 2002.

———. *The Turks and Islam in Reformation Germany*. New York: Routledge, 2018.

Moeller, Bernd. "Tauler und Luther." In *La Mystique Rhénane*, edited by Jeanne Ancelet-Hustache, 157–68. Paris: Presses universitairs de France, 1963.

Moldenhauer, Aaron. "Analyzing the Verba Christi: Martin Luther, Ulrich Zwingli, and Gabriel Biel on the Power of Words." In *The Medieval Luther*, edited by Christine Helmer, 47–64. Tübingen: Mohr/Siebeck, 2020.

Muhlhan, Brett. *Being Shaped by Freedom: An Examination of Luther's Development of Christian Liberty, 1520–1525*. Eugene, OR: Pickwick, 2012.

Nilsson, Kjell Ove. *Simul: Das Miteinander von Göttlichem und Menschlichem in Luthers Theologie*. Forschungen zur Kirchen-und Dogmengeschichte 17. Göttingen: Vandenhoeck & Ruprecht, 1966.

Nirenberg, David. *Communities of Violence: Persecution of Minorities in the Middle Ages*. Princeton: Princeton University Press, 1996.

Nussbaum, Martha. *Political Emotions: Why Love Matters for Justice*. Cambridge, MA: Belknap, 2013.

Oakley, Francis. "Pierre d'Ailly and the Absolute Power of God: Another Note on the Theology of Nominalism." In *Natural Law, Conciliarism and Consent in the Late Middle Ages*, by Francis Oakley, 59–73. London: Variorum Reprints, 1984.

Oberman, Heiko. *The Harvest of Medieval Theology: Gabriel Biel and Late Medieval Nominalism*. Cambridge: Harvard University Press, 1963.

O'Donovan, Oliver. *The Problem of Self-Love in St. Augustine*. New Haven: Yale University Press, 1980.

Osborne, Thomas M., Jr. *Human Action in Thomas Aquinas, John Duns Scotus, and William of Ockham*. Washington, DC: Catholic University of America Press, 2014.

Otto, Rudolf. *Die Anschauung vom Heiligen Geist bei Luther: Eine systematisch-dogmatische Untersuchung*. Göttingen: Vandenhoeck und Ruprecht, 1898.

Ozment, Steven. *Homo Spiritualis: A Comparative Study of the Anthropology of Johannes Tauler, Jean Gerson, and Martin Luther (1509–1516) in the Context of Their Theological Thought*. Leiden: Brill, 1969.

Pannenberg, Wolfhart. *Anthropology in Theological Perspective*. Translated by Matthew J. O'Connell. Philadelphia: Westminster, 1985.

Pasnau, Robert. "Human Nature." In *The Cambridge Companion to Medieval Philosophy*, edited by A. S. McGrade, 208–30. Cambridge: Cambridge University Press, 2003.

Peters, Albrecht. *Commentary on Luther's Catechisms: Confession and Christian Life*. Translated by Thomas H. Trapp. Saint Louis: Concordia, 2013.

———. *Commentary on Luther's Catechisms: Lord's Prayer*. Edited by Charles Schaum. Translated by Daniel Thies. Saint Louis: Concordia, 2011.

———. *Commentary on Luther's Catechisms: Ten Commandments*. Edited by Charles Schaum. Translated by Holger K. Sonntag. Saint Louis: Concordia, 2009.

Peters, Greg. *The Story of Monasticism: Retrieving an Ancient Tradition for Contemporary Spirituality*. Grand Rapids: Baker Academic, 2015.

Pettegree, Andrew. *Brand Luther: 1517, Printing, and the Making of the Reformation*. New York: Penguin, 2015.

Peura, Simo. *Mehr als ein Mensch? Die Vergöttlichung als Thema der Theologie Martin Luthers von 1513 bis 1519*. Veröffentlichungen des Instituts für Europäische Geschichte Mainz 152. Mainz: Philipp von Zabern, 1994.

Pluta, Olaf. *Die philosophische Psychologie des Peter von Ailly*. Bochumer Studien zur Philosophie 6. Amsterdam: B. R. Grüner, 1987.

Porterfield, Amanda. *Healing in the History of Christianity*. Oxford: Oxford University Press, 2005.

Posset, Franz. *Pater Bernhardus: Martin Luther and Bernard of Clairvaux*. Kalamazoo, MI: Cistercian, 1999.

Prenter, Regin. *Spiritus Creator*. Translated by John Jensen. Eugene, OR: Wipf & Stock, 1953.

Probst, Christopher. *Demonizing the Jews: Luther and the Protestant Church in Nazi Germany*. Bloomington: Indiana University Press, 2012.

Raunio, Antti. "Divine and Natural Law in Luther and Melanchthon." In *Lutheran Reformations and the Law*, edited by Virpi Mäkinen, 21–61. Studies in Medieval and Reformation Traditions. Leiden: Brill, 2006.

———. "Die Gegenwart des Geistes im Christen bei Luther—Korreferat zu Theodor Dieter." In *Der Heilige Geist: Ökumenische und reformatorische Untersuchungen*, edited by Joachim Heubach, 89–104. Erlangen: Martin-Luther, 1996.

———. "Martin Luther and Love." *Oxford Research Encyclopedia of Religion*, October 26, 2016. https://doi.org/10.1093/acrefore/9780199340378.013.333.

———. "Natural Law and Faith: The Forgotten Foundations of Ethics in Luther's Theology." In *Union with Christ: The New Finnish Interpretation of Luther*, edited by Carl E. Braaten and Robert W. Jenson, 96–124. Grand Rapids: Eerdmans, 1998.

———. *Summe des christlichen Lebens: Die "Goldene Regel" als Gesetz der Liebe in der Theologie Martin Luthers von 1510-1527*. Helsinki: University of Helsinki, 1993.

Reinert, Jonathon. *Passionspredigt im 16. Jahrhundert: Das Leiden und Sterben Jesu Chrsti in den Postillen Martin Luthers, der Wittenberger Tradition und altgläubiger Prediger*. Spätmittelalter, Humanismus, Reformation 119. Tübingen: Mohr/Siebeck, 2020.

Risse, Guenter. *Mending Bodies, Saving Souls: A History of Hospitals*. Oxford: Oxford University Press, 1999.

Rogge, Joachim. "Gratia und donum in Luthers Schrift gegen Latomus." *Theologische Versuche* 2 (1970) 139–52.

———. *Johann Agricolas Lutherverständnis: Unter besonderer Berücksichtigung des Antinomismus*. Berlin: Evangelische Verlagsanstalt, 1960.

Rolnick, Philip A. *Person, Grace, and God*. Grand Rapids: Eerdmans, 2007.

Rosemann, Philipp. "Fraterna dilectio est Deus: Peter Lombard's Thesis on Charity as the Holy Spirit." In *Amor amicitiae: On the Love that Is Friendship; Essays in Medieval Thought and Beyond in Honor of the Rev. Professor James McEvoy*, edited by Thomas A. F. Kelly and Philipp Rosemann, 409–36. Leuven: Peeters, 2004.

Rummel, Erika, ed. *The Erasmus Reader*. Toronto: University of Toronto Press, 1990.

Saarinen, Risto. "Einige Themen der spätmittelalterlichen Ethik bei Luther." *Kerygma und Dogma: Zeitschrift für theologische Forschung und kirchliche Lehre* 30 (1984) 284–97.

———. "Ethics in Luther's Theology: The Three Orders." In *Moral Philosophy on the Threshold of Modernity*, edited by Jill Kraye and Risto Saarinen, 195–215. Texts and Studies in the History of Philosophy 57. Dortrecht: Springer, 2005.

———. *God and the Gift: An Ecumenical Theology of Giving*. Collegeville, MN: Liturgical, 2005.

———. *Gottes wirken auf uns: Die transzendentale Deutung des Gegenwart-Christi-Motivs in der Lutherforschung*. Veröfftentlichungen des Instituts für Europäische Geschichte Mainz: Abteilung Religionsgeschichte 137. Stuttgart: Franz Steiner Verlag Wiesbaden GMBH, 1989.

———. "Gunst und Gabe. Melanchthon, Luther und die Existentialle Anwendung von Senecas 'Über Die Wohltaten.'" In *"Kein Anlass zur Verwerfung": Studien zur Hermeneutik des ökumenischen Gesprächs: Festschrift für Otto Hermann Pesch*, edited by Johannes Brosseder and Markus Wriedt, 184–97. Frankfurt am Main: Verlag Otto Lembeck, 2007.

———. "Ipsa Dilectio Deus Est. Zur Wirkungsgeschichte von 1. Sent. Dist. 17 des Petrus Lombarus bei Martin Luther." In *Thesaurus Lutheri*, edited by Tuomo Mannermaa, 185–204. Helsinki: Luther-Agricola-Society, 1987.

———. "Presence of God in Luther's Theology." *Lutheran Quarterly* 3 (1994) 3–13.

———. *Weakness of the Will in Medieval Thought: From Augustine to Buridan*. Leiden: Brill, 1994.

———. *Weakness of Will in Renaissance and Reformation Thought*. Oxford: Oxford University Press, 2011.

Schmidt, Kurt Dietrich. "Christus der Heiland der Germanen." In *Gesammelte Aufsätze*, edited by Manfred Jacobs, 9–23. Göttingen: Vandenhoeck & Ruprecht, 1967.

———. "Luther lehrt Beten." *Luther* 34 (1963) 31–41.

———. "Luthers Lehre vom Heiligen Geist." In *Gesammelte Aufsätze*, edited by Manfred Jacobs, 111–27. Göttingen: Vandenhoeck & Ruprecht, 1967.

Schubert, Anselm. "Libertas Disputandi: Luther und die Leipziger Disputation als akademisches Streitgespräch." *Zeitschrift für Theologie und Kirche* 105.4 (2008) 411–42.

Schulken, Christian. *Lex efficax: Studien zur Sprachwerdung des Gesetzes bei Luther im Anschluß an die Disputationen gegen die Antinomer*. Tübingen: Mohr/Siebeck, 2005.

Schwartz, Reinhard. "Die Umformung des religiösen Prinzips der Gottesliebe in der frühen Reformation: Din Beitrag zum Verständnis von Luthers Schrift 'Von der Freiheit eines Christenmenschen.'" In *Die frühe Reformation in Deutschland als Umbruch: Wissenschaftliches Symposium des Vereins für Reformationsgeschichte 1996*, edited by Bernd Moeller, 128–48. Gütersloh: Gütersloh Verlagshaus, 1998.

Schweiker, William. "Divine Command Ethics and the Otherness of God." In *The Otherness of God*, edited by Orrin Summerell, 246–65. Charlottesville: University of Virginia Press, 1998.

———. "Moral Inwardness Reconsidered." In *The Depth of the Human Person: A Multidisciplinary Approach*, edited by Michael Welker, 351–69. Grand Rapids: Eerdmans, 2014.

Seils, Martin. "Gabe und Geschenk: Eine Zugabe." In *Denkraum Katechismus: Festgabe für Oswald Bayer zum 70. Geburtstag*, edited by Johannes von Lüpke and Edgar Thaidigsmann, 87–108. Tübingen: Mohr/Siebeck, 2009.

Silcock, Jeffrey. "Introduction." In vol. 73 of *Luther's Works*, edited by Christopher Boyd Brown, 3–43. St. Louis: Concordia, 2020.

———. "Law and Gospel in Luther's Antinomian Disputation with Special Reference to Faith's Use of the Law." PhD diss., Concordia Seminary, St. Louis, 1995.

———. "Luther and the Third Use of the Law, with Special Reference to His Great Galatians Commentary." MA thesis, Concordia Seminary, Saint Louis, 1993.

———. "Luther on the Holy Spirit and His Use of God's Word." In *The Oxford Handbook to Martin Luther's Theology*, edited by Robert Kolb et al., 294–309. Oxford: Oxford University Press, 2014.

Simpson, Gary M. "'Putting On the Neighbor': The Ciceronian Impulse in Luther's Christian Approach to Practical Reason." In *The Devil's Whore: Reason and Philosophy in the Lutheran Tradition*, edited by Jennifer Hockenbery Dragseth, 31–39. Minneapolis: Fortress, 2011.

Singer, Irving. *The Nature of Love: Plato to Luther*. Cambridge, MA: MIT Press, 1966.

Skinner, Quentin. *The Foundations of Modern Political Thought*. 2 vols. Cambridge: Cambridge University Press, 1978.

Slenczka, Notger. "Luther's Anthropology." In *The Oxford Handbook of Martin Luther's Theology*, edited by Robert Kolb et al., 212–32. Oxford: Oxford University Press, 2014.

Slotemaker, John T. "Reading Augustine in the Fourteenth Century: Gregory of Rimini and Pierre d'Ailly on the Imago Trinitatis." *Studia Patristica* 69 (2013) 345–58.

Smits, Lieke. "Practice, Process, and Performance: Shaping a Devotional Habitus in the Margins of Bernard of Clairvaux's Sermons on the Song of Songs." *Journal of Medieval Religious Cultures* 47.1 (2021) 1–20.

Stanciu, Diana. "Accomplishing One's Essence: The Role of Meditation in the Theology of Gabriel Biel." In *Meditatio—Refashioning the Self: Theory and Practice in Late Medieval and Early Modern Intellectual Culture*, edited by Karl A. E. Enenkel and Walter Melion, 127–52. Leiden: Brill, 2011.

Stegmann, Andreas. *Luthers Auffasung vom christlichen Leben*. Beiträge zur historischen Theologie 175. Tübingen: Mohr/Siebeck, 2014.

Steiger, Johann Anselm. *Fünf Zentralthemen der Theologie Luthers und seiner Erben: Communicatio-Imago-Figura-Maria-Exempla*. Leiden: Brill, 2002.

———. *Medizinische Theologie: Christus Medicus und Theologia Medicinalis bei Martin Luther und im Luthertum der Barockzeit*. Studies in the History of Christian Traditions 121. Leiden: Brill, 2005.

Stjerna, Kirsi, and Brooks Schramm, eds. *Martin Luther, the Bible, and the Jewish People*. Minneapolis: Fortress, 2012.

Stjerna, Kirsi, and Deanna Thompson, eds. *On the Apocalyptic and Human Agency: Conversations with Augustine of Hippo and Martin Luther*. Cambridge: Cambridge University Press, 2014.

Stolina, Ralf. "Gebet-Meditation-Anfechtung: Wegmarken einer theologia experimentalis." *Zeitschrift für Theologie und Kirche* 98.1 (2001) 81–100.

Stolt, Birgit. "'Herzlich lieb habe ich dich, Herr, meine Stärke' (Ps. 18,2)." In *Caritas Dei: Beiträge zum Verständnis Luthers und der gegenwärtigen Ökumene*, edited by Oswald Bayer et al., 405–21. Helsinki: Luther-Agricola-Society, 1997.

———. *"Laßt uns fröhlich springen!": Gefühlswelt und Gefühlsnavigierung in Luthers Reformationsarbeit: eine kognitive Emotionalitätsanalyse auf philologischer Basis*. Studium Litterarum: Studien und Texte zur deutschen Literaturgeschichte 21. Berlin: Weidler Buchverlag, 2012.

———. "Luther's Faith of 'the Heart': Experience, Emotion, and Reason." In *The Global Luther: A Theologian for Modern Times*, edited by Christine Helmer, 131–50. Minneapolis: Fortress, 2009.

———. *Martin Luthers Rhetorik des Herzens*. Tübingen: Mohr/Siebeck, 2000.

———. *Wortkampf: Frühneuhochdeutsche Beispiele zur rhetorischen Praxis*. Frankfurt am Main: Athenäum Verlag, 1974.

Stopa, Sasja Emilie Mathiasen. "Soli Deo honor et gloria—the Concepts of Honour and Glory in the Theology of the Young Martin Luther." In *Anthropological Reformations—Anthropology in the Era of Reformation*, edited by Anne Eusterschulte and Hannah Wälzholz, 229–44. Göttingen: Vandenhoeck & Ruprecht, 2015.

———. *Soli Deo honor et gloria: Honour and Glory in the Theology of Martin Luther*. Zürich: LIT, 2021.

Talbot, Mark R. "Learning from the Ruined Image: Moral Anthropology after the Fall." In *Personal Identity in Theological Perspective*, edited by Richard Lints et al., 159–77. Grand Rapids: Eerdmans, 2006.

Tauler, Johannes. *Die Predigten Taulers aus der Engelberger und der Freiburger Handschrift sowie aus Schmidts Abschriften der ehemaligen Straßburger Handschriften*. Edited by Ferdinand Vetter. Berlin: Weidmannsche Buchhandlung, 1910.

Taylor, Charles. *A Secular Age*. Cambridge, MA: Belknap, 2007.

———. *Sources of the Self: The Making of the Modern Identity*. Cambridge: Harvard University Press, 1989.

Thiselton, Anthony C. *The Holy Spirit: In Biblical Teaching, through the Centuries, and Today*. Grand Rapids: Eerdmans, 2013.

———. "The Image and the Likeness of God." In *The Emergence of Personhood: A Quantum Leap?*, edited by Malcolm Jeeves, 184–201. Grand Rapids: Eerdmans, 2015.

Tietz, Christiane. *Freiheit zu sich selbst: Entfaltung eines christlichen Begriffs von Selbstannahme*. Forschungen zur systematischen und ökumenischen Theologie 111. Göttingen: Vandenhoeck & Ruprecht, 2005.

Totten, Mark. "Luther on Unio Cum Christo: Towards Model for Integrating Faith and Ethics." *Journal of Religious Ethics* 31.3 (2003) 443–62.

Trelstad, Marit. "Charity Terror Begins at Home: Luther and the 'Terrifying and Killing' Law." In *Lutherrenaissance: Past and Present*, edited by Christine Helmer and Bo Holm, 209–23. Göttingen: Vandenhoeck & Ruprecht, 2014.

Työrinoja, Reijo. "Opus Theologicum: Luther and Medieval Theories of Action." *Neue Zeitschrift für systematische Theologie und Religionsphilosophie* 44 (2002) 119–53.

Vind, Anna. "The Human Being According to Luther." In *Anthropological Reformations: Anthropology in the Era of Reformation*, edited by Anne Eusterschulte and Hannah Wälzholz, 69–86. Refo500 Academic Studies 28. Göttingen: Vandenhoeck & Ruprecht, 2015.

Wannenwetsch, Bernd. "A Love Formed by Faith: Relating Theological Virtues in Augustine and Luther." In *The Authority of the Gospel: Explorations in Moral and Political Theology in Honor of Oliver O'Donovan*, edited by Robert Song and Brent Waters, 1–32. Grand Rapids: Eerdmans, 2015.

———. "Luther's Moral Theology." In *Cambridge Companion to Martin Luther*, edited by Donald McKim, 120–35. Cambridge: Cambridge University Press, 2003.

Wawrykow, Joseph. *God's Grace, Human Action: "Merit" in the Theology of Thomas Aquinas*. Notre Dame, IN: University of Notre Dame Press, 1996.

———. "The Sacraments in Thirteenth-Century Theology." In *The Oxford Handbook of Sacramental Theology*, edited by Hans Boersma, 218–34. Translated by Matthew Levering. Oxford Handbooks Online. Oxford: Oxford University Press, 2015.

Weinrich, William. "*Homo theologicus*: Aspects of a Lutheran Doctrine of Man." In *Personal Identity in Theological Perspective*, edited by Richard Lints et al., 29–44. Grand Rapids: Eerdmans, 2006.

Welker, Michael. "Introduction." In *The Depth of the Human Person: A Multidisciplinary Approach*, edited by Michael Welker, 1–12. Grand Rapids: Eerdmans, 2014.

Wengert, Timothy. "'Fear and Love' in the Ten Commandments." *Concordia Journal* 21 (1995) 14–27.

———. *Human Freedom, Christian Righteousness: Philip Melanchthon's Exegetical Dispute with Erasmus of Rotterdam*. Oxford: Oxford University Press, 1998.

———. *Law and Gospel: Philip Melanchthon's Debate with John Agricola of Eisleben Over Poenitentia*. Texts and Studies in Reformation and Post-Reformation Thought. Grand Rapids: Baker, 1997.

———. "[The 95 Theses or] Disputation for Clarifying the Power of Indulgences." In vol. 1 of *The Annotated Luther: The Roots of Reform*, edited by Timothy Wengert, 13–46. Minneapolis: Fortress, 2015.

White, Graham. *Luther as Nominalist: A Study of the Logical Methods Used in Martin Luther's Disputations in the Light of Their Medieval Background*. Schriften der Luther-Agricola-Gesellschaft 30. Helsinki: Luther-Agricola-Society, 1994.

Whiting, Michael S. *Luther in English: The Influence of His Theology of Law and Gospel on Early English Evangelicals (1525–35)*. Eugene, OR: Pickwick, 2010.

Wicks, Jared. "Catholic Encounters with Martin Luther." In *Luther Refracted: The Reformer's Ecumenical Legacy*, edited by Piotr J. Malysz and Derek R. Nelsen, 1–20. Minneapolis: Fortress, 2015.

BIBLIOGRAPHY

———. "Living and Praying as *Simul Iustus et Peccator*: A Chapter in Luther's Spiritual Teaching." *Gregorianum* 70 (1989) 521–48.

———. *Luther's Reform: Studies on Conversion and the Church*. Mainz: Philipp von Zabern, 1992.

Wieneke, Josef. *Luther und Petrus Lombardus: Martin Luthers Notizen anlässlich seine Vorlesung über die Sentenzen des Petrus Lombardus, Erfurt 1509/11*. Theologische Reihe 71. St. Ottillien: EOS, 1994.

Wingren, Gustaf. *Luther on Vocation*. Translated by Carl C. Rasmussen. Philadelphia: Muhlenberg, 1957.

Witte, John, Jr. *Law and Protestantism: The Legal Teachings of the Lutheran Reformation*. Cambridge: Cambridge University Press, 2002.

Wrede, Gösta. *Unio Mystica: Probleme der Erfahrung bei Johannes Tauler*. Stockholm: Almqvist & Wiksell International, 1974.

Yeago, David. "Gnosticism, Antinomianism, and Reformation Theology: Reflections on the Costs of a Construal." *Pro Ecclesia* 2.1 (1993) 37–49.

Zimmerling, Peter. "Einleitung." In *Wie man beten soll, für Meister Peter den Barbier*, edited by Ulrich Köpf and Peter Zimmerling, 9–36. Göttingen: Vandenhoeck & Ruprecht, 2011.

Zumkeller, Adolar. *Erbsünde, Gnade, Rechtfertigung und Verdienst nach der Lehre der Erfurter Augustinertheologen des Spätmittelalters*. Würzburg: Augustinus-Verlag, 1984.

Zur Mühlen, Karl-Heinz. *Nos extra nos: Luthers Theologie zwischen Mystik und Scholastik*. Tübingen: Mohr/Siebeck, 1972.

Index

absolution, 34, 35n18, 63, 63n82, 65
Adams, Marilyn McCord, 192
admonition, 26-27, 84, 88n184, 89-91,
　95, 97-98, 100-101, 100n1,
　110-15, 120, 130, 133-34, 136,
　143-47, 148, 164, 168, 169, 179-
　80, 188-90
affection, 3, 13, 28-29, 31-33, 94, 103,
　109-16, 119, 124, 130, 134-36,
　140, 142-43, 145-47, 152, 159-
　60, 162-63, 165-67, 170, 172,
　177, 184, 190-91, 194
Agricola, Johann, 4-5, 18, 22-23, 26-27,
　30, 37-44, 47, 49, 55-59, 56n46,
　56n49, 56n52, 57n54, 57n56,
　57n58, 58n64, 62, 66n93, 66n94,
　67n98, 69n113, 7374, 78, 81, 85,
　89, 92, 94-99, 110, 117n60, 122,
　127, 145, 156, 167, 173, 187-88,
　191
Althaus, Paul, 9-10, 10n31, 15, 15n58,
Anderas, Phil, 18, 61n69, 93n211,
　94n219, 101n3, 103n6, 114n49,
　115n53, 118n65, 131n110,
　164n63, 191-92
animo, 92
anfechtung. See temptation
affection, 3, 13, 28-29, 31-33, 94, 103,
　109-16, 119, 124, 130, 134-36,
　140, 142-43, 145-47, 152, 159-
　60, 162-63, 165-67, 170, 172,
　177, 184, 190-91, 194

anthropology, theological, 2, 5, 10-11,
　16, 18, 25, 29, 105, 148, 150, 160,
　163, 171, 173, 184-85, 187-88,
　192-94
antinomian, 4, 22, 25, 38-42, 47-48, 50,
　56-59, 80, 94, 96-97, 102, 122,
　141, 143, 156-57, 159-60, 178,
　187, 191
Aquinas, Thomas, 31, 92n206, 108n34,
　162n57
Aristotle, 120-22, 131, 161-62, 166
Aristotelian causality, 27-28, 37, 54n40,
　57, 65-66, 78-80, 86, 88, 93,
　96-99, 105, 107, 121-22, 138,
　148, 149n3, 158, 161-63, 170n90,
　172, 184-85, 190-91
armament, spiritual, 174, 176, 180
attrition, 64-65, 92, 151
Augustine of Hippo, 20, 69-71, 74,
　76n139, 104, 127, 131n110, 152,
　154, 161-62

battle, spiritual, 29, 38, 84, 90, 121, 140,
　156, 160, 174-83, 185, 191
Bayer, Oswald, 16n60, 35n18, 52n27,
　102n4, 119n70, 129n104,
　133n118, 139n151
Bernard of Clairvaux, 128, 175-76
Biel, Gabriel, 33-36, 64-65, 77-78,
　92-94, 102-3, 108n34, 117-18,
　117n60, 131n110, 141, 151-52
body and soul relation, 1-3, 9, 64, 69-71,
　104-5, 149n3, 157, 162, 179, 185

INDEX

Catechism
  Large, 21, 24
  Small, 131, 136
Christ
  after, 23, 72, 75–78, 83, 148, 189
  as gift, 35, 51, 69–74, 84–86, 94n219, 95, 158n41, 189–90
  as example, 69–73, 76, 84–85, 89–91, 98, 123n83, 127–29, 137, 140, 169, 170
  as physician, 101, 104–8, 105n14
  as sacrament, 69–71
  before, 26, 75–82, 85–86, 92, 96–97, 102, 148, 189
  as teacher of the law, 72, 72n129, 83
  under, 26, 75, 77–78, 80–87, 89–91, 93–97, 100, 102, 104, 108–9, 111, 116, 123, 125–26, 134, 138–39, 141, 148, 168, 180, 189
Christian
  militant, 150, 173–74, 177–78, 180, 182, 184, 191
  soldier, 29, 141, 173–83, 185
  youth narrative, 90, 93, 101, 110, 112–13, 115, 120, 123, 133, 135, 138, 142–44, 147, 160, 166, 168–69, 173–74, 180–81, 183
Christology, 19, 108, 149n1, 194
Christus medicus, 104–6, 109, 160n47
  Diagnosis of, 107
complacency, 4, 138–39
conscience, 6–9, 13, 40n37, 41, 51, 52n27, 63–64, 66, 69, 69n113, 81n154, 88, 99, 157, 180
concupiscence, 103, 138, 152, 154–55, 159, 166, 174
confession, 63–65, 128–29, 132, 134–35, 150n4
contrition, 63–66, 92n206, 151
controversy, 111, 152
  Antinomian, 4, 23, 26, 30, 38–39, 41, 43, 47–48, 56, 69, 110, 114, 128, 167, 187–88
  Cordatus, 37–38, 49, 59
cooperatio, 114n49, 115, 118n65, 126, 172, 185

coram relations, 12–13, 149n3, 150n4, 153
Crusades, 29, 161, 175–77

D'Ailly, Peter, 32–34, 162–63
decalogue, 33, 40, 60, 72, 91, 134
decision-making, moral, 142, 144, 146, 174, 190
delight in law, 93, 170
despair, 4, 7, 34, 75, 80, 88, 97, 107, 138, 155, 166, 173, 177–81
devil, 71, 80, 136–37, 140, 165, 174–75, 177n121, 178, 180–81
disease, 101, 104, 106, 107, 108, 152
disputatio genre, 19–20
divine command, 7, 32, 35, 126–27, 129, 133–34, 145, 147, 162n57
dominical injunction, 126
donum et exemplum Christi. See Christ

Ebeling, Gerhard, 11–16, 15n47, 19–20, 49, 87n183, 102n4, 121n77, 148–49, 191–92
Elert, Werner, 8–9, 11–16, 45n1, 87n183, 191
emotions, 20–21, 27, 46, 64, 66–68, 110, 112, 114–16, 130, 146, 188, 193–94
Erasmus of Rotterdam, 111, 176n110
exhortation, 26–27, 84, 87n183, 89–91, 95, 97–98, 100–101, 110–14, 116, 130, 136, 143, 161, 179–80, 188, 190

faith, 2, 7–9, 11, 13, 16–18, 24, 35, 37, 45–46, 51, 54–55, 61–62, 67–68, 70, 72, 77–79, 81–82, 84–86, 89, 92–95, 97–98, 108–9, 112, 121, 135, 138, 149, 155, 158–60, 170, 172, 174, 176–79, 181–83, 192, 193
facere quod in se est, 33, 64, 151
flesh, 83–84, 88–91, 110, 112–14, 118–19, 122, 136–37, 140, 142–43, 145, 152–60, 165–72, 174, 177–92, 188

INDEX

gift, 20, 51, 85–86, 92, 95, 155, 159
  of Christ, 26, 35, 51, 54, 61, 69, 70–73, 84–85, 87, 95–96, 98, 188, 189
  of love, 17, 41–42
  of Spirit, 42, 51–52, 61–62, 77, 86, 92–97, 99, 111, 114, 117, 123, 139, 141, 160, 168, 172, 186, 188, 190
Gerson, Jean, 13–131, 142
grace, 6, 13, 18, 25, 30–31, 33–37, 64–65, 67, 75–77, 83, 92, 109–11, 117–18, 141, 147–49, 152, 157, 159, 164, 171, 181, 187
  cooperating (*cooperans*), 31, 93n211, 115n53
  elevating (*elevans*), 25, 36, 92, 115, 130, 140–41, 169, 170n90, 187, 191, 193
  operating (*operans*), 31
  healing (*sanans*), 36, 118n65, 119n70, 160n47, 164n63, 164

hatred, 32, 67, 174
  of God, 32, 50, 138, 166, 173, 177, 179
  of sin, 64, 67, 91–92, 95, 113, 135, 138, 166, 170, 173
healing, 101, 104, 106–9, 118n65, 141, 152
heart, 7, 28, 36, 51, 66–68, 73, 79, 90–91, 3, 110, 115, 120, 123, 132–33, 135, 139, 141–43, 155, 163, 167, 173, 181, 194
hospital, 105–6

imputation, 27, 51, 59, 70, 81–82, 86, 98, 118–24, 146, 155, 189
indwelling, 5, 17, 98, 123, 139, 146, 183
intellect, 1–2, 5, 13, 15, 18, 24, 28, 31, 34, 36, 49, 68, 73, 90, 109, 111, 115–16, 124, 131, 142–43, 145–47, 151–53, 161–65, 167–72, 174, 181, 183–85, 190–91, 194
intention, 4, 12, 27, 47, 63–65, 67–69, 73–74, 84–85, 91–99, 112–13, 118, 135, 139, 143–46, 188, 190

law
  abrogation of, 39, 189
  accusing, 16, 26–27, 51n17, 53–55, 58–60, 66, 69–70, 73–75, 78–79, 81n154, 83–86, 87n183, 90–91, 97–98, 100–101, 104, 107, 109, 111, 116, 118–19, 124–25, 147, 168, 177, 188–89
  admonishing, 91, 95, 97–98, 190
  as enjoyable, 94, 123
  as exhortation, 84, 87n183, 88n184, 89–91, 95, 101, 110, 112–14, 116, 130, 136, 169, 180
  as terror, 8, 69–70, 75, 78–80, 88, 92, 132
  demands of, 35, 45–56, 50–52, 56, 67, 70, 73, 75, 81–82, 86, 125, 127, 129
  fulfillment of, 35, 73, 76, 81, 86, 89–90, 94–95, 98, 100–104, 109, 111, 116, 123–26, 131n112, 144–47, 171, 189, 192
  salutary, 54n39, 87–90, 167–72
  uses of, 14–16, 18, 26, 29, 35, 38, 40–41, 43, 44n52, 47, 49–50, 51n17, 52n27, 56–57, 59, 68n110, 69n113, 84n170, 85, 86n181, 87–89, 91, 98–99, 101, 141n158, 188–89, 192
law after gospel, 5, 14, 43–44, 99, 129
law and gospel, 13–15, 21–24, 26, 35, 37–42, 44–50, 52–56, 58–59, 62–63, 65–66, 69, 71, 73,76, 79, 80, 89–91, 96–98, 116, 146, 148, 154, 187–89
lectio divina, 127–29, 132
Lombard, Peter, 16–17, 31, 36, 41, 52n25, 64, 76–77, 97, 103–4, 151
love, 2–3, 5, 17, 33, 41–42, 44, 51, 65, 112, 130, 132–33, 142, 151, 161–62, 170, 174, 182
  as sin, 2, 33–34, 64, 78, 110–11
  of God, 2, 28, 31–34, 41, 50–51, 64, 67–68, 73, 77–78, 91–96, 98, 103, 111, 113–14, 117, 151–52, 160, 165, 170, 172
  of law, 170, 190
  of neighbor, 41, 54n41, 73, 166, 170

INDEX

Melanchthon, Philip, 14–16, 37, 39–40, 43, 47, 56, 59, 65n91, 87
mimesis, 71–72
merit, 2–3, 6, 30, 33–35, 44, 76n138, 77, 100, 128n100, 153, 157, 164
Muslims, 103, 161n53
mysticism, 3, 17, 20, 27, 35, 127n95, 130–31, 135–37, 145, 190

Nominalism, 19–20, 28, 30, 32–35, 44, 92–93, 102, 117n60, 141, 151–52, 156–57, 160–62, 164–65

Obedience, 2, 9–10, 33, 37, 43, 59, 67, 69, 71n125, 72–73, 93–94, 99–100, 113, 115, 125, 127, 145, 176
Ockham, William, 31–34, 52n25, 77, 113, 117n60, 120, 162–63, 165, 172, 190
oratio. *See* prayer
order
    law then gospel, 13–14, 26–27, 38, 48, 60, 66, 74–76, 78, 134
    faith then works, 67–68, 71
ordo salutis, 74–79, 85, 87, 89, 84, 102, 139n147, 141, 148
Ottoman empire, 29, 176–76

peccatum, 76n139, 102, 102n4, 104, 122n81, 137n132, 165n71, 181
Pelagian, 92, 94, 117n60, 151–52, 156
penance, 35n18, 64, 64n84, 64n87, 99
penitence, 4, 22, 37n24, 40, 62, 63–67, 63n80, 64n84, 65n92, 73–74, 77, 96, 98, 118n65, 139, 160n49
plague, 105–7
pneumatology, 4, 17, 22–23, 26, 41, 43, 44, 59, 61, 95–96, 149, 185–86, 188
poenitentia. *See* penitence
prayer, 21, 24, 27–28, 64, 89, 91, 101, 110, 116, 125–37, 139–47, 150, 175, 177n114, 190, 194

reason, 3–4, 6–7, 11, 21, 31–33, 40, 93n209, 103, 109, 111–12, 116, 130, 146–47, 162–65, 172, 184–85, 193
regeneration, 17, 76
righteousness, 1–2, 5–7, 23, 27–28, 42, 51, 54, 62, 71, 74–75, 81n154, 87, 90, 101, 118, 121, 138, 146, 148, 154–55, 157, 161, 167–69, 171–74, 181, 184–85, 188–89, 191
    formal, 23, 28–29, 87n183, 89, 117, 120–26, 137–39, 145, 150, 154–56, 158–61, 167, 171, 178, 181–85, 190–92
    of Christ, 1, 9, 35–36, 42, 51–52, 57, 73, 75, 81–82, 86, 89, 97–98, 100, 124, 146, 150, 153, 155–56, 160, 181, 183, 189
    of God, 38, 54n39, 58
    of Law, 51, 89, 100, 118, 169
    relative, 23, 27–29, 122, 124, 146, 150–51, 158, 160, 177, 182, 189

sanctification, 4–5, 13, 17, 25, 35, 44, 54n41, 87, 89, 96, 100, 121, 123–25, 132–33, 138, 141, 145, 146–47, 150, 192–93
simul iustus et peccator, 10, 18, 28, 99, 128n100, 147, 149–58, 160–61, 171–73, 177, 177n119, 182, 184, 190–91
    triumphant part, 173, 177–78, 180, 182, 184, 191
Sin
    actual, 23, 27, 89, 101–11, 116–19, 122, 124–25, 137–40, 144–46, 154, 159, 189–90
    cessation of, 114
    consent to, 94, 103, 113–16, 139, 162–63, 166–67, 170–72, 174, 177, 180–81, 184–85
    conviction of, 7, 42, 54, 57–62, 168–69, 180, 188–89
    ember of, 104, 109–10, 112, 116–17, 119, 138, 145, 152, 157–60, 166–67, 171, 177, 184
    inclination to, 27, 29, 88n184, 100–101, 103–6, 109–17, 119–20,

INDEX

124–26, 134, 137–41, 146, 158–61, 166–69, 171–72, 174, 180–81, 183–84, 189–91
original, 2–3, 6, 23, 27, 31, 76, 101–9, 111, 115–16, 118–20, 124–25, 146, 152–53, 157, 159, 165, 189, 193
purgation of, 27, 87, 117–22, 124–25, 128n100, 139, 14–144, 146, 160n49, 190
remission of, 40, 57–58, 65, 67, 70, 75, 80–81, 90, 92, 96, 108, 178, 188–89
to overcome, 28, 34, 101, 110–11, 126, 140, 142, 144, 147, 154–55, 159, 167, 171, 177, 181–83, 190
to take captive, 29, 144, 171, 174, 181–82

sorrow, 4, 27, 63–68, 70, 73–74, 91, 96–97, 112–13, 129, 134–35, 139, 148, 151, 188

soul
form of, 115n54, 146, 148, 156, 158–60, 168, 172, 181, 183
moral powers of, 3, 5, 11, 23, 25, 28, 31, 35, 119n70, 168, 187, 190–91
noetic form of, 161–63, 165, 167, 170

Spirit
as accuser, 55, 86
as bare divinity, 61, 80, 86
as paracletic comforter, 54–55, 61, 81, 96–97
as sanctifier, 61, 86, 92–94
as vivifier, 61, 86, 92–94
author of law, 59–60, 79–80, 85–86, 92, 94–97, 99, 137, 188
gift of (*see* gift, of Spirit)
indwelling of, 5, 17, 92n211, 98, 123, 139, 146, 168n81, 183
punitive office of, 54–55, 58–60

Tauler, Johannes, 117–18, 120, 124, 131–32, 137, 139
temptation, 28, 90–91, 96, 110, 126, 127n95, 133–34, 136–47, 139n148, 166, 168, 177, 190, 194
tentatio. See temptation
terror, 8, 61, 69–70, 75, 78–80, 88, 92, 132
torment, 67, 107, 159, 173
Trinity, 17, 69, 76, 113, 146, 161, 193

vice, 89, 111, 117–18, 120–21, 176
virtue, 64, 72, 111, 117–18, 120–21, 123–24, 137, 169–70, 176, 179
volition, 1, 11, 13, 31, 34, 64, 93–94, 96, 98, 111, 113–16, 120, 124, 131, 141, 143, 147, 151–53, 161–67, 170–72, 174, 181, 183–85, 190–91, 193–94

will, 2–4, 10, 18, 23, 28, 31–36, 66n95, 68n108, 86, 80, 91, 92–96, 103–4, 109–16, 123, 129, 131, 133–34, 141–47, 161–67, 170–72, 176–77, 180–81, 184–85, 190–91

www.ingramcontent.com/pod-product-compliance
Lightning Source LLC
Chambersburg PA
CBHW020409230426
43664CB00009B/1242